Ambiguity in the Western Mind

PETER LANG
New York • Washington, D.C./Baltimore • Bern
Frankfurt am Main • Berlin • Brussels • Vienna • Oxford

Ambiguity in the Western Mind

EDITED BY
Craig J. N. de Paulo
Patrick Messina
Marc Stier

PETER LANG
New York • Washington, D.C./Baltimore • Bern
Frankfurt am Main • Berlin • Brussels • Vienna • Oxford

Library of Congress Cataloging-in-Publication Data

Ambiguity in the Western mind / edited by Craig J.N. de Paulo,
Patrick Messina, and Marc Stier.
p. cm.
Includes bibliographical references and index.
1. Hermeneutics. 2. Ambiguity. I. De Paulo, Craig J. N.
II. Messina, Patrick III. Stier, Marc.
BD241.A45   121'.68--dc22   2005022904
ISBN 0-8204-6380-9 (hardcover)
ISBN 0-8204-6376-0 (paperback)

Bibliographic information published by **Die Deutsche Bibliothek**.
Die Deutsche Bibliothek lists this publication in the "Deutsche
Nationalbibliografie"; detailed bibliographic data is available
on the Internet at http://dnb.ddb.de/.

Cover design by Lisa Barfield

The paper in this book meets the guidelines for permanence and durability
of the Committee on Production Guidelines for Book Longevity
of the Council of Library Resources.

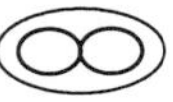

© 2005 Peter Lang Publishing, Inc., New York
275 Seventh Avenue, 28th Floor, New York, NY 10001
www.peterlangusa.com

Contents

Acknowledgments..vii

Foreword
Craig J. N. de Paulo...ix

Preface
Joseph Margolis...xi

Introduction
Craig J. N. de Paulo, Patrick Messina and Marc Stier................1

In Praise of Ambiguity
John D. Caputo...15

Tragic Ambiguity in the *Oedipus Tyrannos*
Robert Guay..35

Is Socrates a Model? Ambiguity in the *Symposium* of Plato
Marc Stier...51

Augustine of Hippo on Seeing with the Eyes of the Mind
Roland J. Teske, S.J...72

St. Augustine's Phenomenology of Confusion
Craig J. N. de Paulo...88

Prudence in St. Thomas Aquinas: Certitude in Ambiguity
John M. Haas...101

"Stay, illusion": Ambiguity in *Hamlet*
Camille Paglia..117

Leo Tolstoy, Russia's Greatest Heretic
Jaroslav Pelikan..131

Hölderlin's *Der Tod des Empedokles: Erste Fassung*
Arthur Grugan..148

Paddling Against Ethics: Huck Finn as Moral Quagmire
Elizabeth Morgan...171

Exploring Ambiguities in the Political Implications of Freud
Bruce Lapenson...181

**Ambiguities in Nietzschean Philosophy:
Problems for Feminism**
Elizabeth Kaufer Busch...191

An Afterthought on Ambiguity
Marc Stier..213

Notes..217

Index..245

Acknowledgments

First of all, we would like to express our sincere gratitude to Dr. Daniel P. Tompkins, Director of the Intellectual Heritage Program at Temple University, without whose support and encouragement we might not have finished this volume at all. We would also like to thank Dr. Susan Herbst, Dean of the College of Liberal Arts at Temple University, for her gracious support of our scholarly endeavors.

We must also acknowledge our sincere thanks to the contributors of this volume, and especially to Professor John D. Caputo, Professor Camille Paglia, Professor Jaroslav Pelikan and Professor Roland Teske. We are also very grateful to Professor Joseph Margolis of the Philosophy Department at Temple University for graciously writing the Preface to this volume.

We would also like to thank Dr. Grant Ward, Associate Director of the Intellectual Heritage Program at Temple University, for his insightful suggestions in revising the Introduction to this volume. We are equally grateful to Dr. Frank Leib, our colleague in the Intellectual Heritage Program, for his gracious counsel concerning the proofreading of this volume. We are also pleased to acknowledge our gratitude to Ms. Linda Tribune, Administrative Assistant in the Intellectual Heritage Program, for all of her kind assistance with this publication. Many thanks are also due to

Catherine Conroy de Paulo for her invaluable assistance with proofreading the entire manuscript of this volume for publication.

We extend grateful acknowledge to the Archbishop Garrity Fund of the Theology Department at Seton Hall University for permission to reprint the 1988-1989 Lecture.

Foreword

Craig J. N. de Paulo
Temple University

This volume entitled *Ambiguity in the Western Mind* is the result of countless conversations among faculty over last years in the Intellectual Heritage Program at Temple University in Philadelphia. As a humanities program, commissioned with the awesome task of introducing the undergraduate to a liberal arts education, the program has been successful in threading the student's experience with a critical appreciation for what is usually discussed in terms of the "Great books" and the ideas that have contributed to the development of Western civilization. With a focus on reading and writing about texts, the program has become an essential element in shaping the critical thinking skills of the student. The program also strives to address the increasing diversity of Temple University (and Western society) by its attention to those issues that have typically been overlooked in traditional readings, which tend to glorify texts without considering the many philosophical, or hermeneutical, difficulties intrinsic to the texts and imbedded in our contemporary interpretations. Hence, this volume considers, or rather *re*considers, the Great books by focusing on textual ambiguities, conceptual equivocity and philosophical tensions that exist within these works, and further considers the hermeneutical challenges in approaching these texts. With contributors from diverse disciplines within the humanities, this volume succeeds in addressing the issue of methodology itself by engaging recent contributions to scholarship by phenomenology and newer forms of philosophical criticism alongside more traditional approaches. The volume begins with a postmodern treatise on ambiguity, followed by a classical consideration of *Oedipus Tyrannos* and a contemporary approach to Plato, challenging some of the very traditional ideas about Socrates. These articles on the Greeks are followed by two on Augustine, one by a medievalist and the other by a phenomenologist. The role of prudence in the thought of St. Thomas Aquinas is taken up by a thomistic moral theologian, addressing some pressing bioethical issues today. The article on *Hamlet* provides a social and political critique of Shakespeare's famous play, calling into question its religious assumptions among other things. The next article by a religious historian deals with Tolstoy's conflicts with Orthodox religiosity, attempting to identify a model of Christian piety. The following article attempts a Heideggerian analysis of the poetry of Friedrich Hölderlin. This article is followed by a deconstructionist approach to *Huckleberry Finn*. The next article provides a psychoanalytic analysis of the political life, inspired by the thought of Sigmund Freud. The last article of this collection provides a feminist critique of power structures by way of insights from Friedrich Nietzsche.

Finally, this volume has a philosophical commitment to nurture questioning and the proposition that these classic texts are still worthy of our speculation. In fact, the "greatness" of these texts might even reside in the fact that they continue to excite the minds of scholars and students alike and inspire generation after generation of thinkers.

Preface

Joseph Margolis
Temple University

The variety of papers in this appealing collection is so wide-ranging that, in introducing it, I find myself obliged to review its theme for my own sake. I do so without the luxury of being sure that its likely readers would welcome any such presumption or opportunism. I don't address the question, however, with the intention of adding another entry from a vantage of special privilege. I have in mind, rather, reflecting a bit on the collection's title: *Ambiguity in the Western Mind*. The phrase "the Western mind" is also, of course, "ambiguous"; and ambiguity is itself an ambiguous term. Some of the papers offer garden-variety specimens of what they call "ambiguity" in speech and deed and situation and the literary arts; and others tend to favor what they suggest, implicitly or explicitly, touches on the "ambiguity" at the heart of the human condition. I like the ring of the second reading, which, I think, can accommodate, as instructive and variously focused sub-species, whatever may be collected under the terms of the first. But, I'd like to adjust our sights a little by reading the phrase "the Western mind" in a way that reflects a very large orienting feature of Western thought itself, a feature that bids fair to house all the senses of "ambiguity" that we might contribute—in a way that draws attention to at least one commanding vision of the world—and of our understanding of the world and ourselves as effective creatures in the world.

"Ambiguity" has a fairly narrow as well as a wider sense. We say, for instance, that a remark or an expression used in a remark is ambiguous when we are aware that what is said could be taken in various senses, where we are not sure what the right sense is. A wicked example, a favorite of W. V. Quine's, who made a lot of the difference between "mass nouns" and "count nouns," is this: "Mary had a little lamb." But if there are, say, two determinate senses that we can supply, where we suppose the speaker has somehow implicated both, whether deliberately or not, we usually speak of equivocation rather than of ambiguity (as with Mary's lamb). The reason is that ambiguity is marked by a certain vagueness affecting a logical or semantic or grammatical distinction, whereas equivocation is usually quite determinate—as determinate as language ever is.

Hence, when we remind ourselves of the sort of caution just invoked—"as determinate as language ever is"—we realize that we need to speak even more penetratingly of potential ambiguity, possibly, then, of vagueness, which also has a narrower and a wider sense. "Vagueness," chiefly among the logicians of the semantic, centers on the inapplicability of the so-called law of excluded middle: that is, the rule that holds that any a is either F or not-F, disjunctively. (Think of baldness.) The wider sense of "ambiguity" thereupon spreads out in a number of directions but begins to touch on what, from various vantages, we are prepared to treat as "the human condition." Here, we realize that we cannot ordinarily say that there is a uniquely valid determinate answer to the question, "What is the human condition?" We don't want to say that the answer is vague or equivocal or indeterminate, or ambiguous in the narrow sense; so that if we favor a wider sense of "ambiguous," we might be willing to substitute a more perspicuous term if we could find one. My sense is that what we mean to say is that we are reasonably clear about the general sort of answer that we'd be willing to take seriously, but we doubt we could settle on any single or exclusionary vision of the generic answer though no one would be satisfied with a merely general answer. Under such circumstances—and in various senses—we speak, say, of what is valid, *qua* "determinable," but not, very probably, uniquely valid as a "determinate" instance of the determinable answer—in spite of the latter's being valid *as* a specific determination of the determinable (answer) among other possible such determinations; or, alternatively, as not determinate (as "indeterminate" perhaps) *as* to validity, in the same strong sense in which the determinable *is* objectively valid. Though, of course, if one must live with an answer, it will be a "determinate" answer, without disallowing other different determinate answers! The trick is that we normally lack a determinate rule by which to determine the valid determinations of the general answer, though we're prepared to debate the comparative reasonableness and adequacy of competing options. Questions of justice and human rights are, peculiarly, questions of this sort.

There's a certain "practical ambiguity" here that I suggest cannot be overcome—for at least the reason that we might be prepared to change our arrangements with the drift of historical circumstances; so that what, at time t, might be an acceptable determination might not be acceptable at some time later than t—which we are normally unable to fix by any antecedent rule. Now then, the extraordinary thought begins to dawn that everything humans are interested in is infected with this sort of practical ambiguity. There's no form of precision adequate to ever escaping such "ambiguity." That *is* the human condition! You will find evidence enough, for instance, in the mere effort to extend the pertinent application of any general predicate—"red" just as much as "democratic"—whenever new would-be instances cannot be convincingly shown to be indistinguishable from our paradigm cases, though they may and must at times, be decided. I suggest that there is an enormously fruitful inquiry waiting to be pursued here, as to how to extend the lesson: rightly amplified, it promises (or threatens) to affect everything we might wish to say. This is not the occasion to fill out the suggestion, but it begins to show the elastic nature of the collection's title.

You see how complicated matters can become. Let me pin down my intuition just a tad. I would say, for instance, that we might agree that all citizens should be treated as equals; and you might ask, "Well, what would you propose regarding Medicare provisions for the elderly in the way of drugs and medicines?" Agreement on the first matter may be said to concern a certain determinable condition (equality), and a decision on the second may be said to be a determinate solution to a problem falling under the generic terms of the first. One might be willing to say, then, that the first question entails a certain indeterminacy or vagueness or ambiguity in the wider sense (though you're bound to wonder whether it's the right term). Significantly, you likely to think that equality (the determinable but not determinate status) affords a valid policy in a way that is more assured than any variable but determinate provisions we could ever possibly support. We might settle, *ceteris paribus*, for one determinate resolution rather than another, in spite of the fact that we couldn't have equality at all (in the pertinent sense) if we didn't have it in one determinate form or another. My suggestion is that, in practical matters of this kind, we seek a *modus vivendi* rather than a specific judgment, which is determinable first but not determinate, and then settle for one determinate form rather than another, which cannot be directly derived from our agreement about the first.

If you concede that "equality," here, is vague or ambiguous "in the wider sense," then I would claim to see a way to enlarge the sense of "ambiguity" in a way capable of addressing the deeper questions that are associated with the analysis of the human condition itself.

Let me add one last tantalizing thought. If you reflect carefully on language—therefore, on thought and the world we think and speak about, including ourselves—you cannot fail to be struck by the fact that a great deal of language cannot be determinate at all in the way actual things and acts are said to be, and that wherever language is determinate it is determinate only to a degree, in a being, finally, determinable rather than determinate (merely or completely determinate) in the sense just mentioned. For instance, proper names cannot name things singly or exclusively, though they (that is, we, using names) do mean to name them uniquely. Predicates are always open to extension to new cases they were not originally (determinately) intended to apply to. Contexts and intentions and frames of reference are variably described and identified, though we have no rule for doing so. Meaning depends on our changeable and disputable sense of the point of whatever we say. And no one has a set of rules for determining the meaning of what either we or others do say. Yet we claim to understand one another—and do! If you add to this the grand idea that whatever we take to be the objective characterization of "what there is" depends on how we view the world and talk about it—which is open to dispute in the ways just mentioned—then what, for argument's sake, I have been calling "ambiguity in the wide sense," or "practical ambiguity, " must be ubiquitous. Not only that, but it yields a lesson that can be independently drawn (perhaps more powerfully) from the decisive philosophical work that spans Kant and Hegel at least. If you grant all this, then you must see just how important it is to analyze what we mean by "ambiguity in the Western mind."

Now, read on!

Introduction

Craig J. N. de Paulo, Patrick Messina and Marc Stier
Temple University

Each article in this collection in some way seeks to revisit the Western tradition, which is in itself an ambiguous endeavor since the idea of the "West" and its "tradition" is not something static, but historical and always changing when the political, geographical, religious, cultural and literary "boundaries" are challenged and redefined. On the one hand, the Western tradition seems to imply something to most people regarding its philosophy, religious commitments, art and architecture, its so-called "canon" of classics. Yet, on the other hand, we can see that the origins of its philosophy derive from the Greeks; its religion is from the Near East; its art and architecture essentially derives from the Greeks and the Romans, having been over and over reinterpreted with Christian ideas—both Latin and Byzantine-for over a thousand years; then, back to "Classical" ideas. As for our "canon" we find that it is entirely defined by each individual "canonist"—that is, the one who decides which book is in, which out that particular year. One certain thing persists, however, that the Western tradition is something equivocal.

The title of this volume, *Ambiguity in the Western Mind*, could also have been called *Ambiguities* of the Western Mind in addition to other possibilities, emphasizing other aspects or dimensions of the concept of ambiguity intrinsic to our consideration. Actually, there is not merely one ambiguity of the Western mind, but rather a multiplicity of ambiguities of, around and in whatever we may refer to as the Western mind. Since we are essentially dealing with "mind," we find that even this ordinary term is quite complicated and equivocal, having as many meanings as the philosophers, theologians and poets who use it to write about everything from that part of the soul that is rational, to that which constitutes the rational soul itself, to sometimes meaning "spirit" (but this term alone would constitute a volume), to its association with thinking and, today, confused with the brain and its material, or neuro-electrical, functioning. Indeed, the term "mind" is wrought with seemingly endless ambiguities that continue to confound philosophers and thinkers within nearly every branch of learning.

This challenging volume can be approached through almost any discipline, which would result in various and different volumes pursuing this arduous task of hermeneutics because this entire endeavor is a matter of interpretation. Our collection, however, is an inter-disciplinary work, which is also a kind of methodological ambiguity. Our collection considers two plays, one Ancient Greek and the other Shakespearean, Plato's dialogue the *Symposium*, Augustine's *Confessions*, Thomas Aquinas' *Summa Theologiae*, two novels, one by the Russian thinker Leo Tolstoy and the other by the American Mark Twain, Freud's psychoanalytic treatises, the verses of the German poet Friedrich Hölderlin, Nietzsche's aphorisms, and the philosophical essays of Michel Foucault. This is a complex and diverse volume, not only in its historical and cultural ambitions, but, more specifically, in the diversity of its texts. This collection was founded on that the idea that texts like these in the Western tradition require a commitment by scholars to de-mythologize such texts by their lifelong re-reading of them that would confront the inherent ambiguities as a means to understanding them. What results from our effort is the development of a *concept of ambiguity* as a methodological tool for understanding Ancient as well as contemporary texts. Thus, this volume is above all a kind of hermeneutics of ambiguity, which will mostly interest philosophers and theologians, but it pertains to all of the arts and sciences concerned with texts and understanding the Western mind.

John D. Caputo aptly begins our volume with an article "In Praise of Ambiguity" that presents an original philosophical treatise that also provides the tone and the direction for the entire volume. This invitation to appreciate the multivalent character of not only our texts but our lives is a striking indication of the change in philosophical temper that makes a collection of this sort possible. Most of the canonical authors in the Western tradition have, at least in their standard interpretation, sought not ambiguity, multiplicity, and undecidability but clarity, unity, and certainty. To recognize, search for, and see the importance of ambiguity in our canonical texts is, then, to begin to break free from one of the themes—or shall we say obsessions—that have dominated our tradition.

Caputo's article shows us that the very qualities and capacities that the tradition has most highly valued are made possible by their opposites. Decision is only possible where indecision first exists. Change, and even progress, is only possible if multiplicity and plurality characterize the contemporary moment. Artistic innovation is only possible when the standards by which we evaluate art can be called into question. Moral choice is only possible when there are genuine alternatives that each carry some weight with us. The pursuit of righteousness in politics or faith is only possible if one recognizes the righteousness of those with whom one disagrees. And the devotion we give to the classic texts is only possible because they carry rich and multivalent meanings, meanings that can bear the weight of our endless rethinking them. Ambiguity for Caputo is a gift that makes our lives not just difficult but worth living.

In his article "Tragic Ambiguity in the *Oedipus Tyrannos*," Professor Robert Guay plumbs the uncharted regions of ambiguity in this, Sophocles' most enduring masterpiece. Citing the authority of Arnold Hug, Guay offers the well-established recognition of ambiguity in *Oedipus* as a springboard to unearthing a unique and hitherto unrevealed array of ambiguities whose depths range from the philological to the philosophical. In showing this expanded range of ambiguous dimension within the play, Guay perhaps succeeds in vindicating not only *Oedipus*, but all of Ancient Greek tragedy from the potential charge of harboring a "superficial" ambiguity; a charge that Guay suggests belongs to a by-gone assessment of Greek poetry replaced, as it were, by a more substantial, contemporary reading of the text. In the final analysis, Guay's own reading of *Oedipus* attempts to reveal ambiguity as the intrinsic, pervasive and revelatory power of Greek tragedy.

In "Is Socrates a Model? Ambiguity in the *Symposium* of Plato," Professor Marc Stier contends that the philosopher who, on the standard interpretation, seeks above all others to escape ambiguity is Plato. The world of forms is, after all, portrayed as an attractive realm precisely because everything is just what it is and nothing else. Yet, at the same time, Plato presents his philosophy as a literary form that, if only we could recognize it as such, is highly ambiguous in nature. In recent years, the importance of the dramatic character of the Platonic dialogue has been widely recognized. Scholars have paid greater attention to who says what to whom and under what circumstances. The irony of having an ironist—Socrates—as one's main spokesman has been duly noted.

Marc Stier follows a few contemporary philosophers in taking this new way of interpreting Plato one step further. He takes seriously the challenge that is put to Socrates in the *Symposium*, a challenge that touches not just his philosophy but his way of life. Along with other new interpreters of Plato, Stier suggests that Plato's ideas may be found not just in Socrates' words but in the speeches of other characters in the Platonic dialogues. Stier, however, goes further in suggesting that, however noble it is, Socrates' life may not be the Platonic model for the rest of us. The picture presented of Socrates in the *Symposium* suggests that he is too different from even the best of other human beings to serve as a model for us. Socrates is a profoundly strange creature, whose qualities suggest that he has partly escaped from the usual circumstances of human life, circumstances that are best presented in Aristophanes' account of how we were mutilated by the gods. As a result, Socrates escapes from human *eros* as well. Yet, because he lives among us, and seeks to understand us in order to understand himself, Socrates must pretend to share a common nature with us. The ambiguity of Socrates' position—and the danger that accompanies that ambiguity—is revealed when Alcibiades bursts into the drinking party and tells tales about his mentor/tormentor.

As the drama ends, the ambiguity of Socrates' position is shown to parallel the ambiguous nature of the dialogue itself, in which tragedy and comedy are intertwined.

From the Greek mind, the collection turns to Latin Christianity with Professor Roland Teske's article, "Augustine of Hippo on Seeing with the Eyes of the Mind," that explores St. Augustine's notion of *intelligere*, or intellectual knowing. As with a great deal of Augustine's thought, on the one hand, this notion appears to be highly influenced by the "Platonists" and, especially Plotinus, which Father Teske refers to as what might be called Augustine's "official version," and on the other hand, we find a more practical, Christian position. In this former position, Augustine gives a rather Platonic description of intellectual knowledge in as much as it is a kind of "seeing with the eyes of the mind" analogous to the way in which one sees things in the world with our physical eyes. Further, just as our eyes require light, the eyes of the mind can boast the Light that is God Himself. But, this is where intellectual knowing seems to be confused, in part, with divine Illumination, according to Professor Teske, who contends that scholars know more about what this does not mean than what it means. The article goes on to point out some interesting limitations to this official position, principally in the fact that this means one must see the divine Ideas in the mind of God, which Professor Teske systematically demonstrates that such a position would result either in reducing intellectual knowledge to intuition or to simply question-begging with regard to Augustine's proof for the existence of God. Then, the article continues by suggesting that there also appears to be another, more "plebeian" position, as Teske puts it, where Augustine offers a more saleable point of view in his own practical counsel, first to St. Jerome, and second, to Consentius, which leads to a more philosophic reading of this ambiguous matter.

The question of ambiguity in Augustine is further addressed in the next article entitled "St. Augustine's Phenomenology of Confusion" by Professor Craig de Paulo, who explores Augustine's own notion of "confusion" while disclosing the various—in fact, almost endless—degrees and levels in which confusion and ambiguity are at work within the thought of the Latin

North African thinker. Relying upon theoretical foundations already established in his previous writings, de Paulo's methodology reveals the complementary relationship that exists between the thought of Augustine and the interests of phenomenology, resulting in what he has termed as an "Augustinian phenomenology of confusion" that will not only interest patrologists, but philosophers and theologians. The article provides insight to Augustine's thought as a whole, but also more specifically in terms of his notion of concupiscence. In short, Professor de Paulo provides an insightful hermeneutics of the *Confessions* that will stimulate both the novice and well-acquainted reader.

Professor John M. Haas takes up the issue of ambiguity by challenging its role with regard to moral certitude in his article "The Virtue of Prudence in St. Thomas Aquinas: Certitude in Ambiguity." The challenge, as it were, does not question the existence of moral ambiguity but the way in which the moral agent acts in the face of it. Drawing upon his expertise as a bioethicist, Haas examines the problem of organ donation and its ethical implications by way of a controversy between the pronouncements of Pope John Paul II and the conclusions of six authors of an article published in *The Catholic World Report* on the topic of determining death in a potential organ donor. The controversy surrounds what these authors perceived as the Pope's departure from the traditional "pulmonary criteria" of determining death (producing absolute certainty), to a "neurological criteria" (producing what the Pope called "moral certitude"). In his analysis, Haas concludes that there is no substantive discrepancy between these two positions, only a misunderstanding of the surety of "moral certitude." In an attempt to resolve this debate, Professor Haas defends the Pope's position on "moral certitude" and reveals its foundation in the Western tradition within a virtue-centered morality guided by prudence.

Relying primarily upon the moral texts of Aristotle and Thomas Aquinas, Haas sheds light on the role of prudence as a "commanding" force in moral agency, navigating an objectively certain course in the wake of the profound moral ambiguities that constitute the seemingly uncertain circumstances of human life. Emphasizing the teleological character of an Aristotelian-

Thomistic ethic, Haas relates the moral reliability of prudential judgment as it constitutes the "lynchpin" between intellectual and moral certainty, relying upon the metaphysical convertibility between Being, Truth and Goodness. Highlighting the Realist tradition, Haas argues against the equation of ambiguity with radical moral subjectivity, or a post-Kantian skepticism.

Haas realizes the ambiguous nature of prudence in admitting that within the Aristotelian-Thomistic tradition it is categorized both as an intellectual *and* moral virtue. The implication of this intrinsic ambiguity of prudence reveals its proper place in the discernment of moral certitude. According to Haas, the perfection of prudence entails a firm decisiveness in the face of ineradicable doubt. Since the Realist position is anything but naïve, it allows for the vestige of doubt in nearly all highly complex ethical circumstances. The persistence of moral ambiguity notwithstanding, Haas reiterates the reliable power of prudence to render a reasonably certain moral conclusion.

Despite the fact that there have been innumerable and diverse kinds of interpretation, Professor Camille Paglia attempts an original and thoroughly modern reading of Shakespeare's *Hamlet* by addressing its intrinsic ambiguities with her characteristic eloquence and keen philosophic insight in her article *"Stay, illusion*: Ambiguity in *Hamlet."* Paglia begins her examination of this famous play by entertaining some of the radical kinds of questioning that it provokes revealing the contradictions and ambiguities surrounding this text. By classifying the ambiguities in *Hamlet* into three groups: the philosophical, political and psychological, Professor Paglia succeeds in elucidating fascinating and perplexing experience from out of the lives of the characters of the play while providing historical commentary as well as psychological and aesthetic analysis almost as enriching as the play itself.

Recognizing Shakespeare's Reformation sympathies, Paglia notes that Hamlet's questioning seems peculiarly Protestant yet reveals an estranged nihilism in an almost regressive, more pagan way of thinking. Paglia suggests that perhaps this religious ambiguity may reveal the influence of the French philosopher Montaigne on William Shakespeare and his depiction of Hamlet. Moreover, Paglia contends that, on the one hand, the play reveals a deeper philosophical ambiguity in Horatio's exclamation "Stay, illusion," in which we find a summary of a perennial obsession in Western thought beginning with Plato until today. On the other hand, in contrast to Plato's own position, the article further explains that the phrase "Stay, illusion" also refers to the artistic desire for the continuance of the play in imagination, and thus, we find that through art we can achieve a deeper sense of reality and truth than what we find in philosophy and science. This longing for illusion also corresponds to the many political ambiguities that exist in Hamlet, paralleling the question of the royal succession that plagued England during Shakespeare's time since Queen Elizabeth was without issue, in effect ending Tudor rule. Lastly, Paglia addresses the several kinds of psychological ambiguities in *Hamlet*, ranging from the prince's forlorn sense of identity to his forbidden fantasies concerning his mother and his sinister desire to rid himself of his father's ghostly dominance and unapproachable model of manliness while at other times subjecting himself to female imagery and self-loathing. Hamlet represents all that plagues the human mind, and this prince-seeking-death reminds us that nothing, however great, remains.

Professor Jaroslav Pelikan in his article "Russia's Greatest Heretic," explores Tolstoy's ambivalence towards Russian Orthodoxy in his complex portrayals of characters in his novels. Tolstoy was clearly *un*orthodox about religion, and Christianity in particular, despising ritual and pious gestures such as the crossing of oneself and the devotion to icons, preferring a more simplistic, Gospel-oriented fundamentalism where the believer encounters the supernatural in everyday faith. Although the character from his novel, *Resurrection*, Katerina Ivanovna, appears at first glance to be the sort of Christian that might win Tolstoy's praise and admiration, Professor Pelikan suggests that Katerina falls short of the Russian ideal according to Tolstoy. Rather, the article contends that we find the celebration and achievement of Tolstoy's authentic Christian to be embodied in Princess Marya Nikolayevna Bolkonskaya from his famed novel, *War and Peace*. This is certainly ironic and confusing since Princess Marya is the epitome of Russian piety, yet she is a true believer and a woman inspired by the Gospel law of love and the theology of self-sacrifice directly linked with the passion and death of Christ. According to Pelikan, Marya represents the bridge between the authentic experience of religion and the habitual practices of ritualistic religion found in Orthodoxy. This princess provides the mean between peasant piety and true Christianity, something akin to the way in which Christ Himself, a king, having been born in a manger and lived as a carpenter, is the Mediator between man and God. As a kind of Christ figure, Princess Marya is a link between the religion of icons and the religion of the Gospel, subjecting her own existential uncertainties and ambiguities to pure obedience and devotion. Perhaps, similar to the writing of James Joyce with regard to the Irish experience of Roman Catholicism, Tolstoy reveals his own desire for a devout Russian Orthodox believer with authentic faith in the character of Marya.

In his article, "Hölderlin's *Der Tod Empedokles: Erste Fassung*," Professor Arthur Grugan attempts a Heideggerian analysis of Holderlin's dramatic play. By Martin Hedegger's own suggestion, Grugan begins his analysis by examining some of Hölderlin's late poetry in order to establish his vehement opposition to the prevailing Cartesian idealism of his day. According to Arthur Grugan, Hölderlin abhorred the radical subjectivism of Descartes' philosophy that ultimately produced the unnatural rupture between man (*res cogitans*) and the world (*res extensa*). Grugan makes clear, however, that Hölderlin was a Modern man, not without sympathies and interest in German idealism. For example, Grugan credits the philosophy of Fichte, and Hölderlin's profound interest with his work, as the inspiration for Hölderlin's optimism for overcoming the Cartesian duality, presumably through the creation of *Der Tod Empedokles*.

Professor Grugan goes on to explain that in Hölderlin's late poetry there is a strong desire to abandon any attempt to relate the German experience of his day with that of the Ancient Greeks. Perhaps emphasizing his Modern commitments, Hölderlin advocated a clean break with the past in favor of an intense focus on the present, presumably to "discover its ownmost essence." In his analysis, Grugan discloses Hölderlin's own preoccupation with the ambiguity of *Zwishenzeit*, the spatio-temporal divide between the past and the future. According to Grugan, it is within this interim period that the modern man finds both his most sufferable and optimistic challenge to find his own way in a world that has been artificially rendered from its natural unity with man.

Moving his analysis to Hölderlin's play, Grugan asserts that in *Der Tod Empedokles*, the character of Empedokles represents both the sins of Cartesian idealism and the repentance of *Zwishenzeit*. In his radical self-absorption and hubris, Empedokles symbolizes the alienating subjectivism of Cartesian idealism; while on the other hand, in his own dramatic conversion, wherein he realizes that he is not a god, Empedokles represents the truly heroic champion of the *Zwishenzeit*, who embraces his ambiguous position as a transcendent being inferior to God. This heroic image is punctuated by Empedokles' resignation to death as the simultaneous means of purification and justification; the latter representative of the restoration of man's proper relation to the world not as the alienated subject of Cartesian idealism, but as being naturally suited to the outside world. Thus, the article suggests that Hölderlin's *Empedokles* stands as the mediator between man's sins of the past and his optimistic transformation of the future, all played out in the drama of that ambiguous present.

In her article, "Paddling Against Ethics: *Huck Finn* as Moral Quagmire," Professor Elizabeth Morgan deconstructs the often misunderstood moral fabric of Mark Twain's enduringly controversial novel to reveal what she calls "a narrative written against ethics." Through her analysis of *Huckleberry Finn*, Professor Morgan attempts to debunk many of the commonly held assumptions about the text that have helped fuel American society's ambivalence toward its perceived racist overtones and its overall moral message. For Morgan, *Huckleberry Finn* tends to defy all attempts at moral categorization. Instead, the novel plays on the complex, somewhat conflicting ambiguities of a post-bellum America struggling to find its moral compass in the throes of the cultural upheaval of the times. Morgan suggests, however, that Twain's lesson of moral ambiguity is not confined to his own time or geography, but extends to "human reality in the post-bellum American South and elsewhere."

Employing Mikhail Bakhtin's *The Dialogic Imagination* as an hermeneutic tool, Morgan assumes the dialogical character of the novel genre, as it reflects what Bakhtin concludes to be the intrinsic dialogic of the human person. In this sense, culture derives from the diverse multiplicity of voices in a given society, marked by conflict, each struggling to be heard, somehow resulting in an amalgam of distinct democratic character. Morgan thus applies the dialogic nature of the novel genre to guide her own deconstruction of *Huckleberry Finn*, revealing what she calls a "disruption of assumed binaries" that expose the profound ambiguous moral character of the text; such as the first of these "binaries" which Morgan calls "Romance vs. Novel." According to Morgan, Twain uses the frontier romance to critique the romantic genre, thereby critiquing the nineteenth-century American promise of romantic freedom. The complexity of ambiguity is furthered by what Morgan suggests is Twain's use of the realistic novel genre to critique such nineteenth-century Southern cultural relics as "mob rule" and "religious rigidity." Thus, the tension between these two forms of the novel genre reveal an equivocal and somewhat contradictory state of the moral climate of the nineteenth-century South.

Professor Bruce Lapenson's interesting and speculative article examines the political implications of ambiguity in the thought of Freud on a number of different levels with particular attention to liberalism and democracy. He demonstrates that ambiguity both by attending to Freud's own work and, even more so, by showing us how Freud's psychoanalysis can and has led his followers to radically diverse political conclusions.

Freud, Lapenson persuasively argues, was a committed liberal who rejected the more extreme critics of liberalism on both left and right. Yet, at the same time, Freud was well aware of the difficulties of liberalism. Freud was dubious about the capacity of liberalism to attain the utopia promised by some of the founders of that doctrine. He believed that the security found in modern societies comes at a very great cost: severe limitations on instinctual satisfaction. Freud also had little hope that limited government or economic growth could free mankind from the wars and other conflicts that have created so much misery, and he feared that excessive restrictions on the instinctual drives created by liberalism would ultimately lead to dangerous outbursts of human destructiveness.

While Freud was critical of liberalism, he had no inclination to embrace the radical left, nor was he in retreat from politics. Freud welcomed efforts to ameliorate the inequalities found in liberal political communities. However, he had no hope that the fundamental tensions between human beings could be resolved by the redistribution of wealth or power. Those tensions were, he thought, far more deeply rooted in human nature than the socialists of his day, or the radical Freudians of our own day, tend to believe.

At a deeper level, Professor Lapenson shows that we can trace ambiguity itself back to the human psyche. The human soul is deeply divided by the conflicting instinctual demands of the "id" as well as by the tension between those demands and the powerful force of conscience created in the "super-ego." These conflicts are the result of still deeper tensions in the child's relationship to the world around him or her and especially in the interaction between the child and his or her parents. Lapenson suggests that it is in large part this ambiguity in our relationship to the world that is exemplified in our ambiguous stance towards most human institutions and ideas.

According to Lapenson, liberalism and democracy are both vulnerable to the very things they foster. As Plato saw, Lapenson argues that democracy can easily fall to the tyranny of the majority and liberalism's thirst for individualism can result in unleashing the "id." This article further indicts the Freudian Left contending that it either fails to acknowledge aggression or fails to deal with it properly.

Some of our authors praise ambiguity in general, or the ambiguity they find in a particular text. Others see in the ambiguity of certain texts a clue to their deeper meaning. Elizabeth Kaufer Busch's article, "Ambiguities in Nietzchean Philosophy: Problems for Feminists" looks at ambiguity in a more traditional manner. In doing so, she perhaps reveals the limits of ambiguity in more polemical discourse. Ambiguity may be delightful and revealing in that it points us to opportunities and potentialities in life and thought. But, when it comes to choosing one path or another, ambiguity can be troublesome, especially when ambiguities are hidden from us, they can lead to confusion or mistake.

That, Busch argues, is the case with some of the contemporary feminists who seek to empower women by deconstructing traditional sex roles. On Busch's reading, the hidden master of these "gender feminists" is Nietzsche, whose ideas about the centrality of the will to power in human life have, by way of Foucault, played a key role in their thought. That the domination of women by men is the central feature of human life; that it has deeply constituted men and women to have certain aims and capacities; and that the personal is political are three key notions of gender feminism that Busch traces to Nietzschean styles of thought.

The central claim of Busch's article is that the ambiguities of Nietzchean thought infect gender feminism and prevent it from developing a coherent or attractive moral position. Gender feminism seems to trade on an ambiguity about the status of the natural differences between men and women. Gender feminists attribute patriarchy to the power seeking of men and imply that the world would be a better place if the good qualities of women were free from that power. Yet they deny that there are any natural differences between men and women. Gender feminists also oscillate between praising women for their freedom from the pursuit of power and calling for women to take power themselves. It is thus not clear whether gender feminism truly seeks democracy and equality or whether that explicit goal is the ruse by which women seek power over men. Feminism, Busch suggests, would be better off with more clarity and less ambiguity. Yet it is only by attending carefully to ambiguity and tension within Nietzsche's thought that Busch can reveal to us the difficulties of modern feminism. Busch's analysis of the troubles with feminism is made possible by her willingness to look for ambiguity and discontinuity in contemporary thought.

The major contribution of this volume to scholarship consists in the treatment of the notion and what has been traditionally conceived as the problem of ambiguity in Western thought. Each essay addresses ambiguity with great seriousness and respect, and in some instances, even reverence, elevating it to a concept worthy of philosophical, theological and literary speculation. The volume is also a scholarly resource for revisiting these well-known and esteemed texts with a new kind of questioning and insight that leads to inexhaustible consideration of the tradition and its positions concerning man and his intellectual, political, spiritual, moral and sexual life with all of its own confusion and ambiguity that, perhaps, best defines the human condition. The volume also presents a hermeneutical approach to whatever may be considered the "Western tradition" as something distinctly interdisciplinary, calling contributors from the various disciplines in the arts and sciences into dialogue over the question of ambiguity and its significance and relevance for contemporary scholarship. Lastly, this volume attempts to promote hermeneutics as a theoretical science and methodology further advanced by this emerging *concept of ambiguity.* Every contributor in the volume agrees that ambiguity is a rather praiseworthy issue that elicits the kind of anguish that assists us in understanding ourselves and our world. Ambiguity is also praiseworthy inasmuch as it calls us to confront ourselves and our fears, our thought of ourselves and of our society, moving us toward the courage to interpret, and *re*-interpret, our lives again and again, more authentically.

In Praise of Ambiguity

John D. Caputo
Villanova University

What could be clearer than that our lives are ambiguous—deeply, provocatively, dangerously, beautifully ambiguous? I am not complaining, for ambiguity is a gift that gives life its interest, its mystery, its passion. Ambiguity lures and entices us, drawing us into the mystery of things, the mystery of one another, the mystery of God. Ambiguity raises the stakes of life; it makes life risky and is liable to lead us astray; that makes life a prize worth winning. Ambiguity leaves us restless, uncertain, questing and questioning, searching and researching; that makes life a treasure worth finding. *Factus sum mihi terra difficultatis*, Augustine said, "I have become a land of difficulty for myself," but it is the very difficulty of life that gives life substance and texture.[1] Whatever is important, valuable, significant is ambiguous—love and death, God and suffering, right and wrong, the past and the future. Just so, if something is unambiguously clear, transparently simple, is that not because its substance is spent, its future is over? Ambiguity is like the blackness of the night sky, which makes the stars glow more brilliantly and leaves us wondering what else stirs in those dark depths from which they shine forth.

Ambiguity is a gift: that is the hypothesis that I will pursue here—in praise of ambiguity, but with all due clarity.

The Principle of Ambiguity: Both/And

Let us begin *in principio,* in the beginning, with a principle of great clarity, for which I turn to Kierkegaard, who launched his career, or rather that of his pseudonyms, with a book entitled *Either/Or,* to which I would like to pay a tribute, or a counter-contribute, entitled "Both/And." I do not in this way mean to defy Kierkegaard but rather to reenforce his position and make it stronger. In my view "both/and" is the other side of "either/or," its complement, the silent partner in the firm of Johannes de Silentio and Victor Eremitus et al. Were I myself bold enough to write in the fanciful manner of the pseudonyms, I would say that my little eulogy to ambiguity today could be called "Both 'Both/And' and 'Either/Or'."

As it happens, that mind bending expression is in fact also a good description of what is called "undecidability" by Jacques Derrida, whose peculiar proximity to Kierkegaard I am constantly insisting upon, instigating, or otherwise insinuating. Undecidability should not be viewed as the sworn enemy of decision, as Derrida's unfriendly critics persist in doing, but rather as its condition of possibility. There is only something to decide when we do not know what to do, whereas when what is to be done is obvious from the start, so that there is little wavering and even less deliberation, then there is very little to decide. However much deliberation is in order, however long deliberation may go on, the actual moment of decision is a leap. Otherwise, deciding is just a question of going through the motions, running the program, connecting the dots. But really to decide something — the root of this word means to *cut,* so that every de-cision is also an in-cision — means to feel oneself pulled in several directions at once, to see the merits of this and the merits of that, of *both* this *and* that, to see that *both* alternatives are right, or perhaps *both* are wrong, or even perhaps that both are right and both are wrong, and to know that nonetheless something, some *one* thing, has to be done. We just can't stand there and deliberate while the city burns. The real decision is urgent; the decisive cut has to be made. So what gives the either/or its passion, its real cutting edge is both/and.

Furthermore, "both 'both/and' and 'either/or,'" which fairly describes what Derrida calls "undecidability," is no less fair a description of *ambiguity*, which comes from the Latin prefix *ambi*, meaning "both," and *agere*, to act or to do. Ambiguity describes a situation in which there is something that must be done but we are of two minds about what to do. Had our linguistic history taken another turn or two, we might have words like ambi-active, ambi-action, or ambi-agile. The German word for ambiguity describes the duality, *Zwei-deutigkeit*, having two meanings or interpretations, but it does not pick up the *agere*. Things get ambiguous precisely when the case for one alternative is as pressing as the case for the other, and we are forced to choose the greater good and sacrifice the lesser, or, alternately, when the case *against* one alternative is as pressing as the case against the other and we are forced to choose the lesser evil and avoid the greater one. Both are right and/or both are wrong, so what is to be done? I hasten to add that I am not complaining about this situation. On the contrary, I, who am a great lover of what the young Heidegger called the difficulty of factical life, intend here to praise ambiguity, to praise "both/and," to praise everything that is ambi-this or ambi-that—ambidextrous or ambi-sextrous or ambivalent—and I look approvingly upon all ambi-tendencies, and this on the general grounds of their wider ambit and more delightful ambiance.

So, with a fear and trembling that befits my humble condition, I stand here, *ich kann nicht anders*, in open defiance of a long and venerable line of thinkers who have preceded me, ready to defend a little thesis or counter-thesis or unconventional hypothesis that ambiguity is a gift, that everything deep and provocative, everything beautiful and mysterious, everything decisive and meaningful, is ambiguous. Ambiguity is not an acid dropped on life's clarity but the veil in which life's *mystery* is kept safe, by which it is protected from the harsh and destructive light of univocity and programmability. My task here is to show that things really have a cutting edge, a meaning that it is worth taking note of, that things are really meaningful, when they are awash in ambiguity, while clear cut and unambiguous matters mostly merit a yawn. Something is really happening when there is ambiguity afoot (with *both* feet, of course). Ambiguity is what makes the great books great, what gives decisions their decisiveness, what gives life its passion, its force, its grip on us. In the classical language of transcendental philosophy, one might formulate my hypothesis by saying that ambiguity is the condition of possibility of everything worthy and important. But if we remember our principle of great clarity, both/and, we would have to refine this into a more ambiguous quasi-transcendental principle: ambiguity is the condition *both* of the possibility *and* of the impossibility of everything meaningful. That means that ambiguity makes our beliefs and practices possible by also making them impossible, that is, ambiguity sees to it that our beliefs and practices are made possible by simultaneously threatening action and menacing meaning, by making them hover over the abyss. Ambiguity is a gift but remember *die Gift vergiftet* and can very well poison us.

Philosophers Against Ambiguity

The case against my hypothesis about the gift of ambiguity among the philosophers—who have long preferred unity to multiplicity, simplicity to complexity, univocity to plurivocity, the one to the many—is formidable and long standing. Ambiguity has been in trouble with the philosophers right from the start, when ambiguity first fell afoul of father Parmenides' passion for monothetic univocity. Parmenides singled out for derision in his poem those "two-headed," (*dikranoi*) types,[2] those deplorable both/and people who wander about saying both "it is" and "it is not," who dwell in the land of *doxa*, which is the sphere of mere opinion and appearance. These woeful ones Parmenides opposed to the clear-headed—by which, of course, he certainly meant the one-headed followers of the way of being, who stick single-mindedly to the "it is," which is the way of "truth" shown by the goddess. But on my heretical account, two heads are better than one, and the dicranial is better than those monocranial, monomaniac, monotonous Parmenidean types. Is it not written (somewhere) that two heads are better than one? Having two heads, or being of two minds, is just the sort of thing that is needed in order to see both sides of the story and to understand the difficulty of a complex situation. In just the way that Kierkegaard tried to write with both hands, to write the signed "edifying" or "upbuilding" works with his right hand, while writing indirect, more seductive and sinistral and pseudonymous works with his left hand, so it is better to be thinking with two heads rather than one, especially when they are combined in one skull. In general, I prefer plurality, plurivocity and pluralism to all this Parmenidean unity, identity and univocity, where being is a well-rounded self-identical and solid sphere, which seems to me uninterrupted, undivided boredom.[3]

In modernity, Descartes made his reputation explaining to us how to clarify our ideas, how to think with methodic precision, how to avoid the abyss of ambiguity in which all our "clear and distinct ideas" are lost like a ship in a fog or a diver in a bottomless sea. Even Heidegger, the great critic of Descartes and the thinker of Being's concealment, denounced *Zweideutigkeit* in *Being and Time* as the refuge of the inauthentic, as the sounding cymbal of those who say they understand something, like the fact of their mortality, precisely when they do not.[4]

Ambiguity is, alas, the Mary Magdalene of philosophical concepts, a woman whose reputation has been unjustly tarnished by the boys just when she may have been the Beloved Disciple herself. Ambiguity is a good woman whose name has been smeared by phallocentric philosophers too much in love with pure Forms, solid substances, clear and distinct ideas, transcendental consciousness, authentic being-unto-death, and other fantasies of an excessively purifying or unifying and very virile frame of mind that has more or less constituted philosophy right from the start. Indeed, philosophy's aversion to ambiguity goes hand in hand with a very virile love of power, of top-down systems with clear directions coming from on high.

Indeed, what is arguably the opening scene of philosophy in the west has Socrates prowling the agora in search of clear definitions of things that most people thought they understood just fine but found they could not define when they came under the fire of Socratic inquisition. Philosophy got off the ground with that kind of passion for purity, pressing for definitions.

Philosophy first opened its doors for business by announcing that it could sort out the clarity of "truth" from the ambiguity of rhetoric, for the only rhetorical skill one needed was the skill to tell the truth (*Apology*). The first act of philosophy ends with a death scene, with Socrates on stage dying for the right to ask his questions.

Nietzsche was the first one to dare criticize Socrates, the first to regard him not as a martyr but a monster, who instead of having an overgrown ear or nose had a grossly overgrown cerebellum. Socrates pressed for well-defined conceptual clarity, Nietzsche complained, just where none was needed or even in order, even as he devalued the importance of the implicit, preconceptual, instinctive capacity to do things, which characterizes everyone who really manages to *do* something. Socrates grossly exaggerated the importance of explicit conceptual definition and precision, precisely the sort of thing prized by professors who are sometimes better at *talking* about things than actually *doing* them.[5]

To that end, and having my own spine stiffened by Nietzsche's audacious critique of Socrates, philosophy's patron saint, I will stick by my perverse philosophical thesis, which is a kind of counter-philosophical thesis or counter-thesis, a hyperbolic hypothesis that will no doubt incite the philosophers against me because it flies in the face of one of philosophy's most fundamental faiths. On the view that I am taking ambiguity is a gift in spite of the fact that, or rather precisely because, ambiguity is a menace that threatens to undermine meaning. Ambiguity is for me the condition that makes meaning possible by making pure and unambiguous meaning impossible. In such a view pure and perfect clarity is an auto-deconstructing event. For if you are completely clear and certain about what you think or what you feel you must do, that is because the life of meaning has gone dead for you, because meaning has stagnated into a settled, dull affair. On the other hand, the more you are stuck and quite bewildered about what the next step is and the more up against a stone wall you are driven, then the more you are really on the move.

The Auto-deconstruction of Univocity

To advance my unpopular cause, let us consider the deadening effects of clarity and univocity, as opposed to the open-ended ambiance of ambiguity. To that end, I take up the opposition, or the "transcendental parallel,"[6] as he calls it, that Derrida stages between Edmund Husserl, the German philosopher who first formulated the method of phenomenology, and as sober a judge as philosophy has ever produced, and James Joyce, the Irish writer whom even the Irish could not tolerate, who raised passions everywhere with his ribald, bawdy and almost unreadably playful prose. Husserl is writing about the history of geometry (a topic about which James Joyce had little to say), and he is insisting that our use of language be unambiguously clear, that no science, geometric or any other, can move forward unless its meanings are formulated in unambiguous expressions that can be passed on from generation to generation, that retain an "ideal identity" that "allows communication among generations of investigators" across the ages. Otherwise, we will be plunged into the night of equivocity. But consider the paradoxical consequence of this notion that Derrida points out, which on the face of it seems otherwise perfectly obvious. History and historical transmission would be possible, on Husserl's account, just on the condition that every trace of historical alteration and deviation is extinguished. The result of this Husserlian demand, Derrida writes, would thus be "to sterilize or paralyze history in the indigence of an indefinite iteration," a repetition of the same that makes for no movement forward, that is, no real movement, no room for movement, no ambiance.

The other alternative is Joyce's, "to repeat and take responsibility for all equivocation itself, utilizing a language that could equalize the greatest possible synchrony with the greatest potential for buried, accumulated, and interwoven intentions within each linguistic atom, each vocable, each word, each simple proposition," a language that instead of trying to translate the common semantic content from one language to another, "circulates throughout all languages at once, accumulates their energies, actualizes their most secret consonances...cultivates their associative syntheses instead of avoiding them," a language that does not avoid complexity but settles within its "labyrinthian field." Nonetheless, without some unity, without some univocity, "the very text of its repetition would have been unintelligible."

In short, historical movement is equally impossible for both Husserl and Joyce, albeit for opposing reasons. Husserl tries to account for history with a power of transmission that is so univocal as to cut off something *new* from happening; nothing different is allowed to be introduced; pure univocity is pure paralysis. But Joyce tries to dominate history from another direction, by exploiting every equivocation, every novelty, so that there is no novelty left that would not be an empty repetition of what Joyce has already deployed. Joyce's pure equivocation makes historical transmission not only unintelligible but unnecessary. What makes history move, what makes movement possible, what makes for historical ambiance, is what Derrida calls "repetition" or "iteration," by which he means the repetition—and the production by repetition—of the different, the mobility of ambiguous transmission, passing along a multiplicity of meanings, multiple associations, more or less loose links, trembling and loose transmissions which are not simply garbled but polyvalent, not confused but polymorphic, not chaotic but astir with a multiplicity of meaning that opens up the future, disclosing possibilities, even as they demand decision and resolution.

Perfect univocity is auto-deconstructing. If a word is unambiguously clear, it has lost its suggestiveness and become a technical term. If a character in a fiction is unambiguously clear, the novel is a bore. If a text is completely readable, completely unambiguous, it would not be worth reading or it would soon lose its interest. Unreadability is the condition of possibility of genuine readability. Progress is made when otherwise smoothly running systems run into an anomaly which forces the system to reconfigure on a higher level. In the sphere of action, of the ethico-political, if someone is unambiguously male or female, white or black, American or anti-American, Christian or Islamic, Republican or Democrat, then God help them and, more importantly, God help the rest of us. If one is faced with a devilishly difficult decision, the only fellow whose advice I would trust is the fellow who does not know what to do, who is absolutely stuck, who sees both sides of the story and is sympathetic with both, and is completely paralyzed by the difficulty of the situation. That is a man whom I admire, someone who is thinking clearly, who is using his head, who is using both his heads, that is, thinking with a clear sense of the ambient ambiguity of the situation.

The Limits of Ambiguity

I hasten to add—before the police of philosophy arrive to cart me off for my civil disobedience—that ambiguity is not imprecision and that I am not simply against precision, clarity and method. Ambiguity is an excess of meaning, a multiplication of too many meanings, so that we find ourselves drawn in several directions at once. Imprecision is not an excess but a lack, viz., a lack of precision where precision is required. Let me be clear that I am unambiguously opposed to imprecision. The most general theory I hold is not about clarity or ambiguity, but about contextuality, according to which everything has a context, and nothing happens outside a context, so that the sense and value of our beliefs and practices are ultimately a function of the context in which they are found. There are clearly contexts in which univocal precision and exactitude are exactly what is in order— when I look at my watch on the way to the airport, balance my checking account, turn the ignition of my car on a dark and freezing cold night far away from home, turn on my computer, or have an MRI or an X-ray of a medical condition that needs treatment. Then I want precision.

So in any discussion of ambiguity, it is necessary to be clear and to make clear distinctions. There are technical instruments and formal systems where unambiguous exactness and precision are a virtue. The lack of virtue is to think that such univocity applies everywhere and to everything, to think that univocity applies univocally to everything. The mistake is to think that such univocity applies to the humanities and the social sciences— although of course even there computer searches not only of ugh of course even there computer searches not only of bibliographies but of the occurrence of words, expressions, etc. are very much in order. It would also be a mistake to think that it applies to the mathematics and the natural sciences at their cutting edge, where theoreticians are breaking new ground when they find themselves faced with paradoxes and aporias that are best met not by method but by imagination. What else is Kuhn's famous account of a scientific crisis if not an account of scientific ambiguity, and what else is a crisis than an opportunity for a revolutionary advance? So the relevant distinction for me is between the formalizable and the non-formalizable. There are things that can be gotten down cold, mastered, reduced to a "method" or "program," so that they can be run with the flick of a switch. There are things that we can calculate, formalize, axiomatize, submit to a methodic procedure that works every time, and there is surely a place for that. When Johannes Climacus distinguished subjective from objective truth, he was not proposing the abolition of the latter, but only that Christianity not be confused with objective truth.

In a similar manner, to the sphere of programmable things I oppose the—in the end—more interesting sphere of things that we cannot formalize or program, master or axiomatize, regularize or normalize, or reduce to a method. It is the latter that concern me here, for it is the latter, I would say, that belong to the avant garde of our beliefs and practices, to the cutting edge of the things to be made or done or known. It is only with the latter more ambiguous things that we reach the point where the gears of our minds are fully engaged. When we hit the point of the unprecedented, the point where we have no guides or guard rails to make safe the way, then we are on our own and must fall back upon the raw resources of raw intelligence. But by the time our beliefs and practices have become crystal clear and precedents point the way, they are more or less spent, worn out, tired, exhausted, on the downward trend in their life cycle. The things that have a future are ambiguous just because we haven't figured them out yet, and their competing possibilities keep the future open. They are ambiguous because they are replete with possibility, tossed and turned about by multiple potentialities, capable of going in many directions at once. When I have to make a first cut into something that I have not encountered before, when I have to think something I have never thought before, or say something I have never said before, or do something that I have never done before, then I am thinking, speaking and acting in a manner worthy of those very worthy names. Otherwise, I am cruising on automatic pilot, half asleep at the wheel.

On my accounting, clarity and ambiguity should not be viewed as simple logical opposites on a timeless spectrum but different stages in the process of making meaning, of producing meaning as an effect. Clarity is a late product, something that emerges at dusk, at the end of the process, when a belief or practice has more or less run its course and has acquired a kind of distilled, stable, settled, literal sense. Then we can write its history, analyze it, formalize it. The ancients said, call no man happy until he is dead; I would say, call no idea clear until it is dead. It has been passed along so long and so easily, is so readily reduced to a formula, that it has been rubbed thin and lost its future. Ambiguity on the other hand belongs to an earlier matinal stage, to a deeper stratum of meaning, where meaning is sending up its first shoots, where things have an irreducible richness that cannot be definitively laid out or decisively nailed down, finally settled or straightened out. Ambiguity is ambi-valent, that is, bristling with multiple values, indeed poly-valent, alive with possibilities that cannot be neatly ordered or contained.

The Ambit of Ambiguity

As a final effort in my uphill battle to make a case for ambiguity, I wish to explore something of the ambit of ambiguity, to investigate something of the varieties of ambiguous experience. To this end, I will take up four revealing cases—the work of translation, the case of avant-garde art, the act of ethical judgment, and the movement of religious faith. Each of these examples reveals a different kind of ambiguity which I hope here to tabulate and elaborate: the ambiguity of the text, the ambiguity of the first or innovative, the ambiguity of the concrete and finally what I will call essential ambiguity.

(1) *Translation and the Ambiguity of the Text.* The late German philosopher Hans-Georg Gadamer, the author of the twentieth century's most important theory of "hermeneutics," says of the process of translation in his magnum opus *Truth and Method* that one of the most important differences between a text in the original language and a translation is that the translation "is at once clearer and flatter than the original" while the original is richer but more ambiguous than the translation.[7] That is because the translator has been forced to decide, to narrow down and determine, to resolve the ambiguity of the original, to translate a word that is astir with multiple associations and connotations with a word that chooses but one association. The translator inevitably emphasizes something that is important to him or herself and downplays other things. The translator must "show his colors" and state clearly how he or she understands something that in the original can be understood in several ways. The translation has thinned out the original and produced a leaner, cleaner, clearer text, while the original retains a dark depth of suggestiveness that inspires multiple translations. That is why texts that Gadamer calls "classics," texts that are great enough, deep enough, *rich* enough to outlive their original context and find a new life in ever-changing times, have to be translated again and again. Classic texts are constituted not by their utter tranquility and harmony, but by their polyphony, by their tensions, equivocations and inconsistencies, by the overrich and overflowing lines of force that compete with each other and keep the text in motion over the ages. We never get to the bottom of what the classics mean, even as they never exhaust what they mean in any one context. That is the gift of tradition, which means to give over (*trans-dare*).

Now it is important to see that for Gadamer translation is not an isolated exercise but illustrative of the general structure of hermeneutics itself, that is, of the structure of reading and consequently of hermeneutic understanding generally, which always means bringing something within the horizon of the reader. To read is to interpret; o interpret is to apply, and to apply is to translate something into the situation of the reader, to appropriate a text and bring it within the horizon of the reader's understanding. What then is a "text?" The text for Gadamer is not a fixed and determinate actuality but a "potentiality," something that is astir with possibilities that are "actualized" only on the occasion of the reading. The best example of a "text" in this sense is a musical score, which is a potentiality that is actualized only in the performance. To read is perform, to actualize, to translate a text that is multivocal, able to be given reality in several ways. As such, as a potentiality, the text is marked by a creative ambiguity, by polyvalent possibilities, which is why a classic text always has a future, and why a text does not so much have a fixed meaning as it has an unfolding history.[8]

(2) *Avant-garde Art and the Ambiguity of the First.* Let us turn now to Lyotard's account of the case of avant-garde art. What makes such art "avant-garde" is precisely what we object to in it, viz., the perplexity--the ambiguity--that it produces, which is such that it leaves the observer wondering whether such a thing is art at all. For Lyotard, the defining and paradigmatic reaction to avant-garde art is that the observer is brought to the point where one is forced to ask, "but is it art?" That is not an objection against avant-garde art or rather that objection is the very thing that constitutes avant-garde art. If anything less happens, if we are not led to object, then it is not avant garde, but part of the rank and file, that is, part of an already constituted style or genre to which we have no objections. The reason for this is that the work is of such novelty that standards of interpretation have not yet been formed. There are no criteria to recognize it either as such and such a kind, or to judge it as a good or bad specimen of its kind. None of that has been produced yet. When once it has, which means, when once a community of judgment has been formed, then artistic judgment becomes a matter of the more or less skillful application of these standards--is this is a good example of expressionism, of a dramatic dénouement, of a classical tragedy, of a modern musical comedy? If a new and hitherto unknown libretto of a Gilbert and Sullivan operetta were discovered, the question would be whether this is a good specimen of the kind, because the kind is well established; that would require a

judgment by those whose taste has been formed by experience with the form. The question provoked by avant-garde art is, as Lyotard puts it, whether a given work of art represents a new move in an old game or the invention of a new game altogether.[9]

Now what is instructive and illustrative to us about this example is that it goes without saying that there is no way to decide in advance whether the piece before us represents a bizarre oddity with no future or a breakthrough to a new level and kind of artistic expression, one that will be imitated and, by being imitated, established as a new style. There are no established rules or criteria to decide that, because rules and criteria are things that are applied within paradigms or genres, whereas the creation of new paradigms or new genres is unformalizable. If the new work is successful, the piece in question is going to establish the rules by which things of its sort are to be judged, but there are no rules to determine what sorts of works will create new paradigms and allow communities of judgment to be formed. But that is not to be taken as a fault or a lack. The ambiguity of the first appearance of the work goes to the essence of *the ambiguity of the first*. Let us say more generally, the ambiguity of the innovation, of what is "first" or "new" or novel, constitutes the first in a positive way; it is an essential feature of the very idea of a breakthrough to something new, not an accidental defect to be removed in a better world. This indeterminability or unregulability—that is, this ambiguity—is so much a defining feature of the first, so much the mark of everything original, innovative or novel, that were we to remove all ambiguity, we would destroy the possibility of original creation.

(3) *Ethics and the Ambiguity of the Concrete*. By the same token, ambiguity goes to the heart of ethical judgment. That is so true that the title of Simone de Beauvoir's book *An Ethics of Ambiguity* from years ago seems to me to pose not a paradox or aporia but a paradigm of good ethical sense, almost a truism. Aristotle recognized this long ago. On the opening pages of the first and, in my opinion, greatest of all the ethics books that have ever been written, Aristotle cautioned us not to look for too much certainty; if it is certainty we are in search of, we should take up mathematics instead, not ethics. That is because ethical judgments

are made in the concrete and the concrete ethical situation is always slightly unprecedented, and oftentimes not just slightly. In ethics, Aristotle said, we can offer the reader only general "schemata," more or less loose fitting paradigms that must be kept essentially vague in order to preserve their flexibility. Ethics can only tell us in a general way about courage, e.g., that in general courage lies in a middle state between cowardliness and rashness. Courage does not consist either in running away from dangers that we should stand and face or in rushing headlong into hopelessly dangerous situations in which there is no chance that we will achieve our goals and every likelihood that we will be destroyed. Yes, yes, we reply impatiently to Aristotle, but precisely what is that middle state? For that, the Philosopher patiently replies, you need a practiced eye, one that has been schooled in sizing up the complexities of the concrete situation and has learned how to make a concrete judgment. But you are being very ambiguous, we complain to the Philosopher. Precisely, the Philosopher would reply. He is being precisely ambiguous or ambiguously precise, for the precision is introduced in the practical application. The virtue of making such practiced practical judgments is what Aristotle called *phronesis* by which he meant, for our present purposes, the power to cope with the shifting sands of practical circumstances, the power to deal with the ambiguity of the concrete.

Aristotle was a superbly sensible philosopher who had the remarkably good sense to see that there was a place for everything, to sort out both a place for *theoria* or *episteme* when it came to unchanging and necessary things, and a place for practical know how when it came to changing and variable things, things that could be otherwise, which is what we mean by the concrete situation. Aristotle had a sharp eye for the hermeneutics of singularity, for the hermeneutics of the concrete, and he had the good sense to know that the concrete situation is always slightly different and a not a little ambiguous.

What we call "postmodernism," if it means anything anymore (which is not certain), means among many other things, an irreducible pluralism, a kind of endless contest of competing paradigms, worldviews, and "incommensurable" differences.

Understood in that way, postmodernism would represent a kind of intensification or radicalization of this Aristotelian point about the concrete or what we today call "singularity." What is "classical" about Aristotle and not postmodern, is that he thought the general schema or paradigm was settled and in place, that we don't choose it but it chooses us, that we are born into it by being born in a particular *polis*, and so the trick to growing up in your culture, in your *polis*, is to get practiced in its vagaries and variable applications. But the more postmodern view, which is more cosmo-politan and multi-politan, would insist not only on the ambiguous *applicability* of the paradigm but on the ambiguity that besets the paradigm *itself*. Aristotle thought there was a more or less identifiable *phronimos*, a prudent man, and that the difficulty lies in learning to imitate him. But the postmoderns locate the difficulty back a step, in coping with irreducible plurality of competing and incommensurable paradigms. For there are a lot of different prudent men, and quite a few prudent women, too, and more than one *polis* to consider which we meet everyday in the media or over the Internet, and so we need a kind of "meta-phronesis" about just what to take as paradigmatic, if indeed there is one at all.[10]

I might add that this idea of postmodern polyvalence would be grossly misused if it were used to stoke the fires of violence by allowing us to dig and balkanize our differences—which is what its critics charge it does. For the whole idea is to provide the key to non-violence. Here is where the idea of ambiguity plays a vital role. We are witness today, and to our regret, to an ancient but it seems almost unlearnable lesson: that ethical and political action is never more dangerous—to oneself no less than to others—than when it is carried out *without* ambiguity. By this I mean an ethics without a sense of self-questioning, without a sense of the multiplicity of ethical perspectives, without a sense that right and wrong, good and evil, are not univocal terms. If we maintain a heightened and salutary sense of ambiguity, we will not dig in about our differences and make them the basis of war, but concede the ambiguity of our respective situations. For ambiguity instructs us that there are many ways to lead the good life, which should make us wary of enforcing our own ideas, which is after all just one idea. The ethics of ambiguity thereby takes an interesting turn and so takes on an additional sense: from the ambiguity of the ethical situation to the ethics of ambiguity. That is, not only is there is something irreducibly ambiguous about ethical judgments—they vary with the variable—but there is an ethical quality in ambiguity, something irreducibly ethical about respecting ambiguity, which respects variation.

(4) *Religious Faith and Essential Ambiguity.* That brings me to my last and final example of ambiguity, the movement of religious faith and what I will call the essential ambiguity of the human situation. In the view that I am defending here, someone who confesses or professes a religious faith is also at the same time confessing to the essential enigma of the human condition; one has faith just because one does not know. To say *credo*, I believe, to confess one's faith, is at the same time to confess to the multiplicity of voices within what we call, by a kind of shorthand, the "self." On this view, the self is made up of multiple selves, of several voices within the same self, at least one of whom—in the case of religious belief—is a firm believer and the other is an ornery disbeliever. What we call the self is like the chairperson of a committee who gets to write up and put his own slant on the committee report, thereby concealing how much dissension there is back on the committee. When I confess, when I say "I believe," I am not quite confessing the whole truth, not quite acknowledging that the "I" is a just a bit of a fiction, a kind of cover for an unruly committee, a condensation of a multiplicity of voices, so that the voice of belief is inwardly disturbed by multiple voices of unbelief that also stir within me and want to make themselves heard. In the end, "univocity" is a fiction, the acoustical illusion of having only one voice; it pretends to speak with one voice, *una voce*, while in fact a keen listener can pick up muffled voices in the background.

To be sure, the multivocity to which I expect the believer to confess is no less a problem for the unbeliever. I think that a truly honest and non-dogmatic expression of disbelief in God would always need to confess that it is haunted from within by competing voices, by a inextinguishable anxiety that one is closing oneself off to another voice, to something deep and important. If the truth be told, one does not know and cannot say if one *is* a believer or a non-believer. That is why Derrida says of himself "I quite rightly pass for an atheist," instead of simply saying "I *am* an atheist."[11] Derrida understands the multiplicity within the subject which makes the subject a kind of corporation or committee or debating society. But as we have seen when Derrida speaks of "undecidability," he does not mean indecision, which makes life easy by sparing us the onerous task of deciding. Undecidability describes the conditions in which the difficulty of a true decision is made and has to be continually remade by being continually exposed to its opposite. In undecidability, the passion of our lives is forged. That is also why Johannes Climacus would never lay claim to *be* a Christian, but to be at most on the way to *becoming* one, which means that he would always confess to a kind of ambiguity about whether or not he is a Christian. "Rightly passing" for this or that is it seems to me the most one can ask for in this ambiguous life of ours.

Once again, this same law of reversibility that sets in when we considered the ethical—that the ambiguity of ethics reveals the ethical quality of ambiguity—is repeated here. For not only must we attach an irreducibly ambiguous character to any religious belief, in order to preserve the diversity and variability of the expression of religious life, the multiplicity of religious paths, the plurivocity of being-religious, but we should also see the essentially religious quality of ambiguity itself, and it is on that point that I wish to conclude. For as Jacques Derrida likes to say, with a devilish gleam in his eye, we do not know the secret. By the secret he does not mean the relative secrets that lawyers learn from their clients, or physicians from their patients, or that priests learn in the confessional, or that the government keeps as classified information, all of which could in principle be revealed under the proper circumstances. We have laws to protect such secrets just because it is entirely possible to reveal them. What Derrida means has to do with what he calls the "absolute secret" that no one could reveal to anyone because it is not known by anyone.[12] He means that we do not know who we are, that our lives are caught up in an irreducible unknowability, and that this unknowability goes to the heart of our human condition.

Derrida is touching upon the deepest ambiguity of all, what I am calling here "essential ambiguity," by which I mean the ambiguity that goes to the heart of the human condition, that envelops what theologian Paul Tillich liked to call matters of ultimate concern, which are also matters of ultimate passion. When St. Augustine asked in his *Confessions, "quid ergo amo cum deum meum amo?,"* "what do I love when I love my God?" (*Confessions*, X, 6-7) that is a question that we lovers of ambiguity take to heart. If by God, we mean the profoundly ambiguous object of our desire, the indeterminable object of our *cor inquietum*, that which provokes the essential restlessness of the human condition, then that is a question that we all can and should ask ourselves all the time. If the truth be told, our lives are shrouded by this most essential and irreducible ambiguity, the essential secret that there is no secret truth, no truth of truth that will show us the way or lift us like a hook out of the flux.

The essential ambiguity of the secret is disquieting and disconcerting, provoking and provocative, but it is a productive unrest and a positive provocation. For the secret is what impassions us, provoking our interpretations, multiplying our translations, our readings, our narratives, our stories. This essential secret is not simply one more ambiguity in the list of four ambiguities that we have been enumerating, but the one that underlies and in part explains the endless translatability of the text, the restlessness of avant-garde art, and the shifting sands of ethical situations. Rightly understood, the secret by which we are all held captive should fill us with compassion for one another, with a sense that we are all fellow travelers in this darkness, siblings of the same dark night. It is this essential secret that injects an irreducible ambiguity into things, into our relationships with one another, into our relationship with God. It is this essential secret that makes it impossible to resolve things into clear and simple essences, as if there were or could be maps or guard rails when it comes to matters of ultimate concern.

Ambiguity is a gift. It is not a fog that settles over things and blurs our vision but a veil that preserves the essential mystery of our existence, that insures that life will not wither under the harsh light of the program or the rule, insuring that life will be an endless provocation, an infinite passion.

Our lives are deeply, disquietingly, dangerously ambiguous, which is why life is what Levinas calls a "beautiful risk" (*beau risque*).[13]   Ambiguity is a gift that gives our lives ambit and ambiance, open-endedness and possibility, danger and riskiness, passion and compassion. The woods of ambiguity are lovely, dark and deep, and we have promises to keep—to the substance of the earth, to the flesh of one another, to the body of God—and who knows when we will ever get to sleep.

Tragic Ambiguity in the *Oedipus Tyrannos*

Robert Guay
Temple University

In a well-known article in the 1872 volume of *Philologus* called "*Der doppelsinn in Sophokles Oedipus könig*,"[1] Arnold Hug iterates the by-then already familiar point that Sophocles' *Oedipus Tyrannos* is exceptional in both the abundance and the type of the ambiguities that it employs. The language of the play, notes Hug, is shot through with double-meanings, and in almost every case only one meaning is accessible to the speaker. In comedies the speaker is often unaware of the full import of his own words, but where ambiguity occurs in tragedies, it is usually a tool of conscious deception. The *Oedipus Tyrannos*, however, is rife with what has come to be called "Sophocles' Tragic Irony:"[2] there are distinct meanings available to the audience that are indiscernible from *inside* the play.[3] Hug offers a catalog of fifty-three instances in which the language of the *Oedipus Tyrannos* forks off in multiple directions, including thirty-eight examples of Sophocles' distinctive brand of ambiguity. We should be grateful for the scholarship that identifies and classifies these features of the play. But such a catalog of the ambiguities in a single play provokes two questions. If there are fifty-three instances in which the language of the play is ambiguous, is the rest of the play completely *eindeutig* or so hopelessly polysemous as to defy analysis? And what is the significance–or what is the point–of such an extraordinary use of language?

In this paper I hope to answer these questions, first by discussing examples of ambiguity that are not mentioned by Hug or, to my knowledge, by anyone else, and then by offering an explanation of what import ambiguity itself has within the *Oedipus Tyrannos*. I shall claim that the play's ambiguity is in no way extraneous to its meaning; on the contrary, ambiguity has a function central to the action of the play, and indeed central to tragedy itself. Ambiguity conveys an understanding of human agency and self-knowledge that is presented in terms of Sophoclean religion, but does not depend on it. In particular, what tragic ambiguity portends is that there is no ground of human agency beyond human experience, but this very ungroundedness, together with the dangers it provokes, can itself constitute a basis for self-affirmation.

Ambiguity

In the *Oedipus Tyrannos*, Oedipus often fails to grasp the multiplicity of his own words. Line 132 is a typical example, identified by the scholiast as having a double meaning:[4]

$$\text{ἀλλ' ἐξ ὑπαρχῆς αὖθις αὔτ' ἐγὼ φανῶ.}[5]$$

Oedipus has just asked the chorus why Laius' murder was not investigated immediately after its occurrence. The chorus pleads that the Sphinx distracted them, to which Oedipus, in line 132 as rendered by Lloyd-Jones, replies:

Well, I shall begin again, and light up the obscurity.

But the verb here, *phanô*, has an alternative absolute meaning: it may be not only "light up the obscurity," but also "shine forth."[6] By the very words that Oedipus uses to assure his subjects that he will solve the crime, Oedipus is thus saying two things:

> Starting back at the beginning [Laius' murder], I shall reveal [who
> the murderer is].
> Starting back at the beginning [my birth], I shall shine forth [as the
> murderer].

I am not suggesting the Lloyd-Jones translation, or any of the similar ones, is incorrect; not only is his rendering a lucid and available one, it is *the* correct one. The alternative meaning makes no sense within the dramatic context: Oedipus can hardly be confessing in line 132. And yet the other meaning is not only available, but it is also *true*. The context decisively favors the expression of confidence, but at the same time it suggests the unknowing confession, which, according to Vernant, has "the ring of a sinister burst of laughter."[7]

Hug offers this interpretation for the remarkable frequency of this sort of ambiguity:

> The Athenian audience seems to have as much as demanded this kind of witty talk . . . from the poet: it wanted to be informed, through etymological interpretations and reinterpretations, about the richness of its language . . . they also wanted their poets, even those of the most serious tragedies, to make use of this newly acquired etymological-grammatical knowledge in order to provide the listening audience with puzzles, which would enable the cleverest among them to guess the course of events in advance.[8]

But one might suspect that this interpretation, coming from a philologist, reveals occupational bias. And not only is such a supposition about the audience dubious, it also takes the ambiguity as accidental: one could eliminate it without affecting any other element of the play, or one could perhaps add it to, say, a Neil Simon play, without incongruity. This interpretation provokes the other, less amicable philologists' assessment of the ambiguity, which perhaps arises from the vocational demand for clarity and determinacy: the ambiguity is "superimposed quite artificially by the author,"[9] it "overthrows the illusion of the play as a real happening,"[10] and it "easily degenerates into a play with words and meaning."[11]

Sophocles' use of ambiguity is certainly deliberate; he even calls attention to it at line 439, when Oedipus exclaims to Teiresias, "How riddling and obscure in excess are all your words!" But such a line as this indicates why the ambiguity should not be taken as ornamental. The meaning of words and signs is itself a central issue of the play, and ambiguity is one presentation of its status. The story of Oedipus presents us with oracles, signs, riddles, clues, rumors, eyewitness accounts, and old wounds, and the action of the play turns on nothing more spectacular than how these are interpreted. And as Charles Segal has pointed out, "Sophocles makes the ambiguity of language impinge inescapably on the ambiguity of personal identity."[12] Oedipus himself is ambiguous, and his ambiguous language is an expression of this. The very name "*Oedipus Tyrannos*" can illustrate this. *Oidipous* suggests both "swollen-foot," alluding to his origin, and "knowing-foot," alluding to his intellectual powers and the answer to the Sphinx's riddle. As the solver of that riddle and the natural heir to the throne, Oedipus both is and is not a *tyrannos*;[13] so here language, as exemplified in the *tyrannos/basileus* dichotomy, fails to capture Oedipus' own multiplicity. Linguistic ambiguity is thus integral to the strangeness of Oedipus, whose mother does not name him until lines 1071f. When Jocasta says, "Ah, ah, unhappy one! That is all that I can say to you . . . ," she uses a word, *proseipein*, that also means "to name;" until identified here as *dustênos*, Oedipus is subject to a name that points to his history and his fate.

So the contemporary interpretation of Sophocles' ambiguity is to see it not as superficial and contrived but as integral to the tragic meaning of the play. In particular, the ambiguity of Oedipus' words shows that "there may be meaning opaque to human understanding":[14] the unconscious double meaningfulness of Oedipus' words shows the operation of powers not subject to human manipulation, powers which Oedipus had failed to acknowledge. Oedipus' fate shows that mundane human agency is entangled with an inscrutable but meaningful realm of powers. Linguistic ambiguity thus conveys a tragic message about the ambiguity of human existence.[15]

But what is the tragic message? Since an article by Eric Dodds,[16] interpreters have been reluctant to say that Oedipus should have acted otherwise, that he is to blame for his lot because of some lack of prudence, foresight, or virtue. Indeed, there is something ludicrously untragic about the idea that one's fate is avoidable, that marginal improvements in judiciousness might eliminate suffering, or that one gets what one deserves. But it has nevertheless been tempting to draw a lesson[17] from Oedipus' failure to recognize ambiguity. Although his case was hopeless, his ambiguity shows that he should have been more sensitive to the plurality of diverse values and viewpoints, and keener to forestall conflict among them,[18] or less confident in the efficacy of his own agency, or more humble in the face of his own wretched finitude,[19] or he should simply not take things so seriously.[20] So in a prominent strand of contemporary interpretation, ambiguity is what shows that one should be more like the chorus, like Creon, like Jocasta, or like Teiresias.

Platonic Ambiguity

One way of understanding the ambiguity of the *Oedipus Tyrannos*, then, is that it presents the depths of that which one must reconcile oneself to in order to achieve a kind of painful enlightenment. This is one meaning that ambiguity could have, but not the only one; another example will help to give a sense of the range of meanings of ambiguity itself. In Book V of *The Republic*, Socrates is questioned about the things of the sensible world, which always participate in both opposites, and about which one opines rather than knows. The question is whether such things are any more what someone says they are than the negation thereof, and Socrates answers,

> No, they are like the ambiguities one is entertained with at dinner parties ... for they are ambiguous, and one cannot understand them as fixedly being or fixedly not being or as both or as neither.[21]

Here the semantic property of ambiguity manifests itself in the world of things. This world is not empty or featureless;[22] rather, it is richly suggestive in divergent ways. The ambiguity of the sensory world is accordingly a kind of contradiction, and so a kind of falsehood. But whereas in language ambiguity results only in self-negation, the world of the substantial kind of ambiguity is permeated with self-destruction: its opposites result in conflict and ruin. Ambiguity is an irreality that menaces us despite its non-being.

The ambiguous character of the sensible world indicates its insignificance *per se*. Ambiguity is a defect and a danger. But even though ambiguity presents meaningfulness in a contradictory way that it is presented at all points to a completely adequate, if unattainable meaningfulness. So the point of Socratic ambiguity, at least in the *Republic*, is to show the defectiveness of a set of values, but also to suggest a solution. On the one hand, ambiguity, through its involvement with transience, appearance, and multiplicity, reveals itself as a kind of corruption. But on the other hand, ambiguity, as corruption, suggests that there is a getting-to-the-bottom-of-things behind the shadow realm of appearances, and that this ground offers stability and security.

teleô and luô

Ambiguity is itself meaningful. What I hope to show below is that the possible meanings mentioned above are not suited to the tragic ambiguity of the *Oedipus Tyrannos*, and that lines 316–7 are the key to understanding this. Lines 316–7, Teiresias' first words of the play, read as follows:

φεῦ φεῦ, φρονεῖν ὡς δεινὸν ἔνθα μὴ τέλη λύῃ φρονοῦντι.

The construction is confusing enough to merit a gloss in every commentary, but a consensus has been built around a reading such as this one:

Alas, alas, how dreadful it is to know when the knowledge does
not benefit the knower.

Teiresias, coming into the presence of Oedipus, thus laments his own condition of useless awareness. Such a strong consensus is compatible with a multiplicity of meaning, however. Words such as *phronein* ("to know") and *deinon* ("dreadful") are always difficult to render, but the *telê-luêi* construction, meaning "benefit," is more intriguing here. There is a common verb, *lusitelein*, that means "to benefit," but the construction that Sophocles uses is not equivalent to *lusitelein* anywhere in extant Greek but here.[23] Kamerbeek speculates that this is "perhaps a reconstruction to be ascribed to Soph. [sic] himself, *in that case a correct one.*"[24]

Whether or not Sophocles has the power to determine correctness, there is no doubt that this is the correct rendering of *telê luêi*: it stands in for *lusitelei*, which means "benefit." Among other considerations, no other reading makes sense in Teiresias' mouth. But a unique, slightly awkward construction merits some attention. "*luô*," the verb, which Sophocles used to mean "benefit," "profit," "solve," and "fulfill," originally meant "loosen" or "dissolve," and therefore also, "undo," "destroy," "annul," or even "refute." "*telos*," the noun, fundamentally carries a meaning similar to that of the ambiguous English word "end:" both "completion" or "finish" and also "goal." The *telos* of human life is accordingly *happiness* in one sense, and *death* in the other; this ambiguity is commonly exploited, for example in the idea of *Zeus teleios*, who both fulfills wishes and brings death.[25] The two basic ambiguities in the phrase *telê-luêi* thus combine to form the following tetrad:

1. How dreadful to know when the knowledge does not destroy death for the knower.
2. How dreadful to know when the knowledge does not destroy ends for the knower.
3. How dreadful to know when the knowledge does not fulfill death for the knower.
4. How dreadful to know when the knowledge does not fulfill ends for the knower.

Sophocles' idiom renders something like #2 the natural one: that is what Teiresias is saying. But the words convey the other meanings at the same time, and indeed, the copresence of these other meanings haunt the rest of the play.

Teiresias to Oedipus

Teiresias speaks these words bemoaning his own misfortune, but he expresses this lament in a universal form, as if invoking a proverbial truth with which we could all empathize. Perhaps none of us can identify with Teiresias' condition, but the universal form does suggest a message that stands independently of Teiresias' circumstances. The tetrad is particularly relevant to Oedipus, the "knowing foot." To know is dreadful if it does not release the knower from death: knowledge carries a cost that does not fall upon immortals but turns out to weigh heavily on Oedipus. To know is dreadful if it does not dissolve one's ends. Teiresias tells Oedipus, concerning the solving of the Sphinx's riddle, "But it is that very happening that has been your ruin"(442); the fulfillment of Oedipus' ends is precisely what leads to his destruction. To know is dreadful if it does not fulfill death: after learning his fate, Oedipus curses the shepherd who, "saved me from death . . . doing me no kindness"(1350-2), and the chorus insists, "better dead than living"(1368). To know is dreadful if it does not fulfill ends. Oedipus sees knowledge as instrumental: it evades prophecies, lifts plagues, solves crimes, and in general fixes problems.[26] So when Jocasta implores him not to know, pleading, "I am telling you what is best for you"(1066), he fails to understand.

Oedipus to Tragedy

So not only do Oedipus' own words reveal his fate at the same time as they express his hopes, others' words also draw from the same semantic reserve: the language of the play in general expresses the duality which both supports and undermines Oedipus' agency and his capacity for knowledge. And as the chorus indicates when it refers to Oedipus as its *"paradeigma"*(1193), this is not only Oedipus' particular condition, but tragic conditionality in general. The tetrad, that is, does not only belong to Teiresias or Oedipus, but to tragedy as such. The tragic tetrad invokes the dread that arises from knowledge that belongs properly to the gods, that occupies a perspective from which human achievement is nugatory, that is painful and ineffaceable, and that is completely distinct from instrumental or craft knowledge. What the tetrad conveys is that tragic conditionality, although seemingly determinate and superable, is in fact so all-encompassing that even Oedipus, by nature the greatest solver of riddles (440), could find no way out.

To know is dreadful when it does not destroy death. Knowledge is something that belongs properly to the immortals; Oedipus could truthfully refer to himself as "unseeing, unknowing"(1484) since mortals at best scrape together bits of history and nature to figure anything out. But tragedy is a story of tyranny: we usurp the gods' sphere of power and partake in divine values even though it is perilous to do so. Part of the peril is willful retaliation. Oedipus' knowing nature puts him at adds with Apollo, who, Teiresias says, "has it in mind to bring [Oedipus' fate] about"(377); elsewhere Oedipus attributes his lot to Zeus (738) or some cruel *daimôn* (828). But the tragic dread stems more generally from the mere aspiration: to be knowing animals who engage in divine pursuits, even though susceptible to being destroyed, and even though we are thereby *made* more susceptible to being destroyed. Knowledge opens us up to doomed attempts to escape our condition and standards of success and failure that we could otherwise ignore.[27]

To know is dreadful when it does not destroy ends. One could, at least in principle, adopt a perspective from which one looks down upon the world in purely theoretical contemplation but never engages in action. From within such a perspective, one is secure from the sort of reversal in which one's very achievements become one's downfall. By becoming involved in the world's affairs and setting ends for oneself, one makes oneself susceptible to the upending of one's endeavors. The danger is not that one fails; mere failure is commonplace and banal. The danger is realizing just the ends that one set, but then to discover that they are empty or, worst of all, have a meaning opposite to the one anticipated. As minimal as our control over the course of events is, our control over the meaning of events is even less. So wherever self-awareness accompanies wanting to achieve something in the world, this is bound to provoke dread.

To know is dreadful when it does not fulfill death. At 1187f, the chorus sings, "Ah, generations of men, how equal to nothingness I estimate your life to be."[28] Such a lesson does not come painlessly, but only with the demonstration that human purposes are vain, human values are groundless, and human lives are insubstantial. And in the face of this recognition, even death is insufficient; what is needed is never to have existed at all.[29] Drawing a terminus to suffering does not eliminate past suffering. The past endures, even if as nothing more substantial than deathless memory. This was indeed the case with Oedipus:

> Alas, alas once more! How the sting of these goads has sunk into me, together with the remembrance of my troubles. (1316ff)

The chorus reacts by exclaiming:

> doubly lament and doubly cry out . . . (1319)

This is one meaning of ambiguity: the double-power of events, to sting us and to sting us once more, from both the goad of misfortune and the goad of memory.

To know is dreadful when it does not fulfill ends. Before the play began, Oedipus was "seen to be wise and approved as dear to the city [*hêdupolis*]"(509f). But this wisdom that pleases the city comes to be replaced by another, completely different kind of wisdom; in the words of the chorus, "A man may surpass one kind of wisdom by means of another"(502f).[30] This contrast between two different kinds of wisdom parallels the contrast between the plague that initiates the story and that of the *Iliad*. Oedipus begins by taking his plague for the latter type. The plague in the *Iliad* is a single incident in a long history. It stems out of an earlier conflict between individuals, which generates a particular grievance. Apollo, in consideration of past favors, intercedes to resolve the grievance by inflicting a harm that will only be lifted upon payment of an appropriate compensation. So there is a problem to be fixed which requires a resolute course of action, and a solution is available. In the *Oedipus Tyrannos*, by contrast, Oedipus, because of completely inscrutable purposes and causes is *himself* a violation of nature so profound that all of existence must strike back without the possibility of any solution or any recourse. The dread of this plague exhausts the power of language and the power of sight: Oedipus' condition is "something terrible [*deinon*], not to be heard or looked upon"(1312). No counsels of prudence could possibly be available here. But there may nevertheless be a wisdom here, one perhaps necessary for living in such a condition.

Hope and Enactment

The ambiguity of the *Oedipus Tyrannos* provokes the question: why bother to proceed in the face of such dread as the tetrad delineates? The question is itself meaningful on several levels. From inside the play, one can wonder, among other things, why fate and the gods conspire against Oedipus as they seem to, why the shepherd who pinned Oedipus to the mountain releases him, and why suicide is not the appropriate response to the oracle, let alone to the final recognition. On the level of the drama, one can wonder why anyone bothers to perform the play, when the conclusion is already established and known. And on a philosophical level, one can wonder why one should bother to live with such a risk. These are distinct questions, but they are all related to at least this extent: Platonic ambiguity and the complex of ideas surrounding it cannot possibly offer a response. If ambiguity manifests a dangerous, if suggestive, irreality, then the characters are at best deluded, the enactment is a waste of time, and life itself is a mistake; one should occupy oneself with something better, or not bother at all. But such a standpoint would seem to have the burden of explaining the persistence of tragic enactments.

The easiest answer is that such an enactment leads outside of itself, to the learning of a lesson that shows that the enactment itself was worthless. The typical lessons from the *Oedipus Tyrannos* are: manage your anger, be nice to strangers, stay away from older women, kill the baby when someone tells you to, if you want a baby killed right, then do it yourself, believe in oracles, do not believe in oracles. These are ridiculous for various reasons, but

Oedipus himself, in one context, completely forecloses any such explanation. After having blinded himself, Oedipus admonishes the chorus:

> Do not try to show me that what was done was not done for the best, and give me no more counsel! (1369f)

Presumably Oedipus' claim is not that his actions were in fact for the best, but that it would be somehow pointless for the chorus to criticize them retrospectively. Oedipus closes off any counterfactual question of failed prudence; there is no general lesson to be learned, even from the suffering, even with the self-infliction of more suffering. The trajectory of Oedipus' hope runs from the confidence that he can make everything all right to the agonized conviction that even though everything done has made things worse, it is nevertheless worthwhile to proceed. But the hope endures.

Making Meaning

This hope is unreasonable. It cannot be redeemed or substantiated in any way; like the track of the killer, it is therefore *dustekmarton* (109), difficult to grasp. The first stasimon, however, like the parodos, a song about hope, provides some information: the chorus declares, "I fly on the wings of hope, seeing neither the present nor the future"(487f). Rather than falling within the scope of usual justification, hope is a propulsion supplied by animal motion; hope lets one coast when other things are more urgent than justification. An example of this comes earlier in the first stasimon:

> . . . all were to follow the track (*ichneuein*) of the mysterious man.
> (475f)

The verb here, *ichneuein*, is something that one usually does to animals[31]: to follow its *ichnê*, footprints or spoors, and so to hunt it down. The insistence here is that the human is animal, and just as Oedipus was propelled by Laius' "double-pointed goad"(809), what propels the hunted away from capture is something beyond justification. The double-pointed goad, further, possesses a tragic aspect in this case: the hunted is also the hunter. We are the animals that hunt ourselves down, that propel ourselves forward, elude ourselves, and sometimes tear ourselves apart. The chorus later observes the cost of this tragic, self-propelled hope:

> The griefs that give most pain are those we bring upon ourselves.
> (1230f)

Our very purposes leave us exposed to sufferings to which other animals are immune.

But to be an animal that pursues itself is no longer to be merely an animal. Thus the question that begins the first stasimon is, "Who . . . is the *telesās*?"(463-6), who is the one who both fulfills and dies, who is capable of bringing things about although ultimately equal to nothing? Although vulnerable, subject to birth and death, Oedipus is godlike before his people. Similarly, any mortal pursuing himself participates in the divine. The tracks that we leave behind are not only animal *ichnê*, but in the play also *semeia* and *sumbola*– meaningful signs. So by making ourselves susceptible to semiotic and symbolic self-pursuits, we make ourselves productive in a way that lets us compete with the gods. We make meanings out of nothing for our animal lives, meanings that subsist even if unreal. The meanings of our lives may be, as the chorus fears, "equal to nothing," but that does not impugn them in any way. Meanings are indifferent to the appearance/reality and animal/god dichotomies. Thus the naïve Oedipus and W.B. Stanford were both wrong. Oedipus, after issuing the curse, nevertheless claims that, "He who is not afraid to do the deed is not frightened by the word"(296). Stanford, implicitly claiming that there is no such thing, postulated a "relic of a superstitious belief in the mystical significance of words"[32] behind Sophocles' ambiguity. But meaning *is* magic. Words and deeds alike have an immense, invisible power to make and unmake human lives.

No One but I

The final ambiguity that this paper presents is line 1415:

For there is no human being who can bear my woes but I.

Dodds's translation emphasizes a common reading of this line: "This horror is mine and none but I is strong enough to bear it."[33] This reading presents us with Oedipus, Supermasochist, whose heroism is ultimately manifest in his amazing ability to endure pain. In the Greek context, one could imagine an *agôn* in which athletes competed to be the best at suffering the worst. But Creon says something strikingly similar to Oedipus' words at the parallel place in the *Antigone*: "This can never be transferred to any other mortal"(1317f). This suggests that what is at stake is less a competition than a claim of individuation: this is *my* pain, *I* am the sufferer of this pain. Pain is real from the mere experience of it, and if this pain is mine alone, then I must be real, too. Recall lines 1331f: "And no other hand has struck my eyes, but my own miserable hand." As a bit of exposition, it is superfluous and silly. But as Oedipus' claim about the fundamental integrity of his person, it is more interesting. Oedipus is staking a claim for the ownership of his actions and thereby his self. The example of Oedipus shows that it is possible to withstand *anything* that fate can bring to bear against one and still preserve, undiminished, who one is.

"There is no human being who can bear my woes but I" is therefore a tremendous affront to nothingness. Oedipus thereby claims for himself some space in which one can be both animal and divine, in which suffering is inevitable, but this very suffering confirms the integrity of one's existence. There is nothing good about suffering, and we would all rather avoid it. But it puts a measure on human agency: it shows the limits beyond which no one can will himself, and thereby provides a horizon for our accomplishments. This is illustrated by a pair of metaphors from the second stasimon, the famous "Ode to Fate." There the chorus sings that a vainly overflowing *hubris* finds itself on a precipice where there is no foothold, but they nevertheless pray for the god not to undo (*luô*) the "wrestler's throw"(880) that brought good to the city. The chorus, prone to fear and debilitation, views any attempt to take control of one's condition as a contravention of cosmic order. In taking control, one elevates oneself up to the gods; the danger here, they warn, is reaching such a height only to find that one has no ground to stand on. The risk of leading one's life is that it is all baseless, that nothing supports one's endeavors. All the same, they wish their "wrestler's throw" not to be dissolved. A wrestler's throw translates leverage into force; they wish for human agency to have some basis and therefore be effective. So what even the chorus perceives is this: we cannot be gods, who can stand on the peaks without risk of the abyss. What is substantive for our lives is grounded in the contingencies, however painful, of this existence. Our condition can only be alleviated by living our own earthbound lives. But in order to take charge of this condition, we must be divine.

Conclusion

The chorus despairs, but the meaning of tragic ambiguity, I suggest, is that we can be both earthbound and divine. The rich and multiple meaningfulness that lies beyond Oedipus' volition and even awareness is a condition of his becoming what he is. Some meaningfulness that transcends the individual must be available for the individual to be; without his fate, he would not be Oedipus. At the same time, this reserve of meaning allows actions to be individually significant: in this way, one can take charge of one's condition, despite the workings of fate. These issues have weight whether one's fate is furnished by history, culture, biology, or some *daimôn* who has it out for you. They are not the product of a specifically Sophoclean religion but of tragic conditionality in general: they arise wherever there are the basic existial worries about how the world works and what, if anything, is genuinely worthwhile. Oedipus must confront these issues against a backdrop of pain, but that does not diminish his achievement. The ambiguity in the person of Oedipus itself comes to represent a resolution, a maintaining of the tension between animal and god. Oedipus asks, at line 99, "*tis ho tropos tês xumphorâs;*" roughly translated, "What is the trope of destruction?" The trope of destruction, in this case, is one of highlighting Oedipus' success despite the most profound disaster imaginable. There is nothing humble, nothing chastened, nothing regretful in the person of Oedipus–only an affirmation all the greater for having withstood fate.

Is Socrates a Model? Ambiguity in the *Symposium* of Plato

Marc Stier
Temple University

On the traditional view of the *Symposium,* and other Platonic dialogues, Socrates is the spokesman of Plato. More recently an alternative has attracted a number of important adherents.[1] It holds that Socrates is one voice among many in this dialogue. And Plato's own view is said to be found not just in what Socrates says, but in what some of the other characters in the *Symposium* say and, also, in both the dramatic context in which they say it, and the dramatic context in which it is presented to us by the narrator Apollodorus who, in turn, heard the story of the symposium from Aristodemus.

I will not argue here for this way of reading the works of Plato. That is a topic for another day. Rather, I will try to extend the work of those who have studied the *Symposium* in this light. After all, the ultimate appeal of any hermeneutic strategy is rooted in what it enables us to discover in a text. The best defense of the way of reading I follow is that it enables us to learn something important from a text.

While most of the works that interpret the *Symposium* as a dramatic work break in one way or another from the traditional view of the place of Socrates in the dialogue, they still take the philosophic life described and exemplified by Socrates as the model of human excellence. It is true that some of these interpreters qualify this view to one degree or another. Still, for all their interpretative daring, most contemporary views of the *Symposium* do not step so far away from the traditional picture of Socrates. Most of them still take for granted that Plato holds Socrates up to us as a role model, that is, as someone whose pursuit of the beauty and the good exemplifies the highest and best form of *erotic* life. In this paper I would like to sketch an interpretation of the *Symposium* that calls this view of Socrates into question.

Here is the central claim of my paper: Socrates is not a model for the rest of us because he is one of a kind. Socrates did not come to pursue the good in itself, the good obtainable only by philosophic procreation, by means of climbing what has come to be called the ladder of love described in his speech. The ladder of love is a portrayal of the struggle of human beings who, with some difficulty, move from lower to higher expressions of *eros*. Yet Socrates did not have to make this struggle himself. We, however, do have to make it. And because we do, we are unlike Socrates in that we cannot live wholly in the upper stories of life. At the top of the ladder of love is a way of life largely freed from all lower expressions of *eros*. But this is not a way of life open to us. Indeed, even to aspire to live as Socrates does is potentially dangerous, not just to our lives but to our pursuit of wisdom.

Socrates and Eros

Let me begin by noting some peculiarities of the portrayal of Socrates in the *Symposium*.

First: Socrates had to learn about *eros* from someone else—that is from a woman named Diotima. Though he calls himself an expert in *erotics*, Socrates seems to have gained his expertise not through his own investigation but by being taught by Diotima. Why is that?

Second: Socrates does not have the bodily desires of other human beings. On military campaigns he needs neither food nor shelter. He is not bothered by cold. He can drink without getting drunk. And he can go for long periods of time without sleep.

Third: Though Socrates pretends to have an erotic interest in the young men with whom he spends his time, Socrates is revealed to have little or no such concern. In particular, he is immune to the beauty of Alcibiades.

What is the explanation of these three peculiarities? Plato's answer, I suggest, is that Socrates is fundamentally different from the rest of us. He does not explain how he is different in his speech. But, if we combine ideas that Socrates presents with those of Aristophanes and look, too, at what Alcibiades tells us about Socrates, we may have our answer. We are justified in combining the accounts of Aristophanes and Socrates because Socrates himself brings Aristophanes' ideas into his own telling of the story of *eros*. (Aristophanes, himself notices this immediately after Socrates' speech.) And Alcibiades provides an important corrective to Socrates' story of himself. This, I suggest, is precisely why Socrates objects to Alcibiades' speech. Socrates does not tell us how different he is from others. Indeed, he seems to go far to keep this difference quiet. But, over Socrates' objection, Alcibiades reveals to us Socrates' true nature.

Aristophanes and Eros

Aristophanes teaches us that erotic desire of the kind we are familiar with is the product of a cataclysm in which the gods ripped our bodies in two. We were once a whole composed of four legs and arms and two faces. It is only because we have been split into two that we so frantically search for our other half and when we find that person, or a suitable substitute we clasp them to ourselves as if to reunite forever. And it is only because the gods have turned our genitals around, thereby creating sexual intercourse, that we can temporarily satisfy our desire to merge with our other half and go on to other things.

Yet, while erotic desire in the narrow sense is a product of our mutilation, something akin to *eros* in the larger sense existed before this transformation in our nature. Aristophanes tells us that, before this cataclysm, human beings were powerful creatures. And he says that the gods mutilated us precisely because we challenged them. The nature of the challenge is not made explicit in the text. But if we think about what the gods have and we lack, the answer should be obvious: immortality. The pre-cataclysmic humans sought, as Socrates teaches us we still do today, to possess the good forever.

The consequence of being divided by the gods is that we human beings are drastically weakened. We need to be clear about exactly how we are made weaker by being split in two. The best way to answer that question is to ask another: After we are split why are we so determined to find our other half? There are two, related answers to this question. One I will talk about here, and the other I will examine later in the paper.

The first answer is that we need our other half because of the physical weaknesses of our bodies. Aristophanes gives us a vision of human beings who, in their original form, lead physical lives that are untroubled. Before we were divided, we human beings were powerful creatures with enormous strength and speed. We had physical needs in our original state—although not the need for sex. But those needs were not difficult to satisfy. Now, however, our lives are plagued by bodily needs that, given our weakened state, are difficult to satisfy. And then, too, there are the possibilities of ill health and natural disaster that were undoubtedly of much less concern to human beings before we were mangled by the gods.

So we seek support from other human beings to make up for our physical weakness. But if the first trouble that leads us to seek our other half is physical, why do we seek particular human beings? Why are we so determined to find our other half? We need to pair up to overcome our physical deficiencies. But why are we so choosy about the person with whom we pair up? Why would any other human being not do?

The answer is that the weakness of our bodies leads to tensions—and worse—in the relationship between human beings. The original human beings seemed to have no trouble working together. Indeed, Aristophanes tells us that, by working together, our four-armed and four-legged precursors challenged the gods themselves.

But, after we split apart by the gods, and were drastically weakened, the physical challenge of staying alive and reproducing is so much greater. Goods that were once easy to obtain are so much harder to come by. While once our human powers gave us plenty, now the danger of poverty is ever present. And, as a result, we human beings struggle not just with nature but with one another to satisfy our physical needs. Simply put, we live in a world that does not have enough good things to go around.[2]

Because we are so physically weakened and our situation is so desperate, we need much help from others. Yet given that we are struggling for a limited supply of goods, tensions between human beings are inevitable. And then the question arises who will support us and who we will support? Who can we count on? And who can count on us? These fundamental questions of politics only arise because we are so challenged by the physical debilities that are the product of the gods mangling of us.

And, of course, politics is not the only product of our weakness. Politics is an imperfect solution to the difficulties we face because the polity may demand some of us to sacrifice ourselves for the good of the political community as a whole. Political survival requires military sacrifice. So we look to deeper ties, not to a group, but to particular other people for whom we are of the greatest importance. We look to our families. And, we create our own families. We pair up because life is too hard to face on our own, and because we can't count on the generality of human beings, or even those with whom we share a political life, to care for us as we care for ourselves.

Pairing up, however, is hard to do. For the complete mutuality of interest and concern we seek is difficult to contrive. That is why we look with such desperation for our other half. We are all searching for that one person who we know will care for us as we care for ourselves.

After we are mangled by the gods, we human beings search for other half. But, Aristophanes tells us, once we have found our other half, we want to stay with them forever. This creates a problem, both for human beings and for the gods. Human beings die because we want to do nothing but hug our other half. And, because we die, the gods do not get the sacrifices they so want.

In what I think is the most charming part of *Symposium*, Aristophanes tells us how and why sex was invented. Sex, it turns out, was invented by the gods as a means by which humans can express their connection to each other in such a powerful way that they can then move on to something else, if only for a time. In sex and especially in orgasm, we become one for a time in so powerful a way that we can temporarily separate knowing that we will want to come back together again. (Of course, as Aristophanes might have added, we don't always want to come back together again. That is why sex can be so disappointing when one is with the wrong person.) Sexual desire, on this account is not primarily for the body but for the soul. It is a means by which we use intense physical pleasure to express and/or create a connection to our other half that is so powerful that we can bear to part with him or her for a time.

As Martha Nussbaum has pointed out, the search for our other half is deeply problematic. As she notes, the comic vision in Aristophanes' speech hides a deeper, more tragic vision. Aristophanes encourages us to look at the desperate search for one's other half from the outside. We are not encouraged—or not initially encouraged—to identify with these mutilated creatures. And thus we find their frantic search humorous. For like all comedy, the humor in this situation is only possible if we distance ourselves from the beings depicted by Aristophanes. We have to see our own situation as superior to that of the mutilated human beings. When, however, we recognize that we are those creatures, when we look at them from the inside, when we identify with them, the tragedy of their lives, and our own, is apparent. It is wonderful to find our other half. But Aristophanes' picture of our lives suggests that doing so is difficult if not impossible. So much can go wrong. What are the odds of finding our other half in a world of billions of people? How can we be sure we won't miss them? And what happens to us when our other half dies before us? Finding our other half is only part of the problem. For, the deeper point of the story is that our mutilation has made true union with our other half profoundly impossible. For the true union we seek with our other half is impossible. We can not be joined together physically. And, as the story of Hephaestus welding us together suggests, physical union is not enough. We are separate individuals and are bound to remain so. We always see others, in large part from the outside, not the inside. It is difficult, if not impossible, to fully share the ends of others. Sometimes we can be as happy when our lover's aims are realized as when our aims are realized. Sometimes our own ends are not competing with our lover's. But it is truly a matter of extremely good fortune when this happens.

What is the source of this difficulty? I have pointed out that the problem is not just that we have separate bodies. The real difficulty is that our souls—our ends and goals—differ. Yet, the issue is perhaps even more complicated. For is it not the split in our once unified bodies that also divides our souls? Because our bodies have been split in two, our souls have taken divergent paths. We each have our own feelings and emotional reactions. And we each have our own bodies about which to be concerned. If we didn't have bodies then, perhaps, we could spend more time together. Then, perhaps, our souls could merge. But the rupture in the unity of our bodies creates a similar rupture in our souls.

Diotima's Teaching

The account of *eros* Socrates gives—which he learned from the priestess, Diotima—fits well with that of Aristophanes but then transcends it. Or perhaps I should say it shows us how we can (partly) transcend it. Socrates' account of *eros* teaches us that our ultimate aim is to possess the good forever. Since we cannot live forever, *eros* leads us to procreate in light of beauty. Procreation is a means by which we try to make something that will endure. And to say we procreate in beauty is to say we try to make something that is noble and splendid and thus deserving of immortality. We are inspired by a vision of beauty and nobility to create something that attains a similar beauty and nobility. Such a creation will last, if not forever, then for a long enough time that it, too, will be an inspiration which stimulates others to procreate as well.

As Diotima describes it to Socrates, our individual pursuit of a good that will last forever can take many different paths. These different paths form what has been called a ladder of love, in which we—or at least some of us—move from lower to higher forms of erotic expression.

We all begin at the lowest level with the recognition of the physical beauty of one person. Physical beauty in one person stimulates a desire to have sex with that person. And sex leads to the procreation of a child who will, we hope, survive us.[3]

The next step is the recognition of physical beauty in many people. We become detached from the beautiful body of one person when we see him or her as just one of many people whose appearance—whose faces and bodies and manner—stimulate our desires. We thus become sexually promiscuous.

It is at this point that a key step up the ladder of love is made, that is, the movement from the pursuit of beauty of body to that of beauty of soul. This is a moment in the *Symposium* that is too often overlooked. One suspects that readers of this work—and not just contemporary readers—are too ready to praise the pleasures of the soul and too quick to overlook the pleasures of the body. There is, however, a serious problem to be resolved here. Even if we accept the Socratic perspective and take the pleasures of the soul to be higher, finer, and better than the pleasures of the body—and we shall see that this claim is far more problematic than Socrates suggests—we still have the difficulty of understanding why someone in pursuit of the pleasures of the body with multiple partners would, all of a sudden, grasp the importance of the soul. That transformation is by no means easy or natural. Indeed, in the *Republic*, a similar transformation is said to require the most intense training over a number of years. How can we account, then, for this important moment in the *Symposium*?

The answer is by no means obvious. Let me suggest, however, that Socrates' argument takes the pursuit of sexual pleasure seriously. As such, it recognizes that sex can be better or worse. And while beautiful bodies do elicit sexual desire, sex with beautiful bodies is not always good sex. Sex with someone who has a beautiful soul is like to be more pleasurable. This is true even if we think of sex as primarily bodily in nature. A person with a good soul is likely to be more giving, more open to our desires, and more interested in pleasing us than a person with an ugly soul. But that is not the whole story by any means. Sex is, as Aristophanes teaches us, not primarily a means of gaining physical pleasure but a means of creating, expressing, and sustaining a relationship between two people. This is not a kind of relationship that people with ugly souls can create and sustain.

Thus it is dissatisfaction with the pursuit of the aims of *eros* at the lower levels that moves us to higher levels. It is precisely in the pursuit of bodily pleasure that we come to recognize the importance of a good soul. And, if we can recognize it, then the object of our erotic pursuits is transformed. We come to treasure beauty of soul rather than beauty of body.

This new direction for *eros* leads us, initially, to the desire to procreate with one other person. We are drawn to procreate children. Yet what concerns us at this point on the ladder of love is not the mere begetting of a child but the creation of a human being who possesses a beautiful soul. At this point on the ladder of love physical and spiritual pleasure are conjoined both in terms of the desires that move us and that which we create as a result of those desires: "...if he meets a beautiful, generous, and naturally gifted soul, he cleaves strongly to the two (body and soul) together."[4]

This is the point reached by men and women according to Aristophanes' account of *eros*. However, Socrates' view is, in important ways, different from that of Aristophanes. Whereas Aristophanes focuses on what is our own, Socrates points instead to that which is beautiful and good. For Aristophanes, we seek our other half. For Socrates the half we seek is one that is good in soul and body. As we will see in a moment, Socrates' account of the love of two people suggests a way beyond the impasse reached by Aristophanes. It points to a way of thinking about intimate love that helps us deal with the difficulty of finding our other half while at the same time transcending intimate love as the ultimate goal of human beings.

We can see how intimate love transcends itself looking to the next level on the ladder of love. At this point body and soul are not disjoined, although the sexual element becomes less important. Just as the appreciation of physical beauty in one person leads to an appreciation of physical beauty in many people, much the same happens with regard to beauty of soul. We are soon lead to recognize the beauty of many souls and perhaps also of the beauty of souls working together. And what beautiful souls produce together is good institutions and laws. Laws are phenomena created by souls but they are realized in our bodily actions. So procreation at this level involves both elements of our nature.

The creation of good laws would seem to be a collective product in which intimate relationships between human beings have been transcended. Indeed, if we were not already prepared to reach this conclusion, we would be led to do so by our reading of the *Republic*, in which Socrates suggests that all intimate ties must be extirpated in the *kallipolis*. But that is not what Socrates says in the *Symposium*. Rather he says that those who love the soul of another are motivated to give birth to offspring such as beautiful deeds, good laws, and, also, works of art. *Eros* works by means of the best men and women who can shape a *polis* and a work of art. Yet, the best men and women are led to procreate in large part by their ties to one another. Socrates gives examples of great men whose individual achievements he honors—Solon and Lycurgus, Homer and Hesiod. Yet he suggests that these are "children" that these individuals "have in common" with another.[5] For reasons we have not yet clearly seen, intimate love does not drop out when we move up the ladder of love. Rather, the love of individuals for one another seems to result in the procreation of "children" of greater importance and permanence than flesh and blood children.

As Socrates understands intimate love, its purpose is not, and cannot be, to restore a unity that the gods have sundered. It is not that Socrates can point to a way in which we can overcome our mutilated state. There is no such way. We cannot restore a unity of body and soul that gave us the strength to challenge the gods. So we must find another way to possess the good forever. If intimate love is focused not on the concrete attributes of our lover but, rather, on the attainments in the world that are stimulated and made possible by intimate love, then our inability to find our other half is less troublesome. For a love that is focused outwards on the laws and works of art we create can produce a unity of purpose between two people that is attainable in no other way. And, procreation of this kind can be stimulated not just by the presence but by the "memory" of those we love. "Whether [the lover] is present or absent, he holds the beautiful one in memory, nurtures with him that which has been generated in common."[6] Thus, if our aim is to procreate things of the soul, it is to our advantage to seek not our other half but someone whose virtue and goodness outshines and stimulates our own.

Why is the procreation of laws and art not something we do entirely on our own—or in conjunction with masses of human beings? We can easily fill in the details. Good laws and good works of art are, for Socrates, the work of one vision, not of the many. At the same time, in our mutilated state no one person has the strength to make good laws and works of art entirely on his or her own. Life is too hard, our needs are too great, to be alone. Even more, even if we work mostly alone, we still need others who understand our aims and purposes and who can share and critique our vision. That reason for intimate ties becomes even evident in the next step up the ladder.

In climbing that next step we are ultimately drawn forward not by beauty of body or beauty of soul but by beauty itself. Now we procreate in light of the form of beauty and we are led by it to contemplate, speak, and perhaps write about that which is most permanent. *Eros* ultimately leads us, then, to philosophy, the love of wisdom. This time, the transformation of *eros* as we move from one level to another is clear. It is imperfections and impermanence of good laws and even of our works of art that lead us to pursue knowledge of that which is prefect and everlasting. It is our capacity to imagine regimes—and worlds—that transcend in beauty any we hope to create or find that leads us to seek to create them in speech.

In discussing the advantages of this pursuit of beauty itself, initially the importance of our attachment to one other person fades away. And yet, immediately after discussing this highest form of erotics, Socrates says that he will "urge on the rest" to follow his path. Why is it important to Socrates to urge philosophy on others?

The answer to this question is connected to the advantages of the philosophic life itself. Why is this form of life higher? And what is the importance to us of procreating in light of a beauty that is eternal and wholly beautiful? We have already seen one answer: the greatest beauty is that which is without imperfection and which is not subject to decay. And what we produce when stimulated by beauty itself is potentially immortal in a way that institutions and laws or even works of art are not.[7]

Another answer is that the life of philosophy is one that, to a large extent, takes us beyond the struggles of human life. Philosophy is the one kind of procreation that transcends the struggle over limited goods. It relieves the tensions between human beings that seem intrinsic to our lives. The good of philosophy is unlimited. There is enough for everyone. We teachers do not lose wisdom if we are so lucky to pass some on to our students. And the tensions between human beings in philosophy are fruitful. In the pursuit of knowledge we seek no one more highly than the person who presents powerful alternative to our own views. No one can teach us more or stimulate us to do better than the person who radically disagrees with us.

Indeed philosophic friendship overcomes to an even higher degree the difficulties of finding our other half. The imperfections of our partners in pursuit of philosophy are less important when we are focused on what we create together than on what we each are. And that is especially true when what we create together is a good that is essentially limitless as opposed to the more limited goods of laws. Philosophy reinstates the element of promiscuity that was given up in the transition from body to soul. We can benefit from having more than one partner in the pursuit of knowledge.

Can We Follow the Socratic Vision?

This is a wonderful vision. Yet the question remains whether it is open to any of us. Can any of us live on the highest rung of the ladder of love? The trouble is that we are not pure souls but embodied beings. We have to care for our bodies. We need material resources in order to live. (We need teaching jobs and grants to philosophize.) We need to reproduce physically so that there are people to teach and learn from and people to read our books. And we also have sexual desires that hold us back from moving up the ladder. Sexual satisfaction may, as Aristophanes suggests, free us from the need for constant contact with our other half. But sexual desire has an independent life as well.

It is likely that this desire will be weakened when we move up the ladder of love. When *eros* is focused on physical beauty or even on the beauty of a single soul, sexual desire is heightened. After all, we know we are really in love with someone when we want to have sex again and again with him or her—as opposed to having sex with many different people. Once this kind of personal attachment is weakened, sexual desire may weaken. But there is no reason to think that sexual desire will disappear.

Indeed, if we ask why *eros* starts at the lowest levels of the ladder of love, the answer is simply that bodies have needs that must be satisfied. Souls develop later than bodies. The physical pleasures are more immediately attractive than the pleasures of the soul. It requires time and patience to learn to appreciate the goods of the soul. Even if it is true that time and patience can also heighten our bodily pleasures, sex has a charm that is immediately obvious to everyone.

Socrates Is Strange

So our doubts about whether life at the heights is open to us are stimulated by our recognition that we have bodies as well as souls. To sustain our bodies may take us from the pursuit of beauty itself. We are further pushed to wonder about whether the life of philosophy is truly open to us when we reflect upon what we learn from Alcibiades about the special nature of Socrates. For it is not at all clear that Socrates is anything like us. In particular, we are led by the speech of Alcibiades, and the action of the *Symposium*, to wonder whether Socrates has the bodily desires of other human beings. As we have seen: On military campaigns he needs neither food nor shelter. He is immune to cold. He can drink without getting drunk. He can go without sleep. And, most importantly, he is immune to the beauty of Alcibiades.

We learn this point from the entrancing yet disturbing story Alcibiades tells us about his pursuit of Socrates. Filled with the madness for another that both Aristophanes and Socrates say is central to love for another person, Alcibiades initially seeks to be *eromenos* or beloved to Socrates. He encourages the presumably shy Socrates to be his lover or *erastes*. Later, Alcibiades pursues Socrates with such passion that he has become the *erastes* or lover. In both poses, Alcibiades comes to understand a deep secret: Socrates is strange. He does not have any of the normal physical desires of human beings. And most especially, he does not have the sexual desires of other men. Alcibiades discovers this when he first wrestles with and later embraces Socrates. It is not so much that Socrates does not want to have sex with him. We would expect Socrates to be able restrain his sexual desires. And, as some interpreters have suggested, doing so would show us what Socrates tells us, that the goods of the soul are worth far more than the goods of the body.[8] What Alcibiades discovers, however, is not that Socrates restrains himself but that Socrates is not aroused by him. When he embraces Socrates he discovers that Socrates is not sexually aroused at all.

Now if Socrates is that different from the rest of us, we can well understand why his vision of *eros* as leading in its highest form to philosophy fits him. But does it fit us? To answer that question we have to know whether Socrates' strangeness preceded his attaining the highest reaches of love or whether it is, instead, a product of his proceeding up the ladder of love. If it is the result of Socrates moving up from one stage to another and then to the highest point of philosophy, then the path is difficult but not unattainable for the rest of us. If, however, Socrates was always a bit different, then at best we can only partially attain the highest form of erotic expression.

The text strongly suggests that Socrates was always different because he always lacked our bodily desires. Indeed, the peculiarity of a naïve and ignorant Socrates learning from Diotima about *eros* suggests precisely this. Diotima has to take him through every basic element of love. And it is not just, or even primarily, the last stage in the procession up the ladder of love that seems new to Socrates. Socrates is perplexed each step of the way, just as someone would be who was a stranger to human desire.

Socrates, then, seems to be a man almost without a body. Even more, throughout his interchange with Diotima and his relationship with Alcibiades he seems rather unerotic in any conventional sense. At the very least his *eros* is not expressed in bodily terms. His well-known ugliness also leads us to see him in this light. And, of course, this is not a new picture of Socrates. In the *Republic*, too, Socrates seems to depreciate the importance of *eros*, especially in its lowest forms.

Why Does Socrates Philosophize?

If Socrates is different from us, then we need to understand how and why philosophy appeals to him. For, if he is not erotic in anything like the conventional sense, there is little reason to doubt that Socrates' love of wisdom is connected to something like the erotic desires to possess the good forever.

One possible suggestion is that Socrates is like the undamaged human beings described by Aristophanes as they were before they challenged the gods. Socrates is in some ways like them. Though he looks like us, his body is as strong as that of human beings before they were mangled. Has Socrates, despite all physical evidence to the contrary, not been sliced in two? Is he whole in a way we are not?

I once thought this. But, now, this no longer seems entirely right. For one thing, there is no indication that human beings philosophized before they were mutilated. Their challenge to the gods, their attempt to gain immortality looks to be physical in nature. Moreover, given what we learn from Diotima via Socrates, it seems that our very weakness in body both hinders us from moving up the ladder of love *and* encourages us to do so. As we have just seen, we are hindered because of our bodily needs. Yet it is perhaps only because the weakness of our bodies makes us so dependent upon others, so desiring of finding our other half, and so consumed by politics that we recognize the difficulties of the pursuit of erotic satisfaction in the love of another or political life. Moving up the ladder of love is moving away from the messiness and dissatisfaction attendant on love of another person or political life.

Pre-apocalyptic human beings do not need to find their other half and do not need politics. However, as a result they do not need philosophy either. They are lacking in the dissatisfactions that result from our mangled state. They are not driven by bodily desires that lead them to grasp the beauty of souls. They are not frustrated by the search for their other half. They do not need a polity to keep them safe and provide the goods they need to stay alive. They also do not need the virtues that makes a good polity possible. And they do not have the dissatisfaction with our intimate, political, and even artistic lives that lead us to pursue beauty itself. Being mangled deepened us. Yet at the same time it created deep tensions within us.

So Socrates is not just like pre-apocalyptic human beings. If he does not need intimate love, he does need politics or at least the protection of a polity. He can be physically harmed and killed. And, most of all, he needs philosophy. As a result, he needs to converse with others about the world around him.

Socrates' erotic desires, at this point, seem general rather than particular. They are oriented not to particular individuals but to goods in general and most of all to wisdom. Or, to put the point another way, Socrates seems to be in between human beings as we know them and human beings before the gods performed their surgery on us. He is lacking in our bodily desires and, it seems, our attachments to particular other people. Yet he shares our need for politics and pursues a good that is only desired by mangled human beings, philosophy.

Socrates, in other words, is the same and different from us. However, he is different enough that his way of life is not one that we can wholly follow. We can pursue philosophy, but only for a time. For we have bodily desires that lead us to seek the comfort and protection of loved ones and sexual desires that can only be satisfied by our lovers.

Procreation in Beauty Requires Partners

But perhaps there is a further complication: Maybe Socrates cannot actually do without other human beings either. After all, Socrates spends his time in the company of others. And, more than that, Socrates pretends to have erotic interests in the young men with whom he associates. If I am correct in doubting that Socrates has any sexual interest in these young men, we need to understand not only why he feigns such interest but why he hangs around them at all.

Once again a comparison with pre-apocalyptic human beings helps us understand Socrates. Aristophanes points out that before they were split in two, human beings were capable of procreating, although the process was closer to the sexual practice of frogs than that of human beings. Aristophanes also gives us an unforgettable picture of a human being who, because of his two faces, is a creature who can converse with himself. Unmangled human beings may not have philosophized, but they could talk, so to speak, among themselves. The power of human beings before we were divided in two is not just physical but spiritual. It is the power of dialogue, embodied in one person.

Socrates needs politics not just to protect himself but to create the possibility of a conversation among friends. Indeed, in the *Apology* he says that he will not leave Athens to avoid condemnation because the philosophic life is impossible if he cannot talk to his fellow citizens. As the Socratic dialogues teach us, philosophy is best practiced by means of debate and discussion. We need the challenge of conversation with those who disagree with us in order to deepen and test our own views.

That is part, but not the whole story of why Socrates needs conversation. It seems that he and we need conversation of a particular kind, intimate conversation in which we reveal ourselves to one another. Early in the text, Agathon tells Socrates to come sit near him so that he can learn from the touch of Socrates. Socrates responds that we cannot learn something in this way. Yet the text shows us that we can. It is in touching Socrates that Alcibiades learns something terribly important about him. And, as we have seen, the importance of the soul is learned by engaging in somewhat promiscuous sex with people who have beautiful bodies.

Of course, it is not just that we need physical contact with others to learn about ourselves. To know ourselves intimately we may have to know others intimately as well. We have to compare our own deepest desires to those of other people. And we have to see ourselves reflected in the eyes of others to be sure we know who we really are. Philosophy requires conversation and philosophic thinking about those things that are most important to ourselves requires conversation in which we explore those parts of ourselves that are so important and hard to know precisely because they are so central to who we are. Again, it may be that the pre-apocalyptic human beings who could talk to themselves could therefore know themselves without close contact with other particular human beings. We, however, cannot.

Surely the point the text makes this deeply true. Socrates may or may not have sex with his friends. But to the extent that he wishes to understand the human condition, he has to understand the most intimate desires of human beings. Socrates sometimes contemplates by himself. Perhaps he can understand what is in the sky and below the earth by himself.[9] But though he can contemplate by himself, he does not just stay by himself. To understand human life he has to partake in it. At the very least, he has to at least become the confidant of his friends. Perhaps he has to become their lovers or at least act like an *erastes* or *eromenos* around them so that they reveal their desires to him. Socrates does reject Agathon's notion that we can learn from others by touching them. But he plays along with Alcibiades nonetheless. And maybe he does sleep with them on occasion, for philosophic not sexual reasons.

Of course, sexual and philosophic reasons may not be so easy to prise apart. Sartre is reputed to have said that he never really knows a woman until he has slept with her. I have always thought this one of the great pickup lines of all time. But, perhaps what makes it so good is that there is a good deal of truth to it. One reason we want to sleep with others—one source of infidelity that is too little remarked upon—is the desire to know and be known by another.

During the speech of Alcibiades we see Socrates upset and discombobulated. There are few if any other places in the Platonic corpus where we see him so out of sorts. By now, the reason for this should be clear. Socrates' cover has been blown. His erotic interest in the young men who follow him around has been revealed as a pretense. And, for a moment Socrates seems like a lonely figure. And we can well understand why, prior to meeting with Diotima, Socrates lacked knowledge of erotics. At the end of the *Symposium* Socrates seems to be a man who is incapable of forming real intimate ties, not just because he lacks sexual desire but because he cannot fully reveal himself to others. His irony is a protective device. It is also a device that distances himself from others.

Perhaps we see Socrates in this way only because we project our own hopes and desires onto him. We desire to be known and loved by particular others and we see that Socrates cannot hope for this. Perhaps a true philosopher can make do with a simulacra of intimacy. We, in our weakness and vulnerability, cannot. We need another person who cares for us as we care for ourselves, who will be there for us when we are troubled or ill, and who can tell us when we are not making sense to ourselves or others. Even in our political or philosophic partnerships we need some promise of permanence or, at the very least, some hope that the relationship will be more than a one-night stand.

Socrates and Alcibiades (and Us)

In different ways, Nussbaum, Bloom, and Rosen have all suggested that the *Symposium* points us to the problem of understanding how and why Alcibiades went off the rails. Nussbaum's intriguing suggestion is that the *Symposium* takes place on the night Alcibiades profaned the Eleusinian mysteries and smashed the statues of Hermes with their erect phalluses. All three interpreters suggest that the events of the *Symposium*—and those recounted within—show us that what drives Alcibiades to despair is his relationship with Socrates.

With this conclusion I concur. With these other interpreters, I would suggest that what troubles Alcibiades is not just that he cannot have Socrates. The trouble is that, for the first time, Alcibiades recognizes that the wholeness he desires, the good he seeks, is beyond him. He cannot be like Socrates—he cannot live a life of philosophy alone—because he is like the rest of us. Human beings are weak in both body and soul. We need the support of others to sustain ourselves physically. And we need to know and be known by a particular other person in order to come to know ourselves. The political life Alcibiades leads is one way to satisfy the urge to be known by others and also to enter the lives of others.[10] Yet it is not enough for Alcibiades as it cannot wholly substitute for the intimate ties he seeks with the one person who he suspects will truly teach him who he is. Yet he cannot have Socrates either. And getting close to Socrates teaches Alcibiades more than he can deal with. He comes to recognize that the pursuit of honor and fame will never give him all that he wants because fame and honor are so imperfect and fleeting. And yet Alcibiades' all too human desires for intimate and political connection with others makes the life of Socrates, the life lived in pursuit of an abstract good, impossible for him. For that life that is only open to Socrates, the one person who lacks the physical weaknesses and desires the rest of us share.

The profanation of the mysteries and smashing of the statues suggest Alcibiades'—and our own—frustration with how the gods have left us. Perhaps Plato does blame Socrates, in part, for this terrible event. Socrates let someone, or more accurately the wrong person, get too close and see him as he really is. We see this as we get closer to Socrates and come to understand how different Socrates is from the rest of us. The closer we get to Socrates, however, the more we recognize that he does not wholly escape from these difficulties either. Though he lacks our physical desires, Socrates needs a kind of intimacy with others. Yet he cannot have it in part because he does not fully share our nature and, in part, because of the dangers involved in revealing himself to others.

Seeing Socrates as he really is helps reveal to us who we really are. And what is revealed to us is the source of our erotic desires and erotic dissatisfaction. We learn that to be mutilated by the gods was not just a terrible consequence, as it gave us the depth we could attain in no other way. But, at the same time, it created not just a split between us and our other halves but, also, a split in our very nature. We long to possess the good forever. Yet each of the paths by which we might pursue that good has its own difficulties and problems. None of them are wholly satisfactory. And each way to satisfy our erotic yearning comes into conflict with the others. The one life that seems most free of difficulties and problems—the Socratic life devoted to philosophy—is a life we cannot live because we cannot do without an intimate, erotic connection to other people. And the closer we look, the more we see even the philosophic life is not as trouble free as it first looks. Even Socrates has a need for intimate connections with others, a need that he cannot wholly satisfy.

The ambiguity of Plato's presentation of Socrates therefore teaches us that there is ultimately no real solution to our difficulties. We each have to find our own way to balance the competing goods to which we, in our mutilated state, cannot but be attracted.[11]

Augustine of Hippo on Seeing with the Eyes of the Mind

Roland J. Teske, S.J.
Marquette University

For a number of years the question of what Augustine means by intellectual knowing, that is, by *"intelligere,"* has lurked in the back of my mind as one of the topics in Augustine's thought that I considered highly puzzling, ambiguous, and much in need of clarification. Previous attempts on my part to deal with the question rapidly brought me to realize that the topic was beyond what I could handle at that time. I am not sure that I can deal with it even now in a satisfactory manner, but I cannot think of a better topic, nor am I likely to have a better occasion.[1] The topic of intellectual knowing in Augustine is central to much of his thought, but what he says about intellectual knowing is not, in my judgment, always consistent with instances of such knowledge that we find in his writings. My thesis is that there is an official account of what he meant by intellectual knowing, that is, the sort of account that he did give of what it is to know intellectually, and that there are serious problems with that account of knowing, problems that are not found at least in some instances in which we can observe Augustine's activity in knowing intellectually or in bringing someone else to some instance of intellectual knowledge. If my thesis is correct, the conclusion will throw some light on several problems or debates that have occupied some of the best contemporary Augustine scholars. I mean, for example, how we are to understand those passages in Book Seven of the *Confessions* that Pierre Courcelle described as *"vaines tentatives de l'exstase plotinienne"* or failed attempts to ascend to a Plotinian vision of God.[2]

Hence, this paper will have three parts and a conclusion: 1) Augustine's official account of intellectual knowing, 2) some difficulties with that account, 3) some actual instances of intellectual knowing, and 4) some concluding reflections, which, I hope, may cast some light on this ambiguous issue.

The Official Account

Augustine's account of intellectual knowing is highly Platonic. When, for example, St. Thomas speaks of intellectual knowing in his *Summa of Theology* I, qu. 84, a. 6, he contrasts the positions of Democritus and Plato with that of Aristotle. While Democritus held that all of our knowledge was sensory and that what we know are only bodily things, Plato distinguished the intellect from the senses and held that the intellect was an immaterial power that did not use a bodily organ and that the intellect knew immaterial forms separated from bodies. Aristotle, on the other hand, distinguished the intellect from the senses and maintained that the intellect, which is an immaterial power, is also a power of a soul that is the form of a body and that the intellect understands intelligible forms that it abstracts from material things by the agent intellect. St. Augustine's view comes very close to that of Plato, as St. Thomas well knew.

Augustine understands intellectual knowing by analogy with seeing with the eyes of the body. He develops this account of the two forms of seeing and points to the many parallels between them. Thus he says that "to understand is to the mind what to see is for the senses."[3] Hence, Augustine identifies seeing God with understanding God.[4] So too, we have eyes of the mind just as we have eyes of the body.[5] And we see with the mind as opposed to seeing with the body.[6] But in order to see something with the eyes of the body, it is not enough to have eyes. Our eyes must also be open and healthy, and they must look in the right direction. There must also be something there to see, that is, a object that can be seen. So too, there must also be light to make the object visible. Similarly, the eyes of our mind must be open and healthy. In Book Seven of the *Confessions*, for example, Augustine describes how his face was so swollen with pride that the eyes of his mind could not see God.[7] In the *Soliloquies* he says that the eyes of the mind are healed by faith, hope, and love.[8] With the eyes of the body it is one thing to look and another to see; so it is with the mind.[9] The mind's gaze or look is reason, and reasoning is the movement of the mind over things that the mind gazes upon.[10]

Furthermore, just as for the eyes of the body to see anything, there must be some visible object present, so for the eyes of the mind to see anything there must be an intelligible object present. Augustine tells us in *Answer to the Academics*, one of his first extant works, where he presents a summation of the history of philosophy, that Plato's great achievement was the realization that there are two worlds. "After all," he says, "it is enough for what I want that Plato held that there are two worlds, one an intelligible world, where the truth itself dwells, and this sensible one, which we obviously perceive by sight and touch."[11] In another early dialogue, *On Order*, Augustine has the chutzpah to instruct his saintly mother, Monica, in the rudiments of philosophy and to claim that Christ himself taught that there were these two worlds. "Christ himself," Augustine said, "indicated well enough that there is another world far removed from these eyes, which the intellect of a few healthy human beings sees. For Christ did not say: 'My kingdom is not of the world,' but: 'My kingdom is not of this world'" (Jn 17:36).[12]

And Augustine, of course, located the intelligible world in the mind of God. After some speculation about whether Plato was the first to maintain that there were such Ideas or Forms, Augustine located them in the divine intelligence. "For," he says, "the principal ideas are certain forms or stable and immutable patterns of things, which are not themselves formed and are, for this reason, eternal and always existing in the same way, and they are contained in the divine intelligence."[13] They are principal ideas, I think, in the sense that they are principles or ἀρχαί of things in this sensible world. "Only a rational soul," Augustine tells us, "is permitted to gaze upon them by that part of itself by which it is excellent, that is, by the mind and reason, as if by its face or by its interior and intelligible eye."[14] Not every rational soul is suited for that vision, but only one that is holy and pure, "that is, one that has its eye, which sees these ideas, healthy, pure, clear, and like these things that it strives to see."[15] Furthermore, Augustine concedes that there are good and religious persons who cannot, nonetheless, gaze upon these ideas. He, however, claims that believers must maintain that there are such ideas in the mind of God if they are to hold that God knew what he was doing when he created the world and that he governs it providentially.[16]

Bodily eyes that are open, healthy, and looking in the right direction still do not see a object that is present unless there is light that makes the object visible. So too, the eyes of the mind need an intelligible light, and for Augustine God is that light of our minds. He says, "There is a certain ineffable and incomprehensible light of minds. Let this ordinary light teach us as much as it can how that light acts."[17] For some people have such healthy and strong eyes that they merely have to open them to see the sunlight, while others have to be gradually brought to see things the sunlight illumines until they are strong enough to look upon the sunlight itself. The light of minds is the Wisdom of God,[18] the true light that enlightens every human being who comes into this world, as St. John said.[19] Just as the light of the sun makes other things visible by its light and is itself visible, so the intelligible light makes other things intelligible and is itself intelligible. "And so," Augustine says, "as in this sun we can observe three things: that it is, that is bright, and that it illumines, so in that most hidden God whom you want to understand, there are three things: that he is, that he is understood, and that he makes other things to be understood."[20] In prayer Augustine addresses God: "O God, the intelligible light in whom and by whom and through whom all things are intelligibly bright that are intelligibly bright."[21]

Contemporary scholars are more in agreement about what this divine illumination cannot mean than they are about what it does mean.[22] Scholars universally agree that Augustine's theory of divine illumination does not mean that God produces concepts or knowledge in our minds in the way the Avicennian agent intelligence supposedly caused human knowledge by producing ideas in our minds as it also produced forms in things in this sublunar world. So too, scholars are almost universally agreed that in Augustine's thought God does not act like the Thomistic agent intellect, which abstracts universals from sensible things. For

Augustine has no doctrine of universal ideas or abstraction. Some scholars claim–quite anachronistically–that Augustine held a version of ontologism, somewhat like Père Malebranche in the seventeenth century and like various nineteenth-century Catholic thinkers, such as the Italian Antonio Rosmini-Serbati and the Belgian Gerhard Ubaghs of Louvain.[23] At least one prominent scholar held that it was before their embodiment that human souls were enlightened and that they now vaguely remember what they saw then.[24] But there is, as I said, little agreement about what Augustine saw as the real role of divine illumination. There are certainly texts in which Augustine seems to say quite clearly that at least some human beings in this life can see and have seen the very substance by which God is what he is. Though he explicitly ascribes such a vision only to Moses and Paul, he perhaps extends it to the great Neoplatonists as well.[25] He certainly says that the great philosophers "saw that which is, but saw it from afar."[26] They saw the fatherland where we are to go, but in their pride they refused the way to it, namely, the Word become flesh.[27]

There are other texts in which he says that we can and do see with the mind the eternal patterns or ideas in the mind of God. Etienne Gilson, the great historian of medieval philosophy, classified those texts in which Augustine spoke of a vision of God or of things in God as mystical and classified all the other, less problematic, texts as ones referring to our natural knowledge.[28]

There is one final point of similarity between seeing with the eyes of the body and seeing with the mind that I want to mention. At times things interfere with our bodily vision. For example, clouds or fog can prevent us from seeing even the sun, and gnats can get into our eyes. So too, phantasms, that is, images of bodily things, can like clouds or fog or gnats prevent our seeing with the eyes of the mind. Images rush into our minds like clouds or fog and have to be brushed away like a swarm of desert gnats.[29] Hence, Augustine prays in the *True Religion* for someone who can think without imagining sensible objects.[30]

Thus far I have tried to illustrate Augustine's "official" account of what it is to understand in which he compares the mind's knowing with the eyes' seeing. Bernard Lonergan describes Augustine's theory of understanding as empiricism's most sublime form but faults the bishop of Hippo for supposing that, because seeing is obviously knowing, seeing is obviously what knowing is.[31] Next, I want to turn to and emphasize some of the problems with the "official" account of what it is to know.

Problems with the Official Version

If to know with the mind is analogous to seeing with the eyes, there, of course, have to be intelligible objects that the mind sees. We have seen that Augustine considered Plato's discovery of the intelligible world and the Ideas as one of his great contributions to philosophy and as something that a Christian has to believe in even if we do not ourselves see that world and those Ideas. Furthermore, Augustine located the Ideas in the mind of God. For, as St. Thomas wisely noted, Augustine saw that it was against the faith to leave such creative substances outside of God and, for this reason, placed them in the mind of God.[32] If we listen to Augustine's official version of what it is to know intellectually, it seems to follow inevitably that he held that we know intelligible objects and truths in knowing the divine ideas–and not merely in the way that we see visible things in the light of the sun, but by seeing the divine ideas themselves.

Let me illustrate this point from Augustine's argument for the existence of God, which he presents in Book Two of *Free Choice of the Will*. The basic structure of the argument is a hypothetic syllogism. Augustine gets his partner in the dialogue, Evodius, the future bishop of Uzalis, to agree that, if there is anything higher than the human mind, at least, if that something is eternal and immutable, that something is God, or God exists.[33] Hence, Augustine has to show that there is above the human mind something that is eternal and immutable, and he does this by showing Evodius that there are truths of mathematics and of wisdom that are eternal and immutable. Augustine says to Evodius: "If without the use of any instrument of the body, neither of touch, nor of taste, nor of smell, nor by the ears, nor by the eyes, but by itself, reason sees something eternal and immutable, it must at the same time admit that it is inferior and that that being is its God."[34] Unlike the conclusion of one of the Five Ways of St. Thomas, the term of

Augustine's argument is reason's act of seeing something eternal and immutable, which is reason's God.

Before turning to the truths of mathematics and of wisdom, Augustine spends a number of paragraphs in an *exercitatio animi*, an exercising of the mind, in which he compares the act of seeing with the acts of the other external senses. His aim is to convince Evodius and us that what we see with our eyes can be something common and public for many or all of us to see, while what we taste or smell cannot be common and public in the same way. For, in tasting and smelling something, we change what we taste and smell so that it becomes something private and proper to each of us. Hence, he concludes, "We must understand by 'proper' and 'private' that which each of us alone possesses, which each of us senses in himself, and which properly belongs to his nature. But that is 'common' and 'public' which is perceived by all who sense it without any destruction or change of that object."[35]

Then Augustine says to Evodius, "Come on now, pay attention, and tell me whether something is found that all who reason see in common, each with his own reason and mind, though what is seen is available to all and is not changed for the use of those to whom it is available, like food or drink, but remains incorrupt and whole, whether they see it or not."[36] Evodius mentions "the nature and truth of number,"[37] which is available to all who reason and which every one who calculates tries to grasp by his own reason and intelligence. At this point Augustine has to face the objection "that these numbers are impressed on our mind, not from some nature of their own, but from those things that we attain by the senses of the body, like certain images of visible things."[38] Evodius claims that, even if we perceive numbers by the senses of the body, we do not grasp in that way the laws of addition and subtraction, and he points to the incorruptible truth that seven plus three equals ten. Augustine, nonetheless, proceeds to show that numbers themselves cannot be derived from the senses of the body. He points out that each number is a multiple of one and argues that one cannot be attained by the bodily senses because everything we perceive by those senses is many. Any body we perceive has many parts, such as a right side and a left, a top and a bottom, a front and a back. Hence, he concludes, "And for this reason we grant that no body is purely one, though we could not count so many parts in it unless they were distinguished by a knowledge of one."[39] Augustine is claiming that a knowledge of one is a condition of the possibility of counting the many parts we find in any body. He says that he does not find one in any body and asks, "When, therefore, I know that a body is not one, I know what one is. For, if I did not know one, I could not count many parts in a body."[40]

Having established that a knowledge of one is the condition of the possibility of knowing the multiplicity in any body, Augustine turns to some simple rules of number, such as the double of any number "x" follows "x" numbers after "x." In any case, like "seven plus three equals ten," these truths about number are eternal and immutably true.

So too, Augustine gets Evodius to admit that there are truths of wisdom that are immutable and eternal, such as, that we should live justly, that we should subordinate the worse to the better, that we should treat equals as equal, and that we should give each what is his own, and he insists that these truths are available to all who see them.[41]

And after exploring the relation between number and wisdom, Augustine says to Evodius, "Hence, you will by no means deny that immutable truth exists and contains all these immutable truths. You cannot say that it is yours or mine or any human being's, but is available to and offers itself, like a light hidden and yet public in marvelous ways, to all who see the immutable truths."[42] Augustine still has to argue that the immutable truth is superior to our mind in order to come to the conclusion that God exists and truly exists. But in the passage just quoted there is also the problem that we see many immutable truths (*incommutabilia vera*) of number and wisdom. These truths are contained in the immutable truth, and the immutable truth is God.

What, then, is the relationship between the many immutable truths that we see and the immutable truth that contains them? The relation between *veritas* and *vera*, between the truth and objects that are true, would seem, in so Platonic a context, to be participation. For example, Augustine says in an earlier commentary on *Genesis*, "But chastity is chaste by participation in nothing;

rather, by participation in it whatever is chaste is chaste. That chastity is, of course, in God where there is that wisdom that is not wise by participation, but by participation in which every wise soul is wise."[43] The relation between the immutable truth and those things that are immutably true cannot, however, be the same as the relation between wisdom and wise souls or between chastity and chaste souls. A soul that is wise or chaste by participation can, after all, cease to be wise or chaste; it is not immutably wise or chaste. But the truths of mathematics and of wisdom are immutably and eternally true. They are, furthermore, things that are common and public and that are available to all who use their reason to see them. Hence, I am convinced that participation will not work here to account for the relation between the *vera* and *veritas*, between those truths and the truth.[44]

Augustine says that the immutable truth *contains* the many immutable truths. I suggest that the immutable truth contains the many immutable truths in the way in which a mind contains the many truths it knows. But that leaves us with the problem that our minds or the minds of those whose eyes are open, healthy, gazing in the right direction, etc., literally see those immutable truths in the mind of God, who is the Truth. Now, to say the very least, it is a strange proof for the existence of God that moves from seeing the divine ideas in the mind of God to the existence of God.[45]

By way of confirmation of this, we find in Book Three that Augustine argues that, though there can exist in the world something that we do not think of by our reason, there cannot fail to exist what we think of with a true reason.[46] "Nor can you, after all, think of something better in creation that will have escaped the author of creation. The human soul, in fact, is naturally connected to the divine ideas (*divinis rationibus*), upon which it depends, when it says, 'This would be better than that.' And if it speaks the truth and sees what it says, it sees it in those ideas to which it is connected."[47] With an almost Leibnizian optimism Augustine says that, if with true reason we know that God ought to have made something, even if we do not see that thing with our eyes, we should believe that God did make it.[48] And the reason he gives is that "one would not see in thought that it ought to have been made except in those ideas by which all things have been made. What is not there, no one can see with true thought, and it is not true."[49]

Even in later works Augustine says quite clearly that the mind at least of a few human beings attains the intelligible forms in the mind of God. In Book Twelve of *The Trinity*, for example, Augustine distinguishes wisdom and knowledge and tells us that to wisdom there pertain the eternal intelligible and incorporeal patterns (*rationes*) of things. "They, however, remain, not fixed as if in places like bodies, but in their incorporeal nature they are, like intelligible things, available to the gazes of the mind, just as these visible or tangible things in places are available to the senses of the body."[50] He adds, "To attain to these patterns is the privilege of a few, and when one attains them, to the extent it is possible, the person who attains them does not remain in them, but is driven back, as if his eyes have been struck, and there is produced the passing thought of a reality that does not pass."[51] Given Augustine's official view of intellectual knowing, we are faced with the problem that the mind of a few is able to attain in this life a vision of the divine ideas, at least momentarily. For those eternal, intelligible, incorporeal patterns or ideas are available to the gaze of the mind, just as visible and tangible things offer themselves to the bodily sight and touch.

Augustine's Unofficial Version of What Knowing Is

We have seen what I have called Augustine's official version of what intellectual knowing is, namely, that to understand is to see an intelligible reality with the eyes of the mind. We have seen that there are serious problems with his account of knowing as a seeing. The principal problem is, in my opinion, that the official version entails that, in knowing intellectually, we quite literally see the divine ideas in the mind of God. The official version, therefore, makes his argument for the existence of God at best a sort of intuition and at worst question-begging. Furthermore, the role of divine illumination seems to remain an unexplained and perhaps an inexplicable metaphor. With reference to the various senses of Scripture, scholars have often pointed out that it is necessary to look at what Augustine does rather than merely at what he says. I suggest that with reference to intellectual knowing, we should also look at what Augustine does rather than merely at what he says. Hence, I will examine two instances in which we can see how Augustine tries to bring others to an intellectual knowledge of something, first, from a letter to Jerome, and secondly, from a letter to Consentius.

Jerome and the Incorporeality of the Soul. In 415 Augustine wrote to Jerome in Bethlehem, a holy but cantankerous priest with whom he has earlier quarreled. Augustine asked Jerome for help with the question of the origin of the soul, that is, with the question of how post-Adamic human souls come to be in bodies, a problem that Augustine claims he was never able to resolve to his own satisfaction.[52] In the letter Augustine wanted to show Jerome that he knew some things about the soul, and one of those things that he claimed to know was that the soul was incorporeal. In order to avoid a merely verbal dispute, he first of all clarifies what he means by a body and says that, if every substance is a body, then the soul too is a body. Similarly, if someone wants to maintain that only an absolutely immutable and omnipresent substance is non-bodily, then the soul is a body. "But if only that is a body that stands or moves with some length, breadth, and depth through some area of place, so that it occupies a larger place with a larger part of itself and a smaller place with a smaller part of itself and is smaller in a part than in the whole, the soul is not a body."[53] In order to show that the soul is not a body in this sense, Augustine appeals to the evidence from sensation that the soul is stretched out through the whole body, not by a local diffusion, but by a vital attention. He produces an argument that "the whole soul is simultaneously present through all the parts of the body, not smaller in smaller parts and larger in larger parts, but more intensely in one place and less intensely in another, whole in all the parts and whole in each part."[54] I do not want to examine the argument here in detail, but to focus on what Augustine does to prove to Jerome that he knows that the soul is not a body. He first makes it clear what he means by a body and defines something incorporeal by contrary properties. He appeals to our awareness of ourselves in sensation and claims that the whole soul could not be aware of something that happens in only a part of the body, unless the whole soul were present in each part of the body. For, when I feel a pain in my toe that I stub, my whole soul is aware of the pain in one small part of my body, though the soul continues to animate the rest of my body. And, if I manage to burn my finger while my toe is still hurting, my whole soul also becomes aware of the pain in my finger. Hence, the whole soul is present in the whole body which it animates, but the whole soul is also present in each of the parts, as is shown by my awareness of the pains in my toe and in my finger. He concludes, "Hence, whether it should be called a body or non-bodily, the soul is understood to have a certain nature of its own, created with a substance more excellent than all these elements with a worldly mass, and it cannot accurately (*veraciter*) be thought of in some picturing of bodily images, which we perceive through the senses of the flesh. Rather, it is understood by the mind and sensed by life."[55] That is, the incorporeal nature of the soul cannot correctly be thought of (*cogitari*) by means of any bodily images, but is understood (*intelligi*) by the mind. When he says that it is "sensed by life (*vita sentiri*)," I think that he means that the soul's sensory awareness provides the evidence of the soul's presence as a whole in the whole body and in each of its parts. That the soul is incorporeal in that sense cannot, however, be imagined, but can only be understood by the mind.

This sort of intellectual knowing is hardly a seeing of an intelligible object in an intelligible world. It is rather an insight into the sort of reality the soul must be if we are to account for the evidence provided by sensory awareness, an insight that transcends anything that we can picture and is expressed in a definition of the soul's incorporeality.

Consentius' and Knowledge of God. In 410 a young theologian from the Balearic Isles by the name of Consentius wrote to Augustine, asking for help in how to think about God. Consentius tells Augustine that he is convinced that the truth about God should be sought from faith rather than reason. Otherwise, he fears that "no one except philosophers and professors will attain happiness."[56]

He is, moreover, convinced that heresies all stem from neglecting the authority of scripture and indulging in rational arguments. Like almost everyone in the Latin West prior to Augustine, Consentius was a man who pictured God to himself as a huge sort of body.[57] He tells Augustine that he believes "that God is an infinite magnitude of a certain inestimable light and that the human mind, though it thinks lofty thoughts, is not sufficient to judge its quality nor measure its quantity nor imagine its beauty."[58] God, according to Consentius, is something that "has an incomparable form and inestimable beauty, which at least Christ could see even with the eyes of the flesh."[59] He quotes from one of his writings where he had said, "God is one, and the persons are three. God is undivided; the persons are divided. God is within all things; he is beyond all things. He includes the last things, fills the middle things, and transcends the highest. He is poured out beyond all things and through all things. But the persons subsisting in themselves are distinguished by their proper character and are not mingled in confusion."[60] He adds, "God, therefore, is one and is everywhere, because there is no other besides him and there is no empty space where another could be. All things are filled with God, and apart from God there is nothing."[61]

Consentius clearly thought of God in terms of a Stoic corporealism of the sort that Augustine himself described as his own view early in Book Seven of the *Confessions*, where he says that he had thought that God was "a great corporeal substance, existent everywhere throughout infinite space, which penetrates the whole world-mass, and spreads beyond it on every side through immense, limitless space."[62] Or, to use the image he employs a few paragraphs later, he thought that the whole of creation was like a huge, but finite sponge in the infinite sea of God, who fills every part of the sponge and stretches endlessly beyond it.[63]

Consentius is well aware that Augustine says "that God should not be thought of as some body," not even as "a light a thousand times more bright and more intense than this sun."[64] But Consentius thinks that to think of God as non-bodily means to think of him like abstractions, such as righteousness or piety. For he concedes that we cannot think of righteousness or piety as bodily, unless we imagine some female figures, as the pagans do, but he adds that he "still cannot think of God, that is, of a living nature, as being like righteousness, because righteousness is not living in itself, but in us."[65] That is, if he thinks of God as righteousness or piety, which he admits are not bodily, he finds that he cannot regard such abstractions as living in themselves but only as living in righteous human beings.

Augustine replied to Consentius in Letter 120. He tells Consentius that he should hold that correct faith about the one God and the three persons, even if he cannot understand it, but he also urges Consentius to love understanding very much.[66] He tries to bring Consentius to understand that God is incorporeal and warns him, "When you think of these things, drive away, deny, reject, cast aside, flee from whatever comes to mind with the likeness of a body."[67] One of the ways in which Augustine tries to get Consentius to transcend imagination or picture-thinking and to understand God involves the technique that he learned from Plotinus of bringing together images that clash with each other and force one beyond images.[68] Augustine takes the verse from Isaiah where it says, "The heaven is my throne, but the earth is my footstool" (Is 66:1). He says, "Even if we understand this in a carnal sense," that is, if we picture this, "we ought to believe that he is there in heaven and here on earth, though the whole of him is not there because his feet are here and the whole of him is not here because the upper parts of his body are there."[69] Another passage of scripture, he tells us, "can shake off for us this carnal thought." For Isaiah also said, "He measured the heaven with the palm of his hand and the earth with his fist" (Is 40:12).[70] If one brings the two sets of images together, they clash and shatter each other so that we are forced to transcend them. Augustine says, "Who can sit in the space of the palm of his hand or can put his feet in a space as small as his fist can grasp? Unless perhaps the vanity of the flesh goes so far that it is not enough to attribute human members to the substance of God if it does not also make them monstrous so that the palm of his hand is wider than his hips and his fist is wider than soles of both his feet joined together."[71] Augustine explains that he says this "in order that, when those things that we hear in a carnal fashion conflict with one another, we may be admonished by them and think of spiritual realities in a way that is ineffable."[72]

Thus Augustine tries to bring Consentius to an intellectual grasp of the incorporeal nature of God by shattering one image against the other so that he is forced to transcend the imagination to a grasp of a reality that cannot be pictured or imagined but can only be understood. This sort of intellectual knowing is, in my opinion, a seeing or insight into the nature of God that is much more plebeian than the seeing of the official version, which seems closer to an account of a mystical experience or of the vision of God by the blessed than of a philosophical insight.

Concluding Reflections

There are instances of knowing in Augustine's works that are closer to the official version than to the unofficial version that I have tried to illustrate. I think, however, that it is important to see that not every instance of intellectual knowing in Augustine involves a vision of intelligible things in the divine ideas or a vision of God himself. Furthermore, Augustine's official version of what it is to know intellectually can be misleading and has, I think, misled some students of Augustine. Let me offer an example of this. In Book Seven of his *Confessions* Augustine speaks several times of his coming to a vision of God. He tells us that he was admonished by the books of the Platonists to return into himself and that he entered into his inmost self under God's guidance. He says, "I entered and saw with a certain eye of my soul above the same eye of my soul, above my mind, the immutable light, not this common light visible to all flesh, nor was it a greater light of the same kind. . . . Nor was it above my mind like oil above water nor like the heaven above the earth, but it was higher because it made me and I was lower because I was made by it."[73] Later he speaks of his having imagined God as extended over infinite stretches of space, but God, he says, soothed his head and closed his eyes so that he would not see vanity. He continues, "I withdrew from myself a little, and my insanity subsided. And I woke up in you, and I saw that you are infinite in another way, and this vision was not drawn from the flesh."[74]

If one understands these instances of seeing in terms of the official version, these passages from Book Seven are inevitably interpreted as records of momentary mystical visions that Augustine enjoyed at Cassiciacum in the months before his baptism. If, however, one understands those instances of seeing in terms of philosophical insights, one can understand Augustine's "I saw" in a non-mystical sense, and one can, furthermore, view the later part of Book Seven subsequent to his encounter with the books of the Platonists, not as presenting a series of historical events that occurred over a relatively short period of time but as presenting a set of philosophical or theological insights that sum up his newly found understanding of the Christian faith in the light of what he learned from Plotinus, an understanding that he need not have acquired over a few weeks or months but that he more likely came to over a number of years of philosophical and theological reflection. The latter I suggest is a more plausible reading of these texts, which have troubled students of Augustine for decades. I have not, of course, settled the question of how to interpret what Pierre Courcelle called "vain attempts at Plotinian ecstasy," but I have at least shown that one need not interpret Augustine's words as claims of having seen as a momentary, ecstatic visions of God.

St. Augustine's Phenomenology of Confusion

Craig J. N. de Paulo
Temple University

According to St. Augustine, even the ancient and familiar term "*philosophia*" (love of wisdom) involves some interpretation since both pagan and Christian alike use this word, yet equivocally. Since "God is wisdom," Augustine argues, "philosophy is the love of God," making no distinction between the *eros* for truth by way of reason or faith.[1] Such a distinction arrives rather late in Western thought, as a matter of fact, when the mediæval Scholastics would subject the divine science of the Greeks to the sacred theology of Christianity, rendering philosophy little more than a "handmaiden" (*ancilla theologiæ*). But, in Augustine, we find a more antique experience that neither separates faith from reason nor man from the world. This is also, in part, what phenomenologists and existentialists admire in Augustine, and the reason I have decided to discuss Augustine's notion of confusion as a kind of phenomenology.[2] Philosophically, it appears from his writings that Augustine moves from his experience to abstraction; and without sacrificing eloquence, he is able to describe the human condition with clarity and a profound sense of flesh and blood, which continues to make his passionate thought so attractive even to contemporary, and much more secular readers.

In Augustine, we find that there are various levels of confusion and ambiguity interwoven with his thought, resulting in a highly sophisticated use of terms with phenomenological credibility.   In this article, I intend to concentrate on Augustine's notion of the human being as a being of confusion and restlessness.

Perhaps, we should begin with this famous phrase from the *Confessions* "*et inquietum est cor nostrum*," where Augustine demonstrates his own sense of the confusion that exists between the individual human person and the entire human race, or what we may also discuss as the phenomenological inseparability between any human being and Adam,[3] or the human being and the world. Augustine recognizes that restlessness defines the human condition; and that while it is the most universal way to discuss man, it is also an equivocal term. In this world (Babylon), we are a single heart ("*cor nostrum*"), held together by our restlessness. First of all, and most importantly, the human being is restless for God, the Creator, who made us and for Whom we long (if not emotionally, then ontologically and *in* our very movements and actions). Secondly, the human being suffers a restlessness over sin, which divides us from ourselves and from God. As St. Augustine writes, "When the human race, in the exercise of this freedom of will, increased and advanced, there arose a mixture and confusion of the two cities by their participation in a common iniquity."[4] Finally, the human being is made restless by the supernatural gift of grace that seems to pierce through nature and its corruption converting it back toward God Himself in love and virtue. Restlessness reveals the delicate and ambiguous situation of the human being in its various kinds of duality: it is a duality of flesh and spirit, a duality of turning, duality of selfhood, a duality of will, resulting in a being in between Babylon and Jerusalem,[5] suffering an estrangement from one city and an exile from the other, a citizen of both and neither, wanting and willing peace, yet held by restlessness. Without doubt, our restlessness has been formed—or, rather, *deformed*—by original sin, so much so that on the one hand, we are moved by the past, by Adam, by his righteousness and by his disobedience, and on the other hand, we are moved by the future, by a teleology of salvation, by Christ Himself. Yet, in this confusion, Augustine recognizes the phenomenon of grace and the Christian's experience of faith, hope and love that appears to act as an illuminative summons to us, which assists us in working out the entanglement of the two cities within us. In this present state,

Augustine views the two cities "commingled," and as such, we are drawn to the false, superficial "peace" of Babylon.[6] Thus, in this corrupt and complacent worldly sort of peace, we further confuse Babylon with Jerusalem, which fuels the fires of concupiscence in our heart, making us more a liar as we attempt to justify and rationalize our sins away as savvy citizens of the world. In fact, Augustine actually states that "Babylon means Confusion,"[7] and in as much as the human being is a worldly being, it is very much a being of confusion.

We can discuss Augustine's notion of human confusion in terms of his further elaboration of the confusion of life and death alongside his notion, or what we could easily call his philosophy, of the confusion of time. For St. Augustine, life is not a simple matter.   With a keen observation on our mortal existence, he writes, "For no sooner do we begin to live in this dying body, than we begin to move ceaselessly towards death."[8] Augustine understood that life and death are also a commingled reality. Although human life can boast of an "innate nobility" having been made in the "image and likeness" of God,[9] spiritually speaking it is also a kind of nothingness to which God has granted being.[10] Augustine viewed human life as a gift, and our entire life, therefore, ought to be conceived as a single expression of gratitude. But, the reality of sin and its native ingratitude reveals the truth about death, another equivocal term. Of course, death refers to our mortality in the natural end of the physical, corruptible body, but Augustine defines this as "the first death," which is not nearly as deadly as "the second death."[11] The second death refers to the death of the soul, or death everlasting, and this sort of spiritual death actually begins in our worldly life. The obstinacy of the will in its refusal to take up God's divine grace and do the good leads to a life of mortal sin, which is only a life in appearance, for Augustine, since such a life is more akin to death. True life is wedded to conversion and to Christ Himself, which has little regard for this world and its pleasures since it is life defined by the notion of pilgrimage toward Eternity.[12] Furthermore, in Augustine's original articulation of time we find yet another, more universal, phenomenology of human confusion. According to Augustine, the human being is always experiencing a "presence of the past" and a "presence of the future" in the "presence of the present" since it is an historical being and a futural being. In other words, the human being is a being *in between* an "Adam past" and an "Adam future," always moving from out of its limitations of dust and ashes toward spiritualization, from mortality to salvation, and all of this not only occurs in history, but in hundreds of moments everyday of every individual's life whenever there is instance of free choice. Following the insights of the Apostle St. Paul, Augustine affirms "as we have borne the image of the earthly, we shall also bear the image of the heavenly."[13]

A Phenomenology of Human Duality

Torn and fascinated with his own interior contradictions, Augustine's thought has numerous kinds of existential tensions that we shall discuss here in terms of "dualities."[14] In Augustine, we find that each experience corresponds to its opposite, revealing the complex and compound condition of the human being as a being of confusion and an admixture of two ontological communities—the city of God and the city of man. Relying on the Scriptures, Augustine's mature thought makes a serious, philosophical departure from Platonism toward the development of his own Christian philosophy especially in the way in which he uses central Biblical terms for understanding his own personal conflicts and, more universally, for understanding all of humankind. Perhaps, the most universal of such terms for considering human duality would begin with Augustine's Scriptural division between the city of God and the city of man. First of all, these divisions come from above, from revelation, and they are supernatural divisions resulting from revealed history, from the fall of the angels and the division between the blessed and the damned, which, according to Augustine, has become intermingled with nature and human history. Since the time of the Fall, the human being has suffered this dual citizenship, having origins in the nobility of a heavenly breath and in the "dust and ashes" of the earth. As a worldly and fallen creature, the human being has also been subject to the all too alluring influence of the "evil one," who exercises a certain perverse governance over the world. Nevertheless, for Augustine, there is a definite world order and hierarchy that exists that acknowledges the supremacy of the Creator and good over evil in the fact that the city of God is theoretically and ultimately superior. In us, however, our spiritual citizenship is more often than not obscured by the everyday experience of being in the world, having a body, and living according to the flesh.

Following St. Paul, Augustine further recognized the depths of human duality by the supernatural division that persists between the "flesh" and the "spirit," which defines the experience of conflict within the human will and the significance of love as the singular source of our becoming, of identifying ourselves with either the heavenly or the worldly. Yet, inasmuch as we remain living in the world, we remain confused and a real ambiguity persists within us, having a desire for transcendence alongside a worldly predilection for things more akin to nothingness than to being. While, on one hand, the confusion of the will does not prevent our ability to become resolute; on the other hand, our resoluteness does not destroy the alterity of the will. Rather, we become resolute fully aware of the other side of our will, resulting in the experience of having two wills and sensing ourselves as a "house divided against itself." Corresponding to the warfare between the spiritual city of God and the diabolical city of man, and the way in which "the flesh lusts against the spirit, and the spirit against the flesh,"[15] Augustine insists that the experience of human volition occurs in the phenomenon of two wills. He writes: "Thus did my two wills, the one old, the other new, the first carnal, and the second spiritual, contend with one another, and by their conflict they laid waste my soul."[16]

From the instant Augustine begins to speak about this conflict of will which "laid waste [his] soul," we are immediately introduced to his own personal interiority and probably the first time in Western philosophy where we encounter the exposure of the innermost dynamics of the human soul beyond the achievements of the philosophical speculation of the Classical Greeks. Augustine does not hesitate to reveal the intimacy and anguish that surrounds human choice in its impotencies and in its possibilities disclosed by the limitations of the past and the uncertainties of the future. Augustine's *Confessions* is a confession of praise, a confession of faith and a confession of sin, disclosing a person who comes to realize his radical dependence upon God in the disturbance and restlessness of conversion. The existential characteristics of the conflict of the will, which are entirely directed toward conversion, begin in what Augustine describes as the "call of conscience."

Again, unlike the Greeks, we find in Augustine that human choice is not merely a matter of virtue and vice, but an agony in the garden of the will where the individual is deafened by the noise of the world and its distractions, and the triumph of truth of self and goodness is never gained without the overcoming of the temptations of the lies of the false self. The false self, according to Augustine, is our everyday sense of ourselves, sometimes exaggerated, sometimes deprecated, but always formed—or, rather, *de*formed, by pride, which is all of the stuff of original sin recycled in us. Although the call of conscience is in fact the voice of Christ in us, deep within the *ego interiora*, it is a silent voice disclosing the war between the spirit and the flesh, between Jerusalem and Babylon. The call is a summons to true selfhood and authenticity in recognizing oneself as a being for God in the midst of its being absorbed by the confusion of the world. Like Jesus calling Lazarus from the dead, the call of conscience summons the true self to resurrection, recovering its original uprightness and dignity.

Conversion, according to Augustine, is full of visions and voices, and continence is one of the greatest combatants against the false self and its worldly illusions. As a manifestation of conscience, continence silences the noise of sensuality exhorting the true self to "turn deaf ears to those unclean members of yours upon the earth so that they may be mortified."[17] But, this is exactly what frightens the true self and keeps it fleeing from the dictates of conscience, fearing its death from its ordinary self, from everybody else, from the world, from its comforts and from "its trifles and vanities."[18] Here, we find another duality, the duality that seems to exist between continence and concupiscence. Having its origins in original sin, concupiscence keeps us "down to earth," so to speak, but inordinately attached to the things of this world. Concupiscence is our bond—or, rather, our bondage, with the world, and it defines Augustine's notion of spiritual fornication, which is an illicit love and a lust according to the flesh.[19] Concupiscence and its perverse inclination toward the flesh disclose another duality regarding the inordinate love of the world, which Augustine discusses in terms of "*uti*" and "*frui.*"[20]

These two forms of love ultimately disclose the tensions that exist between divine love (*caritas*) and worldly love (*amor mundi*). Once again, however, it ought to be said that "*caritas*" exists in the individual alongside worldly love, which is also discussed by Augustine as "*cupiditas*" as well as by the more developed term "*concupiscentia.*" Further, just as the spirit is at war against the flesh, Augustine views the love of *caritas* in opposition to *cupiditas*, which extends to that rivalry between use (*uti*) and enjoyment (*frui*). Augustine writes: "*Quo modo enim radix omnium malorum cupiditas, sic radix omnium bonorum caritas est.*"[21]

The Confusion of the Heart

Although there is little debate over the fact that for Augustine there is certainly a primacy of the heart (*cor*) in his philosophy, there is also a definite confusion of his notion of the human heart with his notion of mind (*mens*). In fact, when we consider this confusion that exists between the heart and mind in Augustine, we find that it further opens up what we have termed as his *phenomenology of confusion*.

While Augustine sometimes uses mind (*mens*) interchangeably with intellect (*intellectus*), he also employs the term "*animus*' and "*anima*" equivocally, the former also referring to the mind and the latter typically identifying the soul as such.[22] There is further confusion over the fact that he uses the masculine form of the term to discuss the thinking aspect of the soul, which is otherwise viewed as something feminine, probably referring to the relationship between the soul (the bride) and Christ (the bridegroom) from his interpretation of the Scriptures inspired by the Apostolic tradition.[23] Furthermore, Augustine also speaks of the soul as "one mind" (*cor unum*), which he explains is the "memory, understanding and will," neither making any distinctions between these faculties nor between those activities ordinarily associated with either the mind or the heart.[24]

This confusion of mind and heart extends to the ambiguity of the will that characterizes Augustine's notion of love (*amor*) with regard to his discussion of concupiscence and sensuality.[25] Augustine writes: "Not with doubtful but with sure knowledge (*conscientia*) do I love you, O Lord. By your Word you have transfixed my heart, and I have loved you."[26] In this passage, we can clearly see the way in which Augustine describes the will in its own existential ambiguity, having *both* the aspect of knowing *and* loving. First of all, the term "*conscientia*" is kind of a middle term between the will and the mind since it is a peculiar kind of knowledge, yet it pertains mostly to informing the will, and, in this case, even as far as loving God. Secondly, we see that God's Word (Christ Himself, which is considered inseparable from the Gospel) pertains mostly to the correction, striking and piercing (*percussisti*) of the heart resulting in the conversion of worldly love (*amor mundi*) toward loving God. But, this passage further infers that Augustine's various usages of the word "love" are also equivocal, stratifying the meanings of these terms from the sensual to the divine. Here, Augustine relies upon the traditional Latin term "*amor*" to describe the love of God, without any mention of the Christian term "*caritas*." Although this is in part due to the limitations of Latin and its conjugations of this term, it nevertheless appears that the term "*amor*" is used by Augustine as another kind of middle term between the divine love "*caritas*" and the more sensual terms like "*cupiditas*" (corrupt love) and "*libido*" (lust, or erotic love).[27] The term "*amor*" is also used by Augustine to express what is, perhaps, the most interesting aspect of love in its movement, fluidity and natural inclinations where he writes "*pondus meum amor meus.*"[28] This famous expression describing love as a kind of spiritual weight directly thrusts us into his entire understanding of the will in its restlessness of love and in its absolute yet ambiguous attraction to the good. It is only in love that the person—the whole person—one's past and future, can be understood and articulated once and for all, as a totality, as "one mind," hopefully, in the end, in God. Love reveals our confusion with the two rival communities commingled within us, with the Church and with the world, falling in the flesh and rising in the spirit.

The Confusion of Concupiscence

In love, we also encounter the *confusion of concupiscence* in the very fabric of the will's struggle for the good, the "real" good, in the double-sidedness of its directionality, as that which reveals our ontological attraction and indebtedness to God, the supreme Good, while sensing an attachment to the world and its illusory horizon of "goods" commingled with evil. In other words, the otherness of the will is equally confused with the world, subjecting our choice making to the influence and corruption of every "other" in this world and the next, a serpentine commingling of the two cities constantly falling and turning, and spiraling through our everyday deliberation. The confusion of solitude constitutes the entire phenomenon of human relations since, as we have already mentioned, Augustine clearly understood that there is a phenomenological inseparability between man and the world. Nevertheless, because friendship is viewed by Augustine as fundamental to us and, more specifically, as a kind of "spiritual otherness,"[29] in the experience of friendship we can more properly examine the confusion of concupiscence with regard to human alterity and love.

But, friendship, too, is a complicated matter. After all, since we are ourselves a composite of two cities, having a kind of ontological and volitional "friendship" with both of these realities in us, Augustine makes a fundamental division between worldly friendship, often viewed as perverse in various degrees, on the one hand, and spiritual, or true friendship, on the other—the first, the result of our bonds with the world, and the second, resulting from the grace of charity. Nevertheless, both of these friendships involve confusion, and this simple division can only be appreciated in abstraction since as Augustine noticed "in this life, we frequently mistake an enemy for a friend, and a friend for an enemy."[30]

In his consideration, or remembrance, of perverse friendship, which he experienced prior to becoming resolute about conversion to Christianity, Augustine confesses some startling revelations about his own personal weaknesses and cravings often resulting in what he defines as "inordinate love." In the *Confessions*, Augustine writes:

> What was there to bring me delight except to love and be loved? But that due measure between soul and soul, wherein lies the bright boundaries of friendship, was not kept. Clouds arose from the slimy desires of the flesh and from youth's seething spring. They clouded over and darkened my soul, so that I could not distinguish the calm light of chaste love from the fog of lust. Both kinds of affection burned confusedly within me and swept my feeble youth over the crags of desire and plunged me into a whirlpool of shameful deeds.[31]

Always drawn by the passionate gravity of love and loving (*nisi amare et amari*), Augustine forlornly recounts this breach of friendship, which ought to have been a spiritual bond between two minds (*ab animo usque ad animum*). Attributing this fall from friendliness to the "slimy desires of the flesh" (*limosa concupiscentia carnis*) and to the uprising of puberty and its novelty of fleshly experience (*scatebra pubertatis*), Augustine allegorically recalls the serpent in the Garden in his use of the term "slimy," indicating his conceptual association of concupiscence with original sin. He further admits here that concupiscence "clouded over" his heart (*obfuscabant cor meum*) so that he could no longer discern the peaceful love of friendship (*serenitas dilectionis*) from the darkness of lust (*caligine libidinis*). In the account above, Augustine explains the precise way in which concupiscence threads straight through our desires (*abrupta cupiditatum*) tearing apart our integrity and mixing both noble and corrupt loves within him in a confusion of self, immersed in a "whirlpool of shameful deeds" (*gurgite flagitiorum*).

Later in the *Confessions*, Augustine tells us that while he was in Thagaste and then again back to Carthage approximately between the years A.D. 373-382, or between the ages of nineteen and twenty-eight, he and his "friends" were involved with "unbridled lusts" (*intemperantiam libidinum*), seducing and deceiving others and one another "by various desires" (*variis cupiditatibus*) for vanity's sake.[32] Augustine's notion of vanity is also a fascinating topic, which leads us back to his days as a student in Carthage, where he defines himself as "overflowing with vanity," linking it with city life and sophistication: "*elegans et urbanus esse gestiebam abundanti vanitate.*"[33] Like his frequent use of the term "Babylon," Carthage, too, is used by Augustine to discuss concupiscence and its confusion not merely as an infection of a single soul, but as a city, a community of corruption, an ontological epidemic, where love is confused, commingled and compulsive, as Augustine writes, *"rui etiam in amorem, quo cupiebam capi."*[34] A city dweller quintessentially, Augustine moves from Thagaste to Madauros, back to Thagaste, then to Carthage, to Thagaste again, back to Carthage, to Rome, then Milan, back to Rome, then again to Thagaste and finally to Hippo, back and forth, mapping his restlessness and turnings toward conversion through each of these cities, each one symbolizing their own unique composites of confusion, reflecting the more cosmic commingling of the heavenly city and the earthly city.[35]

In Carthage, Augustine truly abandoned himself to the flesh, bound by the confusion of concupiscence where he begins to experience the duality of himself as someone "in love with love" (*nondum amabam et amare amabam*)[36] unable to distinguish the love of friendship from the lust that "seeks for something to love" (*quaerebam quid amarem*).[37] Unlike that native restlessness of our heart that desires God, this corrupt love is a desire more akin to nothingness than to being, distracted by the means of love and absorbed by sensual pleasure. Augustine writes:

> Therefore, my soul did not grow healthy, but it was ulcered over, and it cast outside itself and in its misery was avid to be scratched by the things of sense, things that would not be loved if they lacked all soul. To love and to be loved was sweet to me, and all the more if I enjoyed my loved one's body. Therefore, I defiled the very source of friendship by the filth of concupiscence, and its clear waters I befouled with the lust of hell.[38]

Here, too, we find another example of Augustine's own phenomenology of confusion in his description of his experience of concupiscence and its contempt of friendship. This whole experience is a kind of sickness, according to Augustine, that attacks the soul and prevents spiritual growth. We can also see the role of ambiguity in the phenomenon of concupiscence since it affects *both* the body *and* the soul. Using a physical analogy, Augustine describes the soul as being "ulcered over" (*ulcerosa*), "cast outside itself" (*proiciebat se foras*), and wanting to be "scratched by the things of sense" (*scalpi avida contactu sensibilium*). Thus, we find that in the experience of concupiscence, the soul seems to lose its own identity, confusing itself with the body, suffering its pain, feeling thrown into the body and plunged into its world of sense. In concupiscence, then, the soul is no longer soul, phenomenologically speaking, because it has become entirely confused with the body. But, this is only the half of it—that is, the ambiguity of it—since the body, too, appears to have lost its own identity, its own sense of itself, and its boundaries. In concupiscence, the body becomes confused with the body of the other, moving according to the desires and wishes of the other's soul. In this way, friendship, which ought to be the bond between souls, is lost to sin and individual freedom, and autonomy becomes an abstract memory alongside its thirst for sensual satisfaction.

Elsewhere, also discussing the confusion of concupiscence with regard to friendship, Augustine goes so far as to compare himself and his dearest friend who had died to the Greek mythic figures, Orestes and Pylades, who enjoyed an inordinate love that led to death.[39] Augustine writes, "I believe that the more I loved him, the more did I hate and fear death, which had taken him away from me, as my cruelest enemy."[40] Unlike Pylades, Augustine explains that he feared death when his beloved friend died. Although he felt incomplete when his "other self" had died, Augustine's sense of death appears to be very different from the experience of Orestes and Pylades. Despite the confusion of concupiscence, death appears to have a definitive illumination for Augustine.[41] He begins to question what he otherwise presumed in concupiscence, and there appears to be a kind of awakening that occurs in his mortal questioning, which summons the soul back to itself and toward its own truth. Augustine writes, "I marveled more that I, his second self, could live when he was dead."[42] Death—and the projection of death—is an illumination of human confusion from which self-identity springs and, ultimately, the single most important kind of fear that accompanies conversion.

Toward a Spiritual Ontology of Confusion

As the renowned French scholar of Augustine, Aimé Solignac, has already put it, Augustine's thought is essentially a "spiritual ontology, which is directly placed on the level of ethics."[43] As we have seen, we could further say that it is also a spiritual ontology of confusion. Confusion constitutively defines the human condition, as we experience it, in our restlessness, in our turnings, and in our commingling with others and even, to some extent, with God. Phenomenologically speaking, Augustine makes no distinction between being and conversion, and he regards "true life" in spiritual terms, ultimately understanding "the human being to be a *religious being*, a being rooted in the divine Being."[44]

Prudence in St. Thomas Aquinas: Certitude in Ambiguity

John M. Haas
National Catholic Bioethics Center

In a national Catholic publication three physicians, a philosopher, and two bishops published an essay asking if organ transplantation were ever morally licit. Among other things, they wrote of the conditions which had to be met before organs could morally be removed from a transplant donor. In accord with medically accepted standards, they appealed to the "dead donor rule," i. e., vital organs may not legally or morally be removed for transplantation unless the donor is dead. In their essay they stated that the transplant team must have "absolute certitude" that the donor is dead before the organs are excised.[1]

Pope John Paul II had also addressed this subject matter to an international conference of transplant specialists almost a year earlier, in August 2000. In his Address, he, too, insisted that the donor must be dead before the organs could be removed and that death had to be determined by a competent physician using either cardio-pulmonary or neurological criteria. But contrary to what one might expect, the Pope took a position which might seem more liberal than that taken by the authors of the aforementioned essay.

Traditionally death has been determined using cardio-pulmonary criteria. When breathing and heart beat cease for such a period of time that resuscitation would be impossible, the person is declared dead. More recently neurological criteria have also come to be accepted by the medical community for the determination of death. When physicians can ascertain the complete and irreversible cessation of all brain activity (in the cerebrum, cerebellum and brain stem) the person can be declared dead. In the United States neurological criteria can be used for the legal determination of death. Most state laws were drawn up to conform to the Uniform Definition of Death Act drafted by the National Conference of Commissioners of Uniform State Laws in 1980 at their national conference. "Whole-brain" criteria of death were first proposed by the "Ad Hoc Committee of the Harvard Medical School to Examine the Definition of Brain Death" in a "Special Communication" published in the *Journal of the American Medical Association* in 1968.[2] These basic criteria have become almost universally accepted, even as they are continually improved.

In his August 2000 Address, the Pope also accepted the legitimacy of neurological criteria for determining death and insisted that there must be certainty of death before a transplant team could initiate their work on the donor. Significantly the Pope did not call for "absolute certitude" in determining the death of the donor as had the authors in the essay mentioned above but rather insisted upon "moral certitude" or what is sometimes referred to as prudential certitude. The Pope wrote:

> Therefore a health-worker professionally responsible for ascertaining death can use these [neurological] criteria in each individual case as the basis for arriving at that degree of assurance in ethical judgment which moral teaching describes as "moral certainty." This moral certainty is considered the necessary and sufficient basis for an ethically correct course of action. Only where such certainty exists, and where informed consent has already been given . . . is it morally right to initiate the technical procedures required for the removal of organs for transplant.[3]

In other words, it seemed that the Pope was more lax than the physicians, ethicists, and two of his own bishops in indicating the kind of certainty which would be required before organs could be removed for transplantation. Indeed, the authors of the essay on the legitimacy of organ transplantation seemed to accuse the Pope of changing his own standards in the course of his Address to the

International Congress on Transplants. Earlier in his presentation the Pope had said that organs could not be removed until the donor was "certainly dead." And in the Address he also posed the question, "When can a person be considered dead with complete certainty?"

The authors of the aforementioned essay accuse the Pope of having changed his teaching in the course of his Address when he comes to speak of "moral certainty." "Here," they write, "the standard of complete certainty used earlier by the Pope has been changed to 'moral certainty'–a lower standard. Moral certainty comes when the individual's judgment is free of all *reasonable* doubt of error but it does not require the elimination of *all* doubt. When dealing with certain absolute rights of a person—especially the right to life—absolute certitude would seem to be required."[4]

However, the authors are confused about a fundamental teaching in their own moral tradition. It must be stated emphatically that within that tradition "moral certitude" is *not* a lower standard than "absolute certainty." It is *the* standard for moral decisions. Prudential certitude is precisely the kind of certitude which one uses in making moral decisions, even life-and-death ones, although in such cases the greatest effort must be made to eliminate as much doubt and ambiguity from the situation as can be reasonably expected. The "complete certainty" to which the Pope had referred earlier in his Address is precisely that to which he referred when he used the philosophically technical expression "moral certainty." He had not adopted a different standard.

It is not that the Pope was more lax morally than the authors of the essay in question. Rather he was appealing to a different kind of certitude than they were, the certitude of prudence. And it is a certitude which is used in ethical decision making and which fully takes account of the ambiguities in human knowledge arising from human finitude and from the virtually endless circumstances which surround any human act.

The virtue of prudence within western thought is that settled capacity to make sound moral decisions in concrete circumstances with all their ambiguity. It is sometimes referred to by German philosophers as "the conscience of the situation" or *Situationsgewissen*. In fact, the "father of situation ethics," Joseph Fletcher, even went so far as to claim that his ethical methodology was nothing other than a contemporary presentation of the teaching of prudence.[5] However, his approach was grounded in utilitarianism, which is simply not compatible with the moral framework within which the western understanding of prudence was developed. The teaching on prudence to which Fletcher wanted to appeal was developed thoroughly within a virtue ethic which formulates objective moral norms derived from the very nature of the human person. Prudence is the settled capacity, or virtue, of an individual which enables that individual to choose the appropriate means toward his chosen goal, but the efficacy of prudence depends on its clear reading of reality rather than on a utilitarian calculus of self-interest which seeks the greatest good for the greatest number when that good is understood as whatever maximizes pleasure and minimizes pain.

While prudence guides the virtuous person in the concrete situation with all its ambiguity, this virtue also looks to universal principles to guide moral choices. "[I]t is necessary for the prudent man to know both the universal principles of reason, and the singulars about which actions are concerned."[6] There is no ambiguity about the moral principles guiding human action of course: pursue good and avoid evil; never directly take the life of an innocent person; be just. However, the more one descends to the concrete circumstances of a given human act, the greater the ambiguity and uncertainty about what will constitute the moral and just act in this case. It is here in particular that prudence plays its critical and essential role.

Aristotle and Phronesis

Prudence had played a very important role in western ethical thought long before it was taken up into the Christian intellectual tradition. When Aristotle (384 to 332 BC) taught his ethical theory, he referred even then to the wisdom of "the Ancients," which included the importance of prudence. This was a wisdom drawn from the very nature of the human person. Aristotle spoke of prudence as practical reasoning. Moral philosophy was seen as a practical science, not a theoretical one, such as metaphysics or logic. It was concerned with providing guidance to individuals in their need to make concrete moral decisions in everyday life. The word Aristotle used for this virtue of practical reasoning was *phronesis,* and he defined it as "a true and reasoned state or capacity to act with regard to the things that are good or bad for man."[7]

Aristotle's ethic is thoroughly teleological, or "goal" oriented, as can be seen in the first sentence of the *Nicomachean Ethics:* "Every art and every inquiry, and similarly every action and pursuit, is thought to aim at some good; and for this reason the good has rightly been declared to be that at which all things aim."[8] But the good toward which human action is to be ordered is not a subjectively perceived good, but a true good (*bonum honestum*) which will lead to human flourishing. Despite the fact that ethics is a practical science, Aristotle still classes *phronesis* as an intellectual virtue which enables an individual to determine what is the good for the human person and what must be done to achieve it. The virtue is primarily concerned with the means to the end, and it must consider those contemplated means in complex and changing circumstances. As Aristotle states: "Most of the things about which we make decisions, and into which we therefore inquire, present us with alternative possibilities. For it is about our actions we deliberate and inquire, and all our actions have a contingent character; hardly any of them are determined by necessity."[9]

In fact, because of the contingent character of our actions in the area of moral judgment, one cannot anticipate the same kind of certitude which we can enjoy, for example, in mathematics. As Aristotle pointed out, the philosopher is to seek "as much clearness as the subject-matter admits of, for precision is not to be sought for alike in all discussions."[10] The nature of a given subject matter allows exactness to the extent appropriate to its nature. Moral certitude, or the certitude of prudence, is the assurance one has about a proposed course of action, which excludes the reasonable fear of being in error. It is impossible to know all the factors surrounding a decision in a concrete circumstance, and if one refrained from acting until every doubt or ambiguity were removed, one would be incapacitated. But the virtuous person must have the sureness that his contemplated action is honorable and just even if every doubt has not been removed. This assurance is provided by *phronesis*.

Thomas Aquinas and Prudence

In the thirteenth century Thomas Aquinas translated *phronesis* as *prudentia* in his moral treatise in the second part of the *Summa Theologica* as well as in his writings on the disputed questions concerning virtue. In *Quaestiones disputatae de virtutibus cardinalis*, prudence is given such prominence that it is called the *genitrix virtutem*, the mother of all virtues. Since prudence is the settled capacity to choose the right means toward a good end, the other moral virtues of justice, fortitude and temperance are all dependent upon it. Prudence "informs" them, i.e., gives them their interior shape, so that the acting person knows with certitude what is just or courageous or temperate in a given situation. The human person has innate dispositions toward rendering to others their due, or overcoming evils and obstacles in the pursuit of the good, or has inclinations toward food and drink for one's own self preservation or toward sex for the preservation of the species. It is prudence which shapes these inclinations in accord with the demands of objective reality so that they become indeed just, courageous and temperate.

The German philosopher Josef Pieper goes so far as to claim that "the whole ordered structure of the Occidental Christian view of man rests upon the pre-eminence of prudence over the other virtues."[11] Pieper holds that Thomas Aquinas is a singular exemplar of this view. This is a bold claim, but it is built upon a conviction that there is a metaphysical foundation to ethics which enables the moral actor to see and know reality and then to act accordingly. It is also a way of affirming the certitude which can be achieved through prudence even when the circumstances may be fraught with ambiguity. The claim is a way of acknowledging the contingent and situational character of prudence without sacrificing the conviction that a judgment achieved through prudence is not merely a subjective perception of a situation but rather is one that is grounded in objective reality, with respect to the acting agent as well as the moral object which has been chosen.

The virtues are hierarchically ordered in the thought of Aquinas and indeed in most Christian writers, with prudence being ranked the highest, thereby allowing the lower virtues to be properly ordered to one another and to the moral object of choice. As Aristotle, Aquinas also ranks prudence with the intellectual virtues. Among the cardinal virtues those which are properly and exclusively moral virtues are justice, fortitude and temperance. However, these three could not be properly moral virtues were they not guided and formed by prudence. Prudence serves as the lynch-pin between the intellectual and moral virtues, since prudence itself is both an intellectual virtue and a moral virtue, along with justice, fortitude and temperance. It is in fact, the intellectual virtue concerned with action. *"Virtus intellectualis circa moralia."*[12] It is the right reason of action, *"recta ratio agibilium."*

Prudence as a Guarantor of Objectivity

The classical teaching on prudence enables moral theory to avoid subjectivism, emotivism or skepticism, since prudence is understood not only as a moral virtue but also an intellectual one, ordered to the real and the objectively true. As Thomas points out, prudence is an intellectual virtue *"sub ratione veri"* and a moral virtue *"sub ratione boni."* It is an intellectual virtue under the aspect of the true and a moral virtue under the aspect of the good. It is here that Pieper sees the hierarchical ordering of the virtues, with prudence being pre-eminent, as reflecting the "whole ordered structure of the Occidental Christian view of man" since it is based on the insight that Being precedes Truth and Truth precedes the Good.[13]

Aquinas quotes Augustine to the effect that "the true is that which is." *"Verum est id quod est."*[14] Since truth is the conformity of mind to reality (*verum est aedequatio mens ad rem*), being must be seen as preceding the true.[15] And the true precedes the good, for as Thomas says, "The good presupposes the true."[16] In the classical tradtion appropriated by Aquinas, truth is the standard for that which is good. In fact, transcendentally *ens et verum et bonum convertuntur*, being and the true and the good are convertible terms. In the created order, being precedes the true and the true precedes the good. Prudence, as an intellectual and moral virtue, bridges the gap, as it were, between the metaphysical and the ethical orders. It enables the acting person to perceive the real (*verum*) and then to act in conformity with it as the will is drawn to it as the good (*bonum*).

There can, for example, be no justice without truth. Since justice is rendering to others their due, before trying to execute an act of justice one must first know the truth about oneself and the other and one's relation to the other. After the collapse of the apartheid regime in South Africa, a program was established to address and overcome the unspeakable injustices of the past. It was named "The Truth and Reconciliation Commission" of the National Unity Government. Truth, or conformity of mind to reality, is a prerequisite for the exercise of any of the virtues, in this case justice. And the apprehension of the truth of a situation with all its variable circumstances is the province of the *intellectual* virtue of prudence. Apprehending the good to be pursued in a situation and directing one's actions toward the attainment of that good is the province of the *moral* virtue of prudence.

In the thought of Aquinas then, prudence enables the human person to be fully human. Human flourishing is achieved when "reason is perfected in the cognition of truth" so that reason can then order and regulate the lower appetites toward the attainment of the *bonum honestum*, toward the attainment of the true good of the person. "*Bonum hominis, inquantum est homo, est: ut ratio sit perfecta in cognitione veritatis, et inferiores appetitus regulentur secundum regulam rationis.*"[17] The good of the human person, exactly insofar as one is human, is the perfecting of reason in the cognition or apprehension of what is true in order that the lower appetites (which are ultimately ordered toward the good of the person) are regulated according to the rule of reason. This provides the foundation for an objective, realist approach to ethics since, as Aquinas states, "the measure and rule of intellectual virtue is not another kind of virtue, but things themselves."[18]

Kant's skepticism led to his conclusion that one cannot come to know *das Ding-an-sich*, the thing in and of itself, while Aquinas on the other hand was confident of the capacity of the intellectual virtue to be able to grasp the *res ipsa*, the thing itself. Skepticism ultimately leads to a morality of subjectivism while the moderate realism of Aquinas offers an objective morality which one can confidently pursue even in the face of a certain ambiguity.

Aquinas refers to prudence as a "cognitive virtue" (*prudentia est cognoscitiva*) as well as a "commanding virtue" (*prudentia est praeceptiva*) applying knowledge to action.[19] Prudence is that perfected capacity to make correct moral judgments which is more commonly referred to today as conscience. Aquinas writes very little of conscience but extensively of prudence, which can indeed be understood as conscience if more modern preoccupations with legal precepts can be eliminated from the concept. In fact, the Latin root of the word conscience points to what has been said of the cognitive (rather than prescriptive) character of prudence: *con-scientia*, i.e., with knowledge. However, the part of prudence which is most properly characteristic of it is "command." The prudent individual will consider a course of action carefully and without undue haste but if one only engages the reflective character of prudence, one is not virtuous, one is not prudent. After cognition and reflection must come action.

Aquinas identifies the cognitive parts of prudence as being memory, reasoning, understanding, docility and shrewdness. The parts which pertain to the "commanding" action of prudence are foresight, circumspection and caution. Foresight refers to choosing that means which is appropriately ordered to the end, circumspection (literally, "looking around") refers to consideration of the circumstances of the matter at hand in all their complexity and perhaps ambiguity, and caution is the part of prudence directed toward removing obstacles toward the attainment of the chosen goal.

The very word prudence, and those parts of referred to as circumspection and caution, all seem to connote irresolution and timidity as they are used today. However, irresolution and timidity would be imprudent and the very opposite of virtue. The prudent military officer is the one who knows his objectives, who assesses the circumstances of his present position, who can judge the chances of success of a proposed tactic, and then moves with speed to execute it. Yet nothing could be further from the true character of prudence than irresolution and timidity. The most characteristic action of prudence, without which it would not be a virtue at all, is properly command (*imperium*), which follows on deliberation and decision. The "chief act" of prudence "is a command about what has been already counseled and judged in matters of action."[20] Indeed, prudence is focused on the contemplated action in the concrete circumstances rather than universal principles. "Prudence consists chiefly, not in the knowledge of universals, but in applying them to action."[21] This is thoroughly within the classical understanding of this virtue. As Aristotle claimed, appealing to the wisdom of the ancients, one should deliberate slowly but carry out quickly the conclusions of one's deliberations.[22] If one has been formed as a virtuous person, if one has repeatedly and customarily done what is just and courageous and temperate, one does not need to scruple over a given action. By "nature", i.e., by nature of one's formation in virtue, one acts in a way which is just and which leads to human flourishing. The virtuous person usually does not have to anguish or scruple over deciding a course of action. A mark of that person's prudence is the alacrity with which he or she acts.

Prudential Certitude

Indeed, even the complexities and ambiguities of the situation do not deter the prudent person from action. The particular certitude leading to action in such circumstances is known precisely as *"certitudo prudentiae"* in contrast to *"certitudo veritatis."* Prudential certitude is not to be seen in opposition to truth but relies on its own particular grasp of truth. It does not, for example, remove every doubt. As Aquinas says, *"non potest certitudo prudentiae tanta esse quod omnino solicitudo tollatur."*[23] Prudential certitude cannot remove every concern about a proposed course of action. But it does remove any concern which would prevent one from acting. And it certainly is not a "lower standard" of truth and certainty being applied to human actions. It is rather the appropriate standard applied to moral action even in the midst of ambiguity. Again, if one waited for absolute certitude one would never act, one would be incapacitated.

As Thomas points out, and as ought to be immediately obvious to us, a person's activities are of almost infinite diversity.[24] He observes that "the good of man changes in manifold fashion, according to the various conditions of men and the times and places, and similar factors."[25] But even with all this diversity of human action, of goals chosen and means executed, the ultimate end of the human person and the goods toward which his appetites or inclinations are ordered are set.

Aquinas is as thoroughly teleological as Aristotle. As he states at the beginning of the section of the *Summa Theologica* dealing with human action: "Every agent, of necessity, acts for an end."[26] But even as the human person is a free agent and the principle of his own action, the ultimate end of the human person is set. Ultimately the end toward which the acting person strives is happiness. Aquinas actually begins his discussion of morality in the *Summa Theologica* with a treatise on the pursuit of happiness, *beatitudo*. "In this matter we shall consider first the last end of human life; and secondly, those things by means of which man may advance towards this end, or stray from the path: for the end is the rule of whatever is ordained to the end. And since the last end of human life is stated to be happiness, we must consider the last end in general; happiness."

Without going into Aquinas' line of argument, he shows that the happiness sought can be realized only when one is in possession of God Himself. "Final and perfect happiness can consist in nothing else than the vision of the Divine Essence."[27] This is the end or goal of the human person which is set. The moral life consists in choosing a veritably endless number of means finally to attain to that end.

The final end is not the only one which is set for the human person; there are also subordinate ends which are set and which comport with his nature for his perfection, such as the consumption of food for the nourishment of the body or the generating functions of the genitalia for the preservation of the species. Chastity, for example, does not mean making no use of the procreative faculties but rather making appropriate use of them according to one's state in life. As Thomas wrote: "For it belongs to chastity that a man make moderate use of bodily members in accordance with the judgment of his reason and the choice of his will."[28]

One may choose whether or not to make use of one's human procreative power in a virtually unlimited set of circumstances but that does not change the fact that the reproductive system and the accompanying appetites are inherently ordered toward children. Therefore, if one is not married, one makes no use of them, for there does not yet exist a marriage bond to provide a family for the nurture of the procreative goods which might result from their use. If one is married, the spouses use their procreative powers "in accordance with the judgment of reason and the choice of will." Here again, couples can be faced with a wide variety of circumstances which could be considered as they consider making use of those powers and acting in accord with those appetites. What is the health of the wife? What are the economic circumstances of the couple? How many children do they already have? What is the emotional state of the spouse?

Such an endless array of questions will face many at the end of life. What is the doctor's prognosis? What is the cost of this treatment? What are the odds of the treatment working? Do the anticipated benefits of the treatment outweigh the burdens? Such questions simply cannot be answered in advance and do depend upon a developed *"Situationsgewissen,"* a conscience for the situation, or prudence. This holds true in virtually every area of human life, from courtship to warfare. Thomas writes that "the means to the end, in human concerns, far from being fixed, are of manifold variety according to the variety of persons and affairs."[29]

Uneasiness with Ambiguity Leads to Legalism, Casuistry

This is one of the truths of the moral life which makes it so dynamic and exciting. The array of goods among which the human person may choose in pursuit of the moral life are virtually unlimited. Yet there are those who are uneasy with this openness and dynamism. They are uneasy with such a "manifold variety." They want every situation addressed ahead of time, and they want all the moral courses of action pre-determined. They suffer, in a word, from scrupulosity.

A very conscientious individual submitted to a bioethics center his "living will" in which he tried to provide direction for every conceivable contingency which might occur as he approached death. This particular "living will" or "advance medical directive" was twenty-seven pages long. The moralist who reviewed the document for the man responded to him that it was not long enough! The point the ethicist tried to make is that it is impossible to determine what all the circumstances will be as one approaches the end of life and consequently impossible to know what decisions will be required of us. To face the circumstances surrounding one's death, one needs to be prudent, one needs already to have developed the settled capacity or the ability to choose the right course of action whenever choices for treatment present themselves. One needs to have developed that virtue for oneself or one needs to designate a health care proxy with power of attorney who is also a prudent person who will make the right decisions for the virtuous individual who has been rendered incompetent. In fact, because of the variety of circumstances which face anyone making decisions, law and medicine make provision for the review of professional actions which is guided by the "reasonable person rule," i.e., what would a reasonable, as it were, prudent professional have done in that situation?

The discomfort with ambiguity and the anxious desire to have laws or precepts to deal with every conceivable situation which one may encounter and which call for a moral decision leads to legalism and a crimping of the moral life. In certain moral traditions it gave rise to casuistry or the discipline of applying "the precepts of the law" to moral cases presented for study. Casuistry can be a useful tool, but when the moral life is defined as adherence to the law rather than reasonable or prudent behavior in ever-changing circumstances, human freedom and growth in the moral life actually become compromised.

Moral manuals were sometimes filled with pages of possible circumstances in which people might find themselves along with an accompanying analysis of possible courses of action. One reads in a moral manual, which was universally used in Catholic seminaries through the middle of the twentieth century.

> It is not a sin to look at one's own inciting parts of the body from necessity or utility, as long as there is not evil intention. To do this out of levity or curiosity is a venial sin, if not done for lust. To look at less inciting parts of one's own body even without cause is not sinful, as long as one does not do this with the intention of venereal pleasure. . . . To look at a statue or an image of either sex which is entirely nude without necessity or great utility, is usually a grave sin; if the look is serious and prolonged, it is a mortal sin. If this is done only transitorily and briefly without a proportionate cause, there is only a venial sin, as long as one does not directly will venereal pleasure. To look at the generating parts of animals from curiosity without any lustful affection, or only for a short time, is only a venial sin.[30]

It is not that the analysis given in this moral manual is wrong, but it certainly is a manifestation of a legalistic preoccupation applied to the moral life and shows the attempt to anticipate and analyze how the commandment against adultery would be applied in almost every concrete circumstance. (The catalogue of actions under "looks" from which the above passage was taken went on for paragraphs.) The chaste, and therefore prudent, person, on the other hand, would by second nature (which is another definition of virtue) simply avoid the actions or circumstances which could conceivably prove morally troubling, and he or she would be able to do so without such a detail of moral pitfalls. Whether in the area of sexual morality, warfare, bioethics, there are those who seek comfort in the letter of the law rather than in a life of morality which is shaped and guided by prudence and its adaptability and openness to changing circumstances.

The Continuing Need for Prudence

Prudence is indeed such a sure and certain guide for moral behavior that it must be followed, even in the midst of ambiguity and even when it makes a mistake. If for some reason, the acting person misreads a situation through no fault of his or her own and therefore draws a wrong conclusion with regard to the proposed action, one is obliged to follow the judgment given by prudence. There is no other guide given, and to refuse to follow its direction would be tantamount to refusing to pursue the good. This of course does not mean that the one following the guidance of prudence is a subjectivist. Each individual, each acting subject, must make his or her own moral decisions, and no one can substitute ethical decision making for another. However, one is saved from subjectivism by one's conviction that we can know reality and the conditions necessary for human flourishing. There are objective standards which can be applied. Even as one follows an erroneous conscience, however, one always stands ready to be corrected, to be brought back into line with reality through the guidance of a friend who may assess the situation more effectively.

There is guidance for the prudent person from the virtually universal understanding of what is behavior becoming of the human person and what is not. For the Jew and the Christian, the Ten Commandments would provide the fundamental guidance as to what actions to avoid in order to sustain one's own integrity and one's own flourishing. There simply are no situations in which certain activities could ever be deemed worthy of a virtuous person. The Roman mind understood the universality of that insight through the natural law. The pagan Greek mind saw it as well as did the Christian Augustine of Hippo or Thomas Aquinas. Aristotle wrote:

> There are some actions and emotions whose very names connote baseness, e.g., spite, shamelessness, envy; and among actions, adultery, theft, and murder. These and similar emotions and actions imply by their very names that they are bad. It is, therefore, impossible ever to do right in performing them: to perform them is always wrong. In cases of this sort, let us say adultery, rightness and wrongness do not depend on committing it with the right woman at the right time and in the right manner, but the mere fact of committing such action at all is to do wrong.[31]

What is generally agreed upon by all concerned with the ethical issues surrounding organ donation is that the dead donor rule remain firmly fixed.[32] If there were not certitude that the potential donor were dead and surgeons proceeded to remove organs for transplantation, one would be faced with one of those actions whose very name connotes baseness as Aristotle observed: murder. What calls for prudential decision-making is the application of the appropriate criteria for declaring someone dead. Currently very rigorous criteria are applied for the determination of death, but until rigor mortis or putrefaction sets in, there might be lingering doubts in the minds of some whether the person is dead. However, waiting for such extreme indications has never been required in medicine and would prove thoroughly impractical and not just for reasons of transplantation. Whether using cardio-pulmonary or neurological criteria, there might in some case be some lingering doubt; in some circumstances there may be some ambiguity. But if in using cardio-pulmonary or neurological criteria it has been demonstrated beyond any reasonable doubt that the person is dead, the physician may legally and morally make a determination of death. The actions which follow upon such a determination, whether the removal of life support, or the filling out of a death certificate, or the probating of a will, or the removal of organs for transplantation can begin without fear of acting immorally.

Some ambiguity will often accompany declaration of death, however, since death is not an empirical event. If someone watches at the bedside of a dying person the precise moment of death is impossible to assess since it is not a physical event. The Pope himself made that clear in his Address to the Congress on Transplants:

> The death of a person is a single event, consisting in the total disintegration of that unitary and integrated whole that is the personal self. It results from the separation of the life principle . . . from the corporal reality of the person. The death of the person, understood in this primary sense, is an event, which no scientific technique or empirical method can identify directly.[33]

Since one cannot empirically observe death, one is dependent on observing biological signs, which follow upon death and it is these that can be scientifically or empirically verified. This simple metaphysical fact about the nature of death, again, means that its determination will often be accompanied by some ambiguity.

But then life has been and always will be filled with ambiguity. It may be time to rehabilitate an ancient virtue, prudence, to provide guidance and freedom to those who seek to pursue a moral life in a day of increasing complexity.

"Stay, illusion": Ambiguity in *Hamlet*

Camille Paglia
University of the Arts

Hamlet begins with a question: "Who's there?" It's midnight on the high, cold battlements of Elsinore, the Danish royal castle, and the guard is changing. The relief sentinel, the officer Barnardo, solicitously urges his fellow soldier, Francisco, to get to bed, but their first exchange is a hostile military challenge. The play's opening bristles with tension, uncertainty, and fear.

"Who's there?" could stand as an epigraph to *Hamlet*. Barnardo's question might be applied to many moments in the play—such as the traumatic scene in the queen's bed chamber where Prince Hamlet stabs a bulging curtain and accidentally kills Polonius, the Lord Chamberlain, or the grisly scene set in a graveyard where Hamlet stares into the hollow eyes of Yorick's skull. "Who's there?" is also the theme of Hamlet's soliloquies, where he questions his own identity and mortality. And finally, "Who's there?" can possibly be understood as addressed to the audience itself—challenging our openness to the artist whose work unfolds before us and asking if and how we know ourselves.

The doubt and distrust on the dark battlements pervade the entire play, so that even small, enclosed spaces feel chill and gusty. Ambiguity blurs or qualifies every theme and character in *Hamlet*. No major work in literary history has been so contested in meaning or subjected to such a mass of alternative interpretations. Criticism has buried the play in questions, while stage and film productions continue to experiment with an astounding variety of readings and settings. No final answers are possible, because the text is embedded with contradictory material. The play seems to have changed every time we come back to it—a mysterious effect that intensifies as we ourselves age. Like Aeschylus' *Oresteia* and Sophocles' *Oedipus Rex*, *Hamlet* reflects back to us our hard-won experience of the great fundamentals of life, which are glimpsed but never fully grasped in youth.

The nagging, teeming questions of *Hamlet* include the following. Why does Hamlet delay and procrastinate in avenging his father the king's murder? Was Queen Gertrude a co-conspirator in her husband's murder? Did she commit adultery with her brother-in-law Claudius before her husband's death? Why is Hamlet depressed at the start of the play? Why does he contemplate suicide? Is he mad or only feigning madness? If both, when is he faking, and when is he genuinely out of control?

What was Hamlet's relationship with his father? Is the king's ghost real? Is it a demon? Does Hamlet believe in God? If he is a Christian, is he Catholic or Protestant? Should Hamlet be king? Exactly how old is he? If he is 30, as the gravedigger claims, why is he still a student? Does he love Ophelia, and did he ever intend to marry her? Why does Hamlet mistrust and abuse women? Why does Ophelia choose her father and brother over Hamlet? What happened to Ophelia's mother? Why does Ophelia go mad? Is her death a suicide or an accident? Do Hamlet's friends—the intellectual Horatio and the sycophantish Rosencrantz and Guildenstern—have a sex life? If so, what is it? What are the Norwegian Prince Fortinbras' motives and goals? Why does King Claudius permit the Norwegian army to cross through Denmark? What is the future of Denmark as a sovereign nation?

I will classify the ambiguities in *Hamlet* into three groups—philosophical, political, and psychological. To the philosophical category, I also assign questions of religious belief as well as language; to the political, matters of law and procedure; and to the psychological, issues of identity, emotion, and sexuality.

For a century, scholarship has connected the philosophical explorations in *Hamlet* to the play's position at a crucial juncture in the evolution of Western thought and science. A contemporary of

Bacon, Shakespeare was writing between Montaigne and Descartes and between Copernicus and Galileo. Hamlet is a student at the University of Wittenburg, a center of the Protestant Reformation. It was in 1517 in Wittenburg that, according to popular legend, the dissident priest, Martin Luther, nailed his 95 theses to the cathedral door, a challenge to authority that dramatized the new, free, inquiring mind. Hamlet's questions go beyond organized religion and its residual medieval dogma to the very existence of God. Holy Scripture is not in his thoughts—at least not in the way that Bible study would become central to evangelical Protestantism from the seventeenth century on. Rather, the codes and assumptions of Christianity seem to be receding and dissolving.

In the immediate intellectual background of *Hamlet* (which is Shakespeare's adaptation of a medieval Scandinavian saga), the bold, questing individualism inspired by the Reformation was intensified by the skeptical spirit of Montaigne, who showed that a new literary genre—the essay—could be a vehicle of philosophical thought. The autobiographical candor and improvisational, associative form of Montaigne's essays can perhaps be felt in Hamlet's soliloquies, although scholars have debated how much Montaigne could or did directly affect Shakespeare. Insofar as Shakespeare belonged to an artistic London milieu that overlapped cultivated court circles, it seems quite possible that he was at least generally familiar with Montaigne's ideas—above all his first principle, "What do I know?" but also his relentless questioning of the traditional underpinnings of certainty and truth.

Hamlet scrutinizes virtually every aspect of human existence—from personal relationships and social organization to the fundamental nature of matter and being. The prince's most famous soliloquy begins, "To be, or not to be: that is the question" (III.i. 56).[1] When Horatio calls out to the ghost stalking the battlements, "Stay, illusion"—that is, "*Stop!*"—he is also summarizing a major argument in Western philosophy (I.i.127). Is reality nothing but flickering illusions—the shadows projected on the wall of Plato's cave of prisoners—or does some stable substratum remain, however it is transformed over time? *Hamlet* frequently describes life with metaphors of "dream" and "shadow" (II.ii.260-69). Though a supernatural visitation, the ghost or "apparition" embodies the delusion of earthly appearances (I.i.28). "Stay, illusion" also expresses the longing of the creative artist—Shakespeare as well as the producer/director Hamlet who co-writes the self-reflexive play-within-a-play—to linger in the realm of imagination, which Hamlet calls "a fiction" and "a dream of passion" (II.ii.562). Through art, life is seen not with scientific or philosophical clarity but with deeper truth.

As attested by his soliloquies, Hamlet is an agnostic about theological issues such as the existence of a hell where sinners are punished and from which demons masquerading as ghosts may fly. At one point, he acknowledges a transcendent being called "the Everlasting" who has published a "canon" of interdictions, including a law against suicide—the "self-slaughter" that Hamlet weighs at his darkest moment (I.ii.131-32). At times, he seems to envision a universe of godless blankness, like the modernist wasteland. Elsewhere, he suggests there is an occult power that cannot be explained in secular terms: "There are more things in heaven and earth, Horatio, / Than are dreamt of in your philosophy" (I.v.166-67). By the end, Hamlet feels "There's a divinity that shapes our ends", a fate inexplicably at work in human lives (V.ii.10). Is that force Christian or pagan or impersonally astrological? Its nature and operations are left ambiguous, even if its effects are felt in a play whose plot seems to lag and surge, then sweep from scene to scene in a way that never ceases to surprise us.

Pondering the link between soul and body, Hamlet wonders whether consciousness survives death. "What dreams may come / When we have shuffled off this mortal coil": the body, entwining or strangling the soul, is shed like a snake skin at death (III.i.66-67). Hamlet strives to reconcile humanity's divided nature—"how noble in reason... in action how like an angel, in apprehension how like a god"—with our gross materiality, "this quintessence of dust" (II.ii.312-17). "What is a man?" he asks elsewhere—simply a "beast" who is content "to sleep and feed"? (IV.iv.33-35). If simply driven by material needs, we are slaves to the flesh and its impermanence. One of *Hamlet*'s obtrusive patterns is its morbid imagery of squalid decay—a common motif of seventeenth-century literature and Mannerist painting. The ubiquity and certainty of decay (one of the few certainties possible in this play) press on Hamlet amid the general implosion of events. In a world of "garbage," foul smells, and decay, objects and identities are continually fracturing—a slow disintegration where the opposite, fertile extreme in the regenerative cycle is either unperceived or undervalued (I.v.57).

Hamlet's theme of universal decay—often flagged by the word "rank," with its implication of putrid dampness—also affects the state of language. Words are Hamlet's vital instruments, his primary medium of engagement with life. This most brilliantly intelligent of all characters in world literature is shown walking onstage while reading a book. But words always betray him, either by dragging him down to despair or luring him outward, as on Elsinore's battlements, into dizzying doubts. (*Horatio*: "These are but wild and whirling words, my lord." [I.v.133]). Words in *Hamlet* are unreliable, slippery. And in the ethically compromised world of Denmark, they are corrupted by lies—the "forgeries" of Claudius and Polonius or the calculating flattery of Rosencrantz and Guildenstern and the unctuous courtier, Osric, which debase language and worsen Hamlet's sense of nausea (II.i.20).

Hamlet wants language to be an escape from subjectivity, but as he ostentatiously puns and quibbles, words seem to multiply on their own and cloud his mind. "Words, words, words," he says satirically of his reading (II.ii.194). As the Romantic poet Samuel Taylor Coleridge may have been the first to argue, Hamlet's mental activity disables him from acting as required in the real world: "the native hue of resolution / Is sicklied o'er with the pale cast of thought" (III.i.84-85). That is, action stimulates the blood, while reading and thinking drain it. When he tries to goad himself into resolution by seeking absolute proof of Claudius' guilt, Hamlet becomes enmeshed in contradiction: he is already convinced of the relativity of perception—illustrated when he contemptuously forces the busybody Polonius to see animal shapes in the mobile clouds (an image that Shakespeare's Mark Antony uses to describe his own search for coherent identity). Hamlet is trapped in a median realm of floating ambiguity and conflicting impulses—impelled by duty toward action while unable to renounce the alluring, infinite qualifications of ever-shifting language.

Now for the political ambiguities in *Hamlet:* As the play opens, there are undercurrents of political instability as well as popular unrest and anxiety in Denmark. Horatio almost immediately notes the political implications of the walking of the late king's ghost: "This bodes some strange eruption to our state"—an image suggesting both ulceration and the tell-tale unearthing of a corpse (I.i.69). On the battlements, the officer Marcellus questions Horatio about the recent frenzy of activity in Denmark portending war or fear of invasion—arms and ship manufacturing going on day and night, seven days a week. The common people are unsettled by these projects, whose purpose is unknown. Political decisions at the top, which have life and death consequences for the masses, are concealed. In a pre-media age, information must come distorted and secondhand via rumor and the grapevine. Hence Marcellus' interrogation of Horatio has a paranoid insistence: there are five questions in nine lines—"why," "why," "why," "what," and "who" (I.i.71-79).

Horatio's long response (a 29-line monologue) is one of the oddest passages in the play, presenting so knotty a problem to actors that it is sometimes shortened or cut out entirely in performance. It chronicles the political background and military rivalry between Denmark and Norway from the last generation to this. Perhaps mindful of the many law students in his London audience, Shakespeare surely intended it as a parody of legal language—abstract, contorted, labyrinthine, and self-interrupting. Norway forfeited land through a compact pledging a personal combat to the death between the Norwegian and Danish kings. That episode, which ended in Denmark's victory, is narrated in labored syntax and obscure locutions from which the current threat, young Fortinbras, son of the slain Norwegian king, bursts "hot and full" (I.i.96). Horatio's tangled exposition of Fortinbras' legal claim says in effect that it is meretricious but potent nonetheless. Thus in *Hamlet* law too distorts language, as it subordinates justice to glib verbal formulations.

"Something is rotten in the state of Denmark," says Marcellus in one of the play's signature lines (I.iv.90). The rot affects not only the state as a political and administrative entity but the state of the nation in spiritual and physical terms: the nation becomes a living organism in medical crisis. Throughout Shakespeare, kings embody or personify their nations and, like dukes, are addressed by the name of their lands. Hence in *King Lear*, the king of France is called "France" and the Duke of Burgundy "Burgundy." In *Hamlet*, as in *Oedipus Rex*, disease at the top trickles downward to all the body's parts. In Sophocles' Thebes, the crops are dying, and women are miscarrying: the pollution upon the land comes from the fact that an incestuous patricide sits on the throne, though he is unaware of his crimes. In *Hamlet*, the king is again a murderer, this time a fratricide, but his crime was committed in cold blood, and his nephew must expose and avenge it. Much of the political turbulence in *Hamlet* ultimately comes from the quaking of the king's uneasy conscience as well as the devious machinations by which he (unlike Oedipus) tries to stop the truth from outing.

Claudius' weak grip on power is betrayed by his raucous, all-night drinking parties, marked by trumpet blasts and gunfire, about which the stoical Horatio questions Hamlet (echoing the sentinels' earlier questioning of Horatio). Hamlet disapprovingly attributes the palace carousing to rowdy Danish tradition, but the audience is led to conclude that the king is drinking to numb himself and revive his flagging spirits. Certainly, Claudius is an awkward, imprudent, and self-absorbed ruler, as indicated at his first appearance by his nervous, distracted deference to a much younger inferior, Laertes. One of the political conundrums of the play is why, after only recently neutralizing Fortinbras' military threat through direct appeal to his aged uncle, the present king of Norway, Claudius allows the Norwegian army to cross Danish territory on the way to Poland, to which the Norwegians have staked yet another questionable claim. This easily overlooked detail puts Fortinbras in Denmark at the play's violent climax, where the entire Danish ruling class destroys itself, bringing Hamlet's dynasty to an end and leaving Denmark under Norwegian occupation.

The structure of Denmark's government or rather the transmission of its power is another unanswered question in *Hamlet*. The matter is left so tenuous that audiences and readers need help from program notes or scholarly explication. Whether Shakespeare intended this ambiguity remains arguable. Denmark's monarchy, unlike England's, is described as elective, but the mechanics of election, as well as the character of the electors, whether oligarchic or popular, are left vague. By murdering his brother, Claudius opened up space for his ambitions, but his election to the vacant throne was by no means certain, for Hamlet and other nobles would also presumably be candidates. Or is there a trace of matrilinearity in the ancient *Hamlet* tale, as some scholars have found in *Oedipus Rex?* Does Gertrude, like Queen Jocasta, confer kingship through her marriage?

The question of succession was a major public anxiety during Shakespeare's lifetime. Elizabeth I, who assumed the throne in 1558, six years before Shakespeare was born, never married, despite determined wooing by a long list of aristocratic and royal suitors in England and Europe. When *Hamlet* was first staged some time in the late 1590s, it was already clear that Elizabeth, then in her sixties, would die without issue. Hence the English foresaw the end of the House of Tudor, a cataclysm possibly paralleled in the extinction of the Danish royal family in *Hamlet*. A justifiable fear throughout the history of monarchies worldwide has been that ambiguity in succession can lead to civil war—a plague on English society during the 32-year War of the Roses of the fifteenth century.

Denmark's elective monarchy in *Hamlet* might seem to avoid the succession problem inherent in royal dynasties, but Shakespeare shows it as equally susceptible to chaos because of its dependence on group thought or mass will. Throughout his plays, Shakespeare is often suspicious and even disdainful of the fickleness of popular emotion. Democracy for him means mob rule—a blind force tending toward anarchy. This is glimpsed in *Hamlet* when Laertes, protesting his father's killing and undignified, perfunctory funeral, leads a mob (the "rabble") who break through the palace gates and shout, "Laertes shall be king!" (IV.v.101-08). In appeasing and defusing Laertes, Claudius hatches his second scheme against his nephew's life—the fencing match where Laertes' rapier will be poisoned. Earlier, Claudius explicitly acknowledges his fear of popular rebellion in conspiring for Hamlet to be murdered in England rather than at home in Denmark.

Does Hamlet have ambitions to be king? Although he sardonically jokes that he is gloomy because "I lack advancement," political ambition does not seem to figure large in his temperament (III.ii.347). As suggested by his delays and hesitations, he prefers the calm, contemplative life. Does he possess the qualities to be a good king? Or is he too impatient for the dull routine of practical affairs? Brooding or mercurial temperaments aren't the best fit for public life—a point occasionally raised in Great Britain over the past quarter century about Charles, Prince of Wales, an amateur painter and botanist. Hamlet is not a playboy prince, like Shakespeare's Prince Hal, who when he assumes the throne must exile his rollicking, fellow fun-lover, Falstaff. But Hamlet does suffer from chronic inhibitions and indecisiveness. Though he can act on impulse—as when he leaps aboard the pirate ship or into Ophelia's open grave—he spends most of the play buffeted or stymied by excess thought.

As a revenge play, a popular, sensationalistic genre in Elizabethan theater, *Hamlet* is also a mystery story or crime drama, paralleled by modern police and detective fiction descending from Edgar Allan Poe. A murder has occurred in Elsinore but been covered up, and Hamlet is the unwilling civilian drafted into service: he snoops around, follows clues, and conducts surveillance and entrapment (the play-within-the-play). Other legal issues in *Hamlet* include the miscarriage of justice when the king, who represents and enforces the law, is a murderer. There is also the vexed question of the disposition of Ophelia's remains: if she is judged to have committed suicide (she falls into a brook when a bough breaks while she is hanging garlands), then according to church law, she cannot be buried in sacred ground. The matter is ambiguous: a Doctor of Divinity sternly calls her death "doubtful" (V.i.229). In a compromise dictated by the king for his own political protection, her grave is dug in the churchyard, but she is given a truncated service—a harshness bitterly protested by her brother. Another ambiguity, played for farce, is the location of Polonius' body, which Hamlet has unceremoniously dragged offstage: can there be a crime if there is no corpse? The frantic courtiers are turned by the king into detectives who find the body only when

Hamlet, sarcastically urging them to follow their noses and snuff the air, tips them off that he has stashed it under the palace stairs.

I group the psychological ambiguities in *Hamlet* into three areas. First is the question of identity. Is there an essential self, a fixed personality, or are human beings simply a collection of masks, exchanged at whim? Hamlet is afflicted and tormented by his own metamorphoses. He has an actor's facility to try on poses, toss verbal darts, and play with mood and tone—which is why he has such infectious rapport with the troupe of traveling players, whom he tutors in stagecraft. But acting for Hamlet can dangerously overlap deceit: he enjoys duping others and shows contempt for their gullibility (as in his weary exchanges with the gossipy, senile Polonius and the slavish Osric). Impersonation comes too easily to Hamlet, leaving him with feelings of disgust and misanthropy.

The soliloquies show Hamlet's search for identity as well as his despair at not finding it: ideas spiral out of control, and his mood darkens, as certain themes keep recurring, obsessively and compulsively. General reflections on existence and the cosmos always seem to circle back to be overwhelmed by Hamlet's family psychodramas. The persistence of these negative thoughts must be weighed in judging Hamlet's mental competence. Early on, he warns Horatio that he will "put an antic disposition on"—and we do recognize such moments, when Hamlet allows us to laugh with him at his naive victims (I.v.172). But Shakespeare leaves other scenes ambiguous: when Hamlet, as described by Ophelia, appears with clothing disarrayed and looks her up and down with tragic sighs, is this another game, or has he temporarily lost his wits? His tumultuous confrontation with his mother in her bedchamber can be played several ways, but the text indicates a rising level of passion and recrimination peaking in hysteria and near violence. The ghost who materializes is seen only by him and not his mother—as opposed to its two visits to the battlements, when there are a total of three witnesses aside from Hamlet. Gertrude is in little doubt: "Alas, he's mad," she says to herself, as if her son can no longer hear external voices (III.iv.106).

A second area of psychological ambiguity is generational relationships. To the original Hamlet story Shakespeare has added the imposing parallelism of fathers and sons: there are Hamlet Senior and Hamlet Junior; Fortinbras Senior and Fortinbras Junior; and Polonius and Laertes. The elder Hamlet and elder Fortinbras were blood rivals, just as the younger Hamlet suffers the rivalry (real or imagined) of the younger Fortinbras and Laertes. What relevance this theme might have had to Shakespeare's interaction with his own father has been discussed by scholars, but biographical evidence is slight. The play asks us to consider the charged issue of fatherhood and its legacy, particularly in families where the father has power and fame as well as a daunting record of achievement.

Hamlet admires his heroic father but feels overshadowed by him. (He was born on the very day that the king slew Fortinbras.) He is unable or unwilling to match that mythic and archaic level of dominant masculinity, devoted to the service of a competitive nationalism. Hamlet occupies the more sophisticated, cosmopolitan world of humanistic Europe. From the birth of psychoanalytic criticism in the early twentieth century, Hamlet's fervid, divinizing praise of his dead father was defined as ambivalent "over-estimation," concealing contrary impulses of hostility or even repressed homicidal wishes. The matching term in the Oedipus complex—incestuous desire for the mother--has also been detected in Hamlet's indecorous over-involvement with Gertrude's sex life, which he pictures with startlingly pornographic exactitude. Modern productions, beginning with John Barrymore, regularly give Oedipal inflections to the play. In strict Freudian terms, Hamlet's delay in exacting vengeance comes from his paralyzed recognition that his uncle has fulfilled the forbidden fantasies of his own unconscious—that is, killing his father and marrying his mother.

But *Hamlet* had a magnetic effect on audiences and readers alike for 300 years before Freudian theory, with all its insights. The ghost is an oppressive paternal presence. His aggressive demand for revenge is an energy-sapping burden that usurps Hamlet's life and identity. The son at first accepts his mission with enthusiasm because of his hatred for his uncle, but the duty soon becomes a tedious and demeaning irritation. The ghost makes him a prisoner of the past, a servant of the king's now, cancelled life.

Fortinbras, in contrast, seems to relish his role as his father's avenger. Hamlet sourly contrasts himself with Fortinbras and lacerates himself with debased female imagery: he, the prince of Denmark, is a "whore," a "drab," a "scullion" (a kitchen maid [II.ii.597-99]). What we see of Fortinbras is limited: his first entrance is in the last minute of the play, when the stage is strewn with corpses. If Fortinbras has self-doubts, we don't know them, though his manic militancy (like Shakespeare's Hotspur elsewhere) might be interpreted as an attempt to surpass his father by dramatizing the latter's failures.

Parental love as an ambiguous form of power and control is shown in Polonius' bullying behavior toward his son. The scene of Laertes' farewell before his return to university in Paris is usually played for humor: the greybeard Polonius taxes his smirking children with hoary old saws and bromides, whose lessons he himself fails to heed. Parental instruction is shown as boring but harmless. Far more disturbing is the scene where Polonius instructs his servant Reynaldo to spy on Laertes in Paris. In his ruthless thirst for information, Polonius tells Reynaldo to slander Laertes' character and then read the response of his auditors. Even the lowborn servant is appalled by such wanton degradation of Laertes' public image and honor. This is another example of poisoned language operating in the play: Polonius spreads it like an epidemic to another country to taint his own son. Overbearing fatherly concern commits murder—this time of Laertes' reputation.

The third area of psychological ambiguity is love and sex, about which Hamlet is tortured throughout the play. Love is an illusion in which he cannot place faith, and he gratuitously savages both his mother and Ophelia for what he perceives as their betrayals—Gertrude for falling under Claudius' erotic spell and Ophelia for behaving like a proper Renaissance girl and following her father's orders rather than the call of her own heart. Hamlet ends up denouncing all women as false—their thick "paintings" of makeup the false faces and fakery of actress-whores (III.i.144). (This was at a time when no women performed on the English stage: respectable ladies did not put themselves on public display.) The theme of women's crafty self-beautification belongs to the play's constant contrast between shadow and substance: woman traffics in illusion, and what she offers is a lie.

Sexual desire itself is delusive for Hamlet, who feels it entrammels the free mind in animality. The language of disgust spewed in his explosive rages is so extreme that commentators cannot agree on its meaning. As the only son of a royal house, it is Hamlet's obligation to procreate, but the play repeatedly obstructs and frustrates his natural relationship with Ophelia, which his mother blesses (as we learn after Ophelia's death) even while her father and brother hootingly proclaim their union impossible on political grounds. Hamlet himself is unable to sustain romantic love. His attachment to Ophelia cannot withstand his own self-involvement and self-hatred: the death force, in other words, conquers the life force in the play. But why? Is Denmark under a curse that blights the future?

The play systematically undermines Hamlet's hold on his own identity. All of his personal relationships, except with the steady, impassive Horatio, founder. Even his early friendships are corrupted by politics: Rosencrantz and Guildenstern, summoned by the king and queen to spy on Hamlet, make themselves tools to royal command. Hamlet jovially questions the pair about their sudden visit to court, but his attitude hardens when they refuse to admit the obvious truth. The interrogation is nearly an inquisition, with Hamlet taking the roles of detective and prosecutor, microscopically studying Rosencrantz and Guildenstern's ambiguities of response and body language and forcing them along a track of self-exposure until they are helpless. Hamlet learns to distrust emotions and social bonds, which the play shows as painfully fallible.

In *Hamlet*, illusions rule. As a landmark of Western literature, the play symbolizes the cultural shift from the orderly absolutes of the scholastic Middle Ages to the flux of the modern era, in which beliefs, disciplines, and institutions are continually remade, with the individual left to a vertigo of free choice. Major works of art whose appeal endures over centuries usually have some elusiveness or indeterminacy of form or content: the ambiguous qualities of Leonardo's *Mona Lisa*, for example, can also be seen in *Hamlet*,

which seems to take place in Leonardo's *sfumato* or smoky shadows and where sex and emotion, as in the *Mona Lisa,* are cryptic.

Hamlet is a truth-seeker who wants to *be* and not *seem*—that is,
to live without illusions. But in order to defeat illusions, he vainly
tries to make them stay or stop. In that instant, their insubstantial-
ity envelopes him and his view of the material world. The play
unfurls in a swirl of ambiguities, destabilizing person, thing,
place, time, and action—which is why, like Heracleitus' river,
Hamlet seems to change with each of our encounters with it. The
play too is an illusion that, to our dismay and pleasure, will never
stay.

Leo Tolstoy, Russia's Greatest Heretic

Jaroslav Pelikan
Yale University

In this year Slavic Christians of all traditions are commemorating the thousandth anniversary of the conversion of *Rus'-Ukraine*, and with the commemoration are paying fresh attention to the religious and theological legacy of all of Eastern Orthodox and Eastern Catholic Christendom, including Orthodox Russia. Ironically, however, the best-known representative of religious and theological thought in Russia history was not a spokesman for the Orthodox legacy at all, but was, by almost any acceptable definition, a heretic: Lev Nikolayevich Tolstoy.[1]

In June 1883, Ivan Sergeyevich Turgenev wrote the following heartrending words to Tolstoy:

> My dear, my beloved Lev Nikolayevich, I have not written to you for a long time, for I have been ill, and I am, as a matter of fact, on my death-bed. I cannot recover, and there is no use thinking that I can. I am writing to tell you how gratified I am to have been your contemporary, and to address one final plea to you: My friend, come back to your work in literature! That gift of yours proceeds from the same Source as everything else does. How happy I would be if I could think that my plea would influence you! . . . My friend, great writer of the Russian land, hear my entreaty!

With this, the last letter he would ever write, Turgenev, as he lay dying in Paris, made one final effort to persuade Tolstoy to give up his obsession with theology and to return to his primary vocation as a creative writer. Turgenev's plea did not succeed in changing Tolstoy's mind, but it did set a pattern that has been followed by most critics of Tolstoy, whether Slavic or Western. Maxim Gorky found Tolstoy's language about Christ to be "peculiarly impoverished, lacking in enthusiasm"; Tomáš Masaryk concluded that "Tolstoy's manner of feeling and thinking are in fact nothing so much as pantheistic"; Thomas Mann characterized Tolstoy's thought after his conversion as *theologische Grübelei;* and my late colleague Henri Peyre described Tolstoy's screed of 1898, *What Is Art?*, as "one of the least intelligent books ever written." Now a theological aesthetic that ends up preferring *Uncle Tom's Cabin* to *King Lear* must, I suppose, be suspect on the face of it. Yet, as in Turgenev's letter, much of the criticism is based upon a dichotomy between the early Tolstoy and the late Tolstoy. Neither of these dichotomies seems very precise in the light of the evidence. For a while he did become more radical as he grew older, it is evident from his diaries that his preoccupation with theology and with the person of Jesus was there almost from the beginning. And an analysis of his most important creative works will show, I believe, that his quest for the true gospel, heretical though it may be, underlies many of his novels and stories as well as his professedly theological writings. It is such an analysis of the gospel in Tolstoy's fiction that I propose to set forth in this Gerety Lecture (which, as will be evident, could be, and perhaps will be, expanded into a small monograph), by examining how he treats certain elements in the faith and worship of Russian Orthodoxy and by relating his conception of the gospel to this.

In *Anna Karenina* Tolstoy used the friendship of Kitty and Varenka as an occasion to contrast the two basic kins of religion: that which Kitty had known in her Orthodox childhood, "a lofty, mysterious religion," which consisted in "liturgies and vespers" and "in learning by heart Slavonic texts with the priest"; in "reading the Gospel to the sick, the criminals, and the dying."[2] Elsewhere one of his characters drew a distinction between a religion of "mysteries" and a religion of "precepts."[3] When Tolstoy put his hand to describing the first of these forms of religion, his eye for detail and his sense of irony combined to give his readers striking insights into the anomalies of conventional piety. Thus in *Hadji Murád*, a work of his old age, he spoke of the liturgical prayers of the Tsar as the place "where God, through his servants the priests, greeted and praised Nicholas just as worldly people did."[4] He was especially fond of noting the ironies created by the political–and, above all, the military–use of religion. Nekhlyudov, in the novel *Resurrection*, was taken aback to find an image of the Crucifixion in a prison, for he thought of Christ as a force of liberation, not for captivity[5]; but later in the same novel, in the warden's office, he saw another such image, which by now had become "the customary appurtenance of all places of barbarity–a large image of Christ, as it were in mockery of his teaching."[6] As a young cadet aflame with his first love, Nekhlyudov had exemplified such an anomaly when, at the Easter liturgy, he had exchanged the traditional Church Slavonic greeting, "Christ is risen! –He is risen indeed!"[7]—but all his thoughts were on the girl Katusha, later to become, as a result of his cruelty and lust, the prostitute Maslova. Thus also in *War and Peace* Nikolay was at his most devout in his prayers while he was yielding to his compulsive lust for gambling,[8] and again while he was waiting for the wolf during the hunt, praying with what Tolstoy called "that passionate compunction with which men pray in moments of intense emotion arising from trivial causes."[9]

But as already noted, Tolstoy reserved his special irony for those instances in which religion served a political, and above all a military, interest. *Hadji Murád* satirized the official and impersonal letter informing the next-of-kin that a soldier had died "defending his Tsar, his Fatherland, and the Orthodox Faith."[10] Repeatedly *War and Peace* referred to "the Russian Orthodox Army."[11] Already in *The Cossacks* Tolstoy had lampooned the practice of Cossack soldiers, who would draw a bead on their target and then would fire while reciting the formula "In the name of the Father and of the Son and of the Holy Ghost,"[12] as well as other such uses of the Trinitarian invocation.[13] Like other observers of civil religion in the service of the military, including above all Abraham Lincoln, Tolstoy was grimly amused by the prospect of both sides after a battle offering up thanksgiving through their clergy for divine blessing on their warfare[14]; and in a superb description of the prayer for Russia's deliverance from the armies of Napoleon, he rehearsed "that clear, mild, self-effacing tone peculiar to the Slav clergy, which acts so irresistibly on the Russian heart" as it invoked the protection of God against "those who hate us and our Orthodox faith."[15]

As in the case of the liturgical prayer for the Russian people under siege, Tolstoy did sometimes manifest a capacity to resonate to the Orthodox liturgy, despite his existential alienation from it. In this respect as in others, he used the character of Levin in *Anna Karenina* to document his own fundamental ambivalences. At the beginning of Part Five, when Levin was urged to go to Holy Communion for the first time in nine years in preparation for his forthcoming marriage, his participation in the liturgy, together with his confession and conversation about religious doubt with the deacon,[16] can be read as a statement of such ambivalence: "Believe he could not, and at the same time he had no firm conviction that it was all wrong."[17] Later, attending the cathedral in Moscow while awaiting the birth of their child, he participated in the liturgy, affirming "I kiss the Cross" and sharing in the worship.[18] Later still, at the birth of their child, he found himself, "for some reason", repeating the words of the liturgy, *Gospodin pomiluy.*[19] Although he continued to have his intellectual difficulties with the Christian faith, he "turned to God just as trustfully and simply as he had in his childhood and first youth."[20] In a parallel to these presentations of Levin's faith which appears in the story of *Father Sergius*, written in 1898, Tolstoy identified the commitment to which Stepan Kasatsky (Stiva) turned when he discovered his fiancée's past as the Tsar's former mistress as "God, the faith of his childhood which had never been destroyed in him."[21] The liturgical scenes in *War and Peace* were likewise shaped by this ambivalence. He had Pierre speak of those who "were growing up and dying with no idea of God and truth beyond ceremonies and meaningless prayers"[22]; he dismissed the Christmas liturgy with a brusque *obiter dictum*[23]; and he had Kutuzov define boredom as being obliged to attend a church service.[24] Yet he could also speak sympathetically of those who took the liturgy seriously, and could have Natasha at an Orthodox liturgy react with a combination of lassitude and fascination to "that hushed solemnity that has so elevating and soothing an effect on the souls of the worshipers."[25]

With the Russian Orthodox liturgy there were certain features that inevitably figured in Tolstoy's narratives. One of these was the so-called Jesus prayer, which consisted in the repetition, over and over, of the name of Jesus, accompanied by breath control and other exercises. It had been developed by the ascetic fathers of the patristic and Byzantine periods, and during the eighteenth and nineteenth centuries it was given wide circulation in Russia and beyond through the efforts of the Ukrainian monk, Paissy Velitchkovsky (1722-94). Such a practice would lend itself to caricature very easily, but almost certainly there can never have been a parody of it more devastating than that which appeared in the censored portions of Tolstoy's novel, *Resurrection*.[26] Set as it was in the context of the imprisonment of Maslova, who because of the injustice she was suffering had ceased to believe in God and goodness,[27] this recitation of the name of Jesus with infinite variations took on an especially bitter irony, which was compounded by the further observation, as Tolstoy observed at the end, that in the Sermon on the Mount[28] Jesus had expressly forbidden all such empty liturgical chatter, which was now being carried on in his name—and even *with* his name.[29] Yet in another work, *Father Sergius*, which was contemporary with the writing of *Resurrection*, Tolstoy was able to treat the Jesus prayer more sympathetically. Here Sergius fought against sexual temptation by praying before an icon of Christ crowned with thorns: "Lord Jesus Christ, Son of God, have mercy on me a sinner" and doing so over and over "unceasingly."[30] He did so again as the temptation intensified[31]; and although the prayer itself proved ineffectual, as indeed even the more extreme ascetic acts of Father Sergius did, Tolstoy here spared us the heavy-handed sarcasm that marked—and, I believed, marred—his account of the liturgy and the Jesus prayer in *Resurrection*.

A similar oscillation between sarcasm and sympathy was evident in Tolstoy's treatment of icons and of sacraments (one could almost say "of icons and of *other* sacraments"). In many scenes of Tolstoy's books, icons were simply part of the furniture, as for example in the prison scenes mentioned earlier or in the scene from

War and Peace after the fire in Moscow, when "all sorts of household goods had been thrown in heaps: featherbeds, a samovar, icons, and trunks."[32] Yet when forced to choose among items of furniture during the evacuation, the Rostov family had left behind the Count's books as "not needed" but had taken along "the most precious [icons], those with which family traditions were connected."[33] Wonder-working icons of the Mother of God were not only a part of folk piety[34]; but the icon of the Mother of God of Smolensk was "our defender" in battle, which Kutuzov kissed "in a naïve, childish way,"[35] as later he was to give thanks before the icons for the salvation of Russia.[36] The icon of the Iberian Mother of God was carried into battle[37] and into hospitals for the wounded after battle.[38] The greatest contribution that the Orthodox Church could make to the war effort was the gift of an icon of Saint Sergius to the Tsar.[39] The alliance of superstition and cynicism in the cult of icons was well described by the character Toporov in *Resurrection*, who, in a tone that is in some ways reminiscent of the Grand Inquisitor, made it clear that he himself did not believe in anything, but that the devotion to the icons, while of course idolatrous, was necessary to keep the common people content,[40] and by Vasily Andreyevich in *Master and Man*, who saw the icons as necessary in church but useless in a crisis.[41]

It is evident from some of these scenes, however, that Tolstoy's attitude toward the worship of icons was not always one of scorn, but sometimes one of condescension or amusement or even sympathy. He was, for example, obviously positive in his treatment of Kutuzov's tearful prayer of thanksgiving before the icons after Napoleon's retreat from Russia: "Lord, my Creator, Thou hast heard our prayer. Russia is saved."[42] He had reported, on the other hand, that an icon of the Pantocrator had been disfigured by a young "smart-aleck."[43] Between these two references to icons in *War and Peace* came the charming vignette of Platon Karatayev, "the personification of everything Russian, kindly, and rotund."[44] After describing how his father had lined up all his children in front of the icons of the saints, Platon himself said his evening prayers, including the petition, "Lord, lay me down like a stone, and raise me up like a loaf," but also prayers to various saints, including two unknown names, who were, as he explained to a puzzled Pierre, "the horses' saints." In one of the prison scenes in *Resurrection* we meet an old woman saying her prayers before her icons,[45] later to be identified for us as Menshova, unjustly imprisoned for arson[46]; her devotion to her graven images, apparently, was not a mortal sin of idolatry but at most a venial one. Later in the same novel Tolstoy introduced Katerina Ivanovna, who was an adherent of an Evangelical sect and believed that the essence of Christianity was belief in justification by faith alone, without ritual or icon or sacrament; nevertheless she kept an icon in every room and did not appear to find that inconsistent. Tolstoy does not seem to have approved of all this, but one gets the sense that her doctrine of *sola fide* offended his view of the gospel more than did her adherence to these vestigial remnants of Russian Orthodoxy.[47] Both of the main characters in *Master and Man* were iconodules; but Vasily Andreyevich was a ritualist, who believed that it was necessary to light a candle to the icons (snuffing it out quickly so that it could be used again), but knew that they were useless when he was dying,[48] while Nikita was a muzhik, whose wish to die at home "under the icons, with a lighted candle in his hand" was fulfilled and who therefore died at peace with his family, with himself, and with his God.[49]

This comfort from the icons as the believer faced death was part of the system of support provided by the Orthodox Church to its faithful especially in that awesome and sacred hour. As such, it belonged with the final confession of sins, with the terminal anointing of holy chrism, and with the last reception of Holy Communion (or *viaticum*, as it was called in the Latin Church). Almost all the references to these last rites in Tolstoy's novels and stories were sympathetic, not least because of Tolstoy's own profound feelings of reverence before the *mysterium tremendum* of death; this is evident, for example, in Kitty's sense of urgency about extreme unction for her brother-in-law.[50] Ivan Ilyich at first rejected the idea of taking Communion and then went along with it to satisfy his wife, but when he did take it he derived a momentary comfort from it and "received the sacrament with tears in his eyes."[51] Although the administration of extreme unction to Count Bezukhov in Book One, Part I of *War and Peace*[52] was quite perfunctory, complete with a priest who called it "an awesome sacrament" as he "ran his hand over his bald head," later uses of sacraments on the deathbed in the novel were significantly more constructive. Thus even Natasha was helped in her convalescence by praying before the icon of the Mother of God and receiving Holy Communion, even though the doctor took credit for the joy and peace she had gained.[53] (Tolstoy's exquisite scorn for clergy was surpassed only by his contempt for physicians.) Her father, filled with remorse over not being able to leave his family a proper inheritance, "received Communion and the final chrism and died peacefully."[54] And her former fiancé, Andrey Nikolayevich Bolkonsky, likewise slipped away from this life peacefully: He took leave of his loved one, said his confession, and received Holy Communion.[55]

By contrast with his treatment of icons and especially of final sacraments, Tolstoy's frequent references to the practice of making the sign of the cross were only rarely positive. Most of the time it was described, for example in the case of Dimitry Olenin in *The Cossacks*, as "an old habit of his childhood,"[56] or in the case of Masha in *Family Happiness* as "an old custom,"[57] or in the case of Kutuzov as "clearly habitual"[58]–although later on, when he made the sign of the cross and said a prayer upon hearing of the death of Prince Nikolay Bolkonsky, it may have been more.[59] At the wake for Ivan Ilyich, Pyotr Ivanovich was not sure what to do; all he knew was that at such a time "it is always safe to cross oneself."[60] The old man at the beginning of *The Kreutzer Sonata* made the sign of the cross three times,[61] as did Nikita in *Master and Man*[62] and Yakov Alpatych, the faithful servant of the Bolkonsky family in *War and Peace*.[63] In *Resurrection*, where the liturgy and piety generally came off very poorly, making the sign of the cross before and after eating was compared to using one's napkin at table;[64] it was explicity described as part of the hypocrisy with which Selyenin deceived himself into reaffirming the Orthodox faith[65]; and in an extended conversation with an old man who refused to make the sign of the cross, Nekhlyudov recognized the difference between such traditional acts of piety and authentic religious faith.[66] Sometimes this practice became more sinister. Balaga Makarin, the speed demon who was about to use his skills as a troika-driver to help the rake Anatol Kuragin in his seduction of Natasha, crossed himself as he entered the room to meet Anatol and Fyodor Ivanyich Dolokhov.[67] For the record it should be noted that there are instances in Tolstoy's writings in which the sign of the cross had a neutral or even a constructive role; for example, the protagonist in Tolstoy's story of 1905, *Alyosha the Pot*, we are told, "did not know how to pray at all. His mother had once taught him the words, but he had forgotten them even as she spoke. Nevertheless, he did pray, morning and evening, but simply, just with his hands, crossing himself,"[68] and he did so with a priest in the hour of his death.[69] And while Andrey was asking her parents for Natasha's hand, we see Natasha herself "pale and dry-eyed, gazing at the icon and whispering something as she rapidly crossed herself."[70] But it is much more characteristic even of *War and Peace* when Tolstoy described the mourners at old Prince Bolkonsky's bier as "crossing themselves, like horses shying, snorting, and jostling around a dead horse."[71]

It is obvious, then, that for Tolstoy Russian Orthodoxy was a false gospel, but his specific treatment of Orthodoxy deserves nevertheless to be summarized, if not belabored. We would expect a remark like the one in *Resurrection* to the effect that all the Germans who belonged to the bureaucracy of the Russian civil service were, of course devout members of the Orthodox Church.[72] But there were three long passages in that book where Tolstoy analyzed Orthodoxy more thoroughly, though not, to be sure, any more favorably. The first of these was a classification of the various reasons underlying the acceptance of Orthodoxy by its several kinds of adherents: the priest who did not believe the dogma of the Church, but how did "believe that one ought to believe it"; the subdeacon who "sang and read what he had to sing and read as a matter of course, just as another man sells wood or flour or potatoes"; the warden and other, who "believed that one must believe in this faith because the higher authorities and the Tsar believed in it"; and the prisoners, including Maslova herself, who believed that the Orthodox ritual "possessed a mystic power by means of which a great many comforts might be obtained, in this life and in the life to come."[73] Although this disquisition was basically an interruption in the narrative even of this extremely didactic novel, the other two discussions of Orthodoxy were integrated more successfully into the story, probably because each of them was part of a total characterization. In the portrait of Selyenin, once Nekhlyudov's fellow student, Tolstoy included a diagnosis of "the great lie" by which he had found his way back to a reaffirmation of the Orthodox faith, through the study of such writers as the lay theologian Aleksei Khomyakov,[74] whom Levin in *Anna Karenina* had also read on the doctrine of the nature of the Church.[75] And the character Toporov in *Resurrection* was a man who himself believed nothing but who adhered to Orthodoxy and enforced it because of his concern about the common people.[76]

Tolstoy also used his narratives to reflect on the relation of Eastern Orthodoxy to other faiths. The contrasts between Eastern Orthodoxy and Roman Catholicism inevitably played a part in his account of the war between the Russians and the French[77]; but the most memorable use of this contrast in *War and Peace* was the conversion of Pierre Bezukhov's frivolous wife Elena to Roman Catholicism, achieved, of course, by Jesuits,[78] which made it "a simple, easy matter from the ecclesiastical point of view" for her to annul her senseless marriage. The differences among faiths also engaged Tolstoy more seriously, however. The old man whom Nekhlyudov met on the raft, the one who refused to make the sign of the cross, listed the various sects of Russian believers and concluded that there were different religions "just because people believe in other people and do not believe in themselves."[79] More profound and more complex was the reflection on this matter by Konstantin Levin in the final part of *Anna Karenina*. Once he had concluded that his sophomoric rejection of all religion was wrong,[80] he had to face the question[81] whether "if the chief proof of the Divinity was his revelation of what is right, how is this revelation confined to the Christian Church alone?" Levin's conclusion was to confess: "To me individually, to my heart has been revealed a knowledge beyond all doubt, and unattainable by reason. [It] has been revealed to me as a Christian. The question of other religions and of their relations to the Divinity I have no right to decide, and no possibility of deciding."[82]

Levin (and Tolstoy) knew, however, that it was simply another form of self-deception if one replaced the claim of Orthodoxy to be the one true faith with a no less absolute reliance on one's own "mystical fervor."[83] There were, as Father Sergius observed, "pilgrims who constantly tramped from one holy place to another and from one *starets* to another, and were always entranced by every shrine and every *starets*."[84] As Tolstoy noted in *The Cossacks*, "a man is never so much an egotist as in moments of spiritual ecstasy."[85] In his novels, as in his public career, Tolstoy strove for justice to the sectarians, Evangelicals, and mystical groups, such as the Dukhobors, who were being persecuted by church and civil state. It was, he asserted through Nekhlyudov in *Resurrection*, a disgrace that the reading of the Gospel by the sectarians had become a criminal offence.[86] But this indignation at persecution did not blind him to the dangers of private mysticism and arcane religiosity. The spiritual odyssey of Pierre in *War and Peace* took him for some time into the labyrinthine teachings of Freemasonry, to which he was introduced by the imposing figure of Iosif Alekseyevich Bazdeyev.[87] In these teachings Pierre found the genuine essence of Christianity, free of the interference of church or state.[88] After a while, however, he began to get the sense that "the more firmly he tried to rest on the ground of Freemasonry on which he had taken his stand, the more it was giving way under him."[89] He did continue to probe various kinds of mysterious formulas and even worked out an exegesis of 666, the number of the Beast in the thirteenth chapter of the Book of Revelation, that identified Napoleon as the Beast and himself as the one destined to destroy the Beast.[90] But this, too, became "incomprehensible and even laughable" to him,[91] and he found that Masonic speculations had lost their interest for him.[92] For he learned "that God was greater, more infinite and unfathomable, than the Architect of the Universe whom the Freemasons acknowledged"–and he learned this from the muzhik Platon Karatayev.[93]

To the false gospel of Russian Orthodoxy Lev Tolstoy opposed what he regarded as the authentic gospel. In several full-length works of theology and biblical study he systematized his beliefs about God, about Christ, about the moral life, and about death and the life to come. In addition to these systematic treatises, Tolstoy also built his rediscovered gospel into his works of fiction, with greater or lesser success, embodying the precepts of the gospel in his characters. It was above all the Sermon on the Mount that performed this function in his stories and novels, so much so that it would be possible to reconstruct a considerable portion of it from the quotations scattered throughout his books. In many instances, moreover, these quotations came at a critical juncture in the development of Tolstoy's plots or characterizations.

The closing pages of *Resurrection* consisted of a kind of homily on the Gospels, which Nekhlyudov read with new eyes, seeing in the Sermon on the Mount "for the first time, not abstract beautiful thoughts, presenting for the most part exaggerated and impossible demands, but simple, clear, practical commandments, which if obeyed (and this was quite feasible) would establish a completely new order of human society."[94] One such commandment in the Sermon on the Mount, which Tolstoy made basic to his theological and ethical thought, was the saying of Christ: "But I say to you, that ye resist not evil; but whosoever shall smite thee on thy right cheek, turn to him the other also."[95] This was the message which Nekhlyudov communicated to the prisoners,[96] but that saying of Christ also played a part in the spiritual evolution of another of Tolstoy's characters, Aleksye Aleksandrovich Karenin. Through the early stages of Anna's infidelities he seemed to be little more than the usual pathetic and ridiculous cuckold, muttering such sentiments as "She is bound to be unhappy, but I am not to blame, and so I cannot be unhappy"[97] and drawing upon his conventional view of Christianity as a justification for his coldness and attitude of moral superiority.[98] The Christian command to forgive did not apply in his case.[99] But as his struggle and his suffering continued, he caught a glimpse that it did apply and that he was to love and forgive his enemies, even his wife and her lover.[100] This he found in the word of Christ, "Turn the other cheek."[101] Ye he continued to have a faith that was "erroneous and shallow,"[102] and so he turned back from his insight about forgiveness to declare with his old pomposity, when his brother-in-law suggested the possibility of a divorce: "I, as a believer, cannot, in a matter of such gravity, act in opposition to Christian law,"[103] If he had acted soon enough and obeyed his deep but momentary insight into what really was the Christian law, the commandment of the Sermon on the Mount, he might have saved his soul, if not his marriage, and might have averted the eventual tragedy.

Even more "exaggerated and impossible" in the opinion of many was the saying of the Sermon on the Mount a few verses earlier: "But I say unto you, that whosever looketh on a woman to lust after her hath committed adultery with her already in his heart. And if thy right hand offend thee, cut it off, and cast it from thee."[104] The references to this saying described in the lives of the desert fathers prompted Yevgenyi Ivanich in *The Devil* to light a candle and put a finger into the flame when he was templted to commit adultery, but he quickly pulled it back and blew out the flame.[105] But Father Sergius in the story of that name did burn his hand to resist temptation, and when that did not work, he obeyed the words of Christ quite literally and chopped off his finger.[106] In *The Kreutzer Sonata* Tolstoy took his reading of these verses even further. For in the *samizdat* version of the story he set forth his exegesis of the words about committing adultery in the heart: They were not only a prohibition of lust for another than one's rightful spouse, but "specially and chiefly" they were directed against lust for one's own wife.[107] The command of the Gospel was complete and utter chastity, even in marriage, and it was to be taken literally. So it was also with the words of the Sermon on the Mount about taking no thought for one's life, but being like the fowls of the air, which sow not, neither do they reap,[108] but it was only at the moment of death that Prince Andrey saw this, and he could not explain it, even to his sister.[109]

If we look for the embodiment of the true gospel in Tolstoy's characters, we must turn to his portraits of various peasants. He was expressing his own conviction, seriously yet playfully, when he had Platon Karatayev in *War and Peace*[110] confuse the words *Krestyanin* (peasant) and *Khristianin* (Christian). Bringing his Father Sergius face to face with his childhood friend Praskovya Mikhaylovna (Pashenka), Tolstoy had him confess the difference between the church's gospel and the true gospel: "Pashenka is what I ought to have been but failed to be. I lived for men on the pretext of living for God, while she lives for God imagining that she lives for men."[111] Another such peasant hero was Nabatov in *Resurrection*, who did not need abstract beliefs about God and immortality but lived in faith and dignity.[112] The most complete of these portrayals of peasant believers was that of Karatayev, who brought to Pierre the revelation of the truth that he had vainly sought in cabbalistic exegesis and Freemasonry. Karatayev lived in practice what the Gospels commanded, even though he could not theorize about it, for he "knew nothing by heart except his prayers."[113] And so his overcoat seemed to Pierre to be a priestly vestment,[114] and his face was marked by "serene exaltation." As Masaryk put it, "in this predicament Tolstoy finds himself saved by the Russian muzhik."

Yet the supreme embodiment of the true gospel and the most complete and profound portrayal of its meaning in the works of Tolstoy was Princess Marya Nikolayevna Bolkonskaya in *War and Peace*. All the elements of conventional Russian Orthodox piety that we have catalogued were present in her. "May our divine Savior and His most Holy Mother keep you in their holy and almighty care" was how she would conclude a letter.[115] After the scene between her father and her brother and her brother's wife, she turned to the door when her brother had left and made the sign of the cross.[116] She was faithful in her attendance at church services, even at vespers.[117] She was devoted to icons, not only having them on the wall of her room as others did,[118] but presenting one to her brother when he left for war: "Andrey, I bless you with his holy image, and you must promise me you will never take it off. Against your will He will save you and have mercy on you: He will bring you to Himself, for in Him alone is truth and peace."[119] When Andrey was wounded, he looked at the icon and remembered her faith,[120] and when she heard that he had been wounded fatally, she too thought of the icon and wondered whether he had come to faith at the end.[121] The heart of her own faith was, as Tolstoy put it, "summed up in the one clear and simple law of love and self-sacrifice, laid down for us by Him who in His life had suffered for all mankind, though He Himself was– God."[122] This was, Prince Andrey said, "the love which God preached to us on earth, and which Princess Marya tried to teach me."[123] When she prayed, as Nikolay Rostov observed, it was not what his prayers and Natasha's had been as children, that snow might turn to sugar, but something "a little frightening" and awe-inspiring.[124] This is not to say that prayer was something that came easily to her; often, in times of crisis, she found that she could not pray as she wanted to.[125]

In the course of his description of Princess Marya, Tolstoy had her (or, as he would probably have preferred to say, since he regarded the characters of his books as real people, *watched* her) blossom also as a person. In the early portions of the novel, she was "awkward and devoid of grace,[126] and even considerably later she was "a timourous maiden, no longer in her first youth, wasting the best years of her life in fear and mortal anguish."[127] Yet she had always been "possessed of an ineffable beauty of sorrow and self-forgetfulness"[128] and so was in fact "really not so plain."[129] As she matured spiritually, her "movements [became] full of grace and dignity" and she "began speaking in a voice that for the first time vibrated with a new, deep, womanly note."[130] For now "all that pure, spiritual inner travail through which she had lived appeared on the surface. All her spiritual searchings, her anguish, her strivings after goodness, her humility, self-sacrifice, and love–all this now shone in those luminous eyes, in the delicate smile, in every feature of her gentle face."[131] Her otherworldliness, which had marked her from the beginning, became even more pronounced; even amid family happiness, she sensed "another happiness, unattainable in this life,[132] for her "spirit was ever aspiring to the infinite, the eternal, the absolute, and therefore could never be at peace."[133] Although she married Nikolay Rostov, she kept this spiritual quality. She had always been sensitive to the potential conflict between the love of Christ and erotic love.[134] Sometimes she had vowed that she would never marry anyone, because her "vocation [was] a different one,"[135] and she had spoken of thoughts about marriage as temptations of the devil.[136] But at other times she had confessed that "There are moments when I would marry anyone!"[137] When her marriage finally came, it only intensified the "spiritual treasures" that she had manifested earlier,[138] and her husband Nikolay was filled with "awe at her spiritually, at the lofty moral world, almost beyond his reach, in which she dwelt."[139]

When I first read *War and Peace* more than fifty years ago, I, like any teenaged boy, fell in love with Natasha. At the ball, you will remember, she herself was not in love with anyone but rather "in love with everyone,"[140] and possessed that quality of intuition about others that would instantly endear her to them.[141] It is obvious that Tolstoy felt the same way about Natasha. But each successive reading of the book has made it clearer to me that he reserved his deepest admiration for Princess Marya, whom he patterned after his mother. It is instructive to watch the relation between Natasha and Marya in Tolstoy's account. Their first meeting was anything but cordial,[142] and Marya wrote to Natasha to voice her concern over their misunderstanding.[143] When the engagement of Natasha and Mary's brother Andrey broke up, Marya could not repress her *Schadenfreude*.[144] Of course both Natasha and Marya were at fault, Natasha because of her flightiness and Marya because of a rather priggish Orthodox piety. But they were reconciled through the death of Prince Andrey, Natasha's former fiancé and Marya's brother, and they found in each other "comrades in grief."[145] They grew together; for "Natasha, who with a serene lack of understanding had formerly turned away from that life of devotion, submission, and the poetry of Christian sacrifice, now, feeling herself bound to Princess Marya by affection, learned to love her past as well and to understand a side of life she had no conception of before," while Marya for her part discovered "another, formerly uncomprehended, side of life: belief in life and its enjoyment."[146] Differences between them there continued to be, but according to Tolstoy "Natasha was sincere in acknowledging Marya's superiority," so long as she could count on the love of her husband Pierre.[147]

How is it that this could end up being Tolstoy's most convincing depiction of the gospel in an individual life? He romanticized the simple piety of the muzhik, but Marya was a princess; he lampooned the beliefs and practices of Russian *Pravoslavie*, but she was thoroughly Orthodox in her liturgical, sacramental, and iconodule piety; he looked beyond the claims of a narrow Christianity to the religions of mankind, but she was content to be what she had been born to be, a devout member of the Russian Orthodox Church. Yet as such, she managed to practice all that Tolstoy celebrated as authentic, because she understood the Gospels. "*You know,*" said Natasha, "*you are always reading the Gospels.*"[148] It was teasing in its tone, but accurate in its description. At the center of Marya's Orthodox piety were the Gospel and the person of Christ.

In our first introduction to her, her letter to Julie, we hear her say: "I have never been able to understand the passion certain people have for confusing their understanding by applying themselves to mystical books that only awaken doubts in the mind and excite the imagination, creating in them a tendency to exaggeration altogether contrary to Christian simplicity. Let us rather read the Gospels and the Epistles."[149] Her image of Christ was Orthodox, combining the Christ of the Gospels with the Christ of icons, but it evoked from her the kind of obedience that Tolstoy saw as the essence of the Christian message. And so she managed to combine in herself what Tolstoy could not hold together himself, what in *Anna Karenina* he called "a lofty, mysterious religion" of "liturgies and vespers" and a religion of compassion[150]–or what she herself called "mysteries" and "precepts."[151] More than any of his theological polemics, more than any of his heresies, this portrait of Princess Marya articulated Tolstoy's vision of life. And so, when Turgenev called him back from theology to literature, he recognized, and yet did not recognize, the essential, if extremely complicated, unity of the gospel according to Russia's greatest heretic, Lev Nikolayevich Tolstoy.

Hölderlin's *Der Tod des Empedokles: Erste Fassung*

Arthur Grugan
La Salle University

Friedrich Hölderlin was born in 1770, and in 1843 he died. Sometime around 1805-1806, the poet fell victim to a madness from which he was never able to recover. During the all-too-few years of his creative life, Hölderlin had figured importantly in the philosophical-poetic determinations of his age. He read and discussed Kant. While a student at Tübingen, he befriended Schelling and Hegel. He admired and received significant support and encouragement from Schiller. He intently followed the lectures of Fichte. He wrote poetry, translated and wrote critical essays about Homer, Sophocles, and Pindar. He studied Protestant theology but could never bring himself to undergo ordination, to the life-long disappointment of his mother. He left behind important correspondence. He published a novel, along with several drafts therefor. And he wrote a play.

In this paper, I intend to restrict my reading of Hölderlin to the first version of his only drama, *Der Tod des Empedokles*. The play exists in three versions. Additionally, Hölderlin wrote an early poem entitled *Empedokles*, a *Frankfurter Plan*, and an essay *Der Grund des Empedokles*. Following the suggestion of Martin Heidegger, I plan to read the play from the context of Hölderlin's later poetry.[1]

During Hölderlin's time, the philosophy of Rene Descartes was continuing to reverberate throughout western thinking. Des-

cartes had privileged reason, as it had never been privileged before, and articulated a radical dualism. As the foundation for truth
and being, Descartes had posited the *res cogitans*, which thinking I
defined as the essence of the human person as a rational being
rather than as a rational animal. Essentially separated from and
opposed to the *res cogitans* was the *res extensa*, the entire order of
the Not-I, which included the human person's body as a non-
essential dimension of the person, and all of nature. Hölderlin inherited the tradition of thought defined by Cartesian philosophy,
a tradition wherein western man struggled to retrieve his belong-
ingness in nature, to reëstablish his connection with the Not-I,
which included God, and to comprehend this difference, the difference between thinking man and his or her animal, sensual dimension, and between the thinking person and the natural world
outside, beyond her thinking consciousness.

Cartesian reason strove towards the ideal of clear and distinct
ideas, so illuminated by the flame of reason that all tenebrosity
would be displaced from them, that all ambiguity would need to
submit to a defining, clarifying light. Yet the clarity of thought
promised by the Cartesian *cogito* was never able to dismiss or
overcome the consequences of the trenchant disjunction which
that same reason caused between man and nature. The Cartesian
will towards a totalizing clarity and an all-mastering concept—a
will to be much developed by the thinkers of German Idealism, in
which thinking Hölderlin was to play a significant role—was de-
fied almost immediately by profound ambiguities engendered by
man's perplexing place outside of nature. Essential questions
emerged from this ambiguity. What is man? Who am I? How can I
get back to where I once was and regain my place in the universe?
Am I restricted, ultimately, to the inward domain of consciousness, "hole[d] up in the refuge of one's own psyche," one result of
which will be "the forsaking of reality?"[2] Is all communication
between the I and the Not-I, between the self and the world impossible? How did this loss, this separation, this difference occur?
Hölderlin sang of the "day, when life / Appears fevered and
chained, / Or by night, when everything blends / Into confusion,
and primeval / Chaos reigns once more,"[3] and of the "wild confusion"[4] that characterized western thought as a result of the essen-

tial rupture that entered it through Descartes, and he expressed the deep loss of bearings that once illuminated and guided man's sense of himself when the poet wrote that "No one knows what's happening to him."[5]

In a preliminary but important essay, Hölderlin berated the thinkers of his own time for deluding themselves that they were educated, original, and autonomous, for believing that the Germans were "saying all kinds of new things and, still, all this is reaction, as it were, a mild revenge against the slavery with which we have behaved toward antiquity."[6] He wrote:

> There seems to be indeed hardly any other choice than to be oppressed by what has been appropriated and by what is positive, or, with violent effort, to oppose as a living force everything learnt, given, positive. What seems most problematic here is that antiquity appears altogether opposed to our primordial drive which is bent on forming the unformed, to perfect the primordial-natural so that man, who is born for art, will naturally take to what is raw, uneducated, childlike rather than to a formed material where there has already been pre-formed [what] one wishes to form.[7]

It was Hölderlin's conviction that the Germans of his time had not found themselves in relation to the Greeks of the past. To come into its own, to initiate a new beginning, a beginning from out of one's own rather than a *recherché* of what belonged to others, the present age could not merely imitate the past. It would need to discover its ownmost essence. Thus, Hölderlin thought on the difference between past and future from out of a present riven with essential opposition and with the drive to "give ourselves our own direction which is determined by the preceding pure and impure directions that we, due to understanding, do not repeat."[8] He often articulated this difference and the struggle to go his own direction by thinking upon what is foreign (*das Fremde*) and what is one's own (*das Eigene*), as he did in his altogether important letters to his friend Casimir Ulrich Böhlendorff.

> We learn nothing with more difficulty than to freely use the national. And, I believe that it is precisely the clarity of the presentation that is so natural to us as is for the Greeks the fire from heaven. For exactly that reason they will have to be surpassed in beautiful passion—which you

have also preserved for yourself—rather than in that Homeric presence of mind and talent for presentation.[9]

Moreover, Hölderlin's poetry is everywhere preoccupied with this tension between what once was and what has not yet eventuated, and with how the poet should thoughtfully and poetically deal with this problematic. In one of his most complicated poems, *Der Archipelagus*, for example, Hölderlin wrote:

Ah, but our kind walks in darkness, it dwells as in Orcus,
          SEVERED FROM ALL THAT'S DIVINE. TO HIS OWN INDUSTRY ONLY
Each man is forged, and can hear only himself in the workshop's
          Deafening noise; and much the savages toil there, for ever
          Moving their powerful arms, they labour, yet always and always
          Vain, like the Furies, unfruitful the wretches' exertions remain
there,
          Till the nightmare ends, and the human spirit, awakened,
          Burgeons, youthfully glad, and love like a gentle warm breath
blows
          Over this new age as often once it would blow over Hellas,
          Blessing her children in flower, and over our brows less con-
stricted
          Nature's spirit that comes to men from far-distant places,
          Calmly abiding, in clouds all golden the god reappears now.
          What, and you hesitate still? And they, though their birth was
divine, still
          Live as they did before, O day, as though lonely, confined in
          Gloomy depths of the earth, while a springtime eternally living
          Glimmers away unsung above the heads of those sleepers?[10]

And in *The River Main*, the poet again sings in images of precisely the vacuity of the present. That poem, in relevant part, sings:

          O once I long to land there, on Sunium's coast,
          Once ask my way to your columns, Olympion,
          And soon, before the northern gale can
          Bury you too in the scattered rubble

          Of temples Athens raised, and their imaged gods;
          For long now desolate you have stood, O pride
          Of worlds that are no more![11]

Further, Hölderlin wrote:

> The temple columns stand
> Forsaken in days of need,
> And though the northern gale's echo
> Resounds deep in the halls
> And rain washes them clean
> And moss grows, and the swallows return
> In the spring season, yet nameless in them
> Is the God, and the cup of thanks
> And the vessel of sacrifice and all the holy things
> Buried against the foe in a place kept secret. [12]

Hölderlin's belief is, therefore, that the past, while in itself remaining alive, has run its course and flourishes in radical independence of and indifference towards the Germans of the present. His *Archipelagus* and his *Germanien* are particularly important expressions of that belief. Thus, the poet sings that new modes of expression must be imagined in order to acknowledge and give voice to the difference that spans between past and future, and then eventually to announce the oncoming of a new beginning. In a draft for the *Concluding Chorus of Act One of Empedokles*, the poet cried out:

> O when, when
> will it break at last,
> the flood, over the parched land.[13]

Hölderlin thinks on the difference between these two worlds both spatially and temporally, and he names this *Zwischenzeit* variously as an interval or a caesura that is horrible,[14] needy,[15] as a time when night, although holy and sacred and healing,[16] reigns, and when God is absent.[17] Faced with the end of the great past of the classical world and the outstanding nature of the future, Hölderlin nourished the fundamental mood of mourning, sadness, and, from out of that mood, he wrote several elegies. In an ode called *Thränen*, the poet sang:

> For too devoutly almost, too gratefully
>> In days of beauty there did the holy serve,
> And furious heroes; and no lack of

Trees, and the cities at one time stood there

> Visible, like a pondering man; now dead
>> Those heroes are, the islands of love defaced,
>>> Disfigured nearly. So for ever
>>>> Love is outwitted, for ever silly.[18]

Hölderlin defined the responsibility and the vocation of the poet in terms of an obligation to stand within this interval, to hold his ground during the *Zwischenzeit*, as the voice of the people, as the poet feels "[t]he shadowy shapes of those who once were here."[19] The space of this interval is not unlike a bottomless abyss, where "primordial disorientation"[20] has displaced Cartesian clarity, where nothing appears to be clear as once it promised to be, where essential ambiguity holds sway, and, in this space, in this meantime, the poet is alone. His fundamental sensation is that of being abandoned, orphaned. What fulfills the lives of nonpoets brings the poet no consolation. For the poet is not "fortunate [as] he who peacefully loving a pious wife / Lives in his praiseworthy home, at his own hearth."[21] Poem after poem sings out of the depth of that solitude.

> Meanwhile, O mighty one, spare
> Him who lonely sings, and give us tunes enough
> Until uttered as we intend it
> Is the mystery of our souls.[22]

> Content the boatman turns to the river's calm
>> From distant isles, his harvest all gathered in;
>>> So too would I go home now, had I
>>>> Reaped as much wealth as I've gathered sorrow.[23]

> Celebrate—yes, but what? And gladly with others I'd sing now,
> Yet alone as I am nothing that's godlike rings true.[24]

But what exactly is this night? What does the attributive adjective *"heilige"* signify? It obviously means sacred and holy, but it also strongly connotes "wholesome" and "healing." Indeed, the night of the absence of God and the gods is a time / space caesura that remains penetrated, transfused, by day and a new presence.

Although the land is arid and parched, it remains, nevertheless, and, at the same time, a land fertile with promise, as *Germanien*, for example, makes clear:

> Not them, the blessed, who once appeared,
> Those images of gods in the ancient land,
> Them, it is true, I may not now invoke, but if,
> You waters of my homeland, now with you
> The love of my heart laments, what else does it want, in
> Its hallowed sadness? For full of expectation lies
> The country, and as though it had been lowered
> In sultry dog-days, on us a heaven today,
> You yearning rivers, casts prophetic shade.
> With promises it is fraught, and to me
> Seems threatening too, yet I will stay with it,
> And backward now my soul shall not escape
> To you, the vanished, whom I love too much.
> To look upon your beautiful brows, as though
> They were unchanged, I am afraid, for deadly
> And scarcely permitted it is to awaken the dead.[25]

Thus, the poetry of aridity and sadness is at the same time the poetry of waters and expectation, of prophecy and promise, and it is to endure throughout this essential waiting that the poet is called until night gives way to day, and absence to a new presence. For the poet will not flee to ancient Greece but will stay with the *Zwischenzeit*, waiting for the flowering and fruition of a future, for the inauguration of a new beginning in a new time, feeling "The shadowy shapes of those who once were here, / The ancients, newly visiting the earth. / For those who are to come now jostle us."[26] The poet sings:

> Meanwhile, however, flower, till our fruition commences,
> Flower, Ionian gardens, no less, and you others, you dear ones
> Green behind Athens' rubble, hide her, lest day see her sadness![27]

And in *Menos Klagen um Diotima* Hölderlin gave further poetic expression to the sadness-become-hope, the emptiness-becoming-fulfillment:

Once, how different it was! O youth, will no prayer bring you back, then,
Never again? And no path ever again lead me back?
Shall it be my fate, as once it was that of the godless,
Bright-eyed to sit for a time feasting at heavenly boards
But to be cloyed with that food, all those fantastical guests now
Fallen silent, and now, deaf to the music of winds,
Under the flowering earth asleep, till a miracle's power shall
Force them one day to return, deep though they lie now, at rest,
Force them to walk anew the soil that is sprouting new verdure—
Holy breath, then, divine, through their bright bodies will flow
While the feast is inspired and love like great flood waters gathers,
Fed by the heavens themselves, on sweeps the river, alive,
When the deep places boom, Night pays her tribute of riches
And from the beds of streams up glitters gold long submerged.[28]

Hölderlin's extraordinary hymn *Brot und Wein* further develops his poetic thinking upon the seriousness of the *Zwischenzeit*, the profound ambiguity it produces, and the responsibility of the poet to address that ambiguity. In *Brot und Wein*, the poet wrote:

Surely, friend, we have come too late. The gods are alive,
Yes, but yonder, up there, in another world overhead.
There they are endlessly active and seem not greatly to care
If we are living or not, such is their lenience.
For a fragile vessel is rarely able to hold them in:
Only at times can man cope with the fullness of god.
So life has become a dream about them. Nevertheless,
Error can help, like sleep, night and distress give strength,
Till heroes enough have grown, in this obdurate cradle, to stature,
And hearts as once have a strength matching the heavenly powers.
Then they will come, with thunder. But for the present, I think,
Sleep may be better than life lived without comrades like this,
Waiting and always waiting; and what's to be done and be said
I do not know, or the object of poets in desolate times.
But, as you say, they are like the sacred priests of the winegod,

> Who from country to country traveled in sacred night.[29]

To address the notion of the interpenetration of absence and presence, of day and night, as well as the matter to be thought of how error can help and how night and distress give strength, I refer to Heidegger's commentary on Hölderlin's poetic thought that God's absence, God's failing actually helps contribute to God's coming to renewed presence.[30]

Yet much is demanded of the poet to evoke the slumbering fertility of the night as it wakens into flowering day. Specifically, the poet must be ever mindful of measure, must never forget the difference between himself and the gods but hold that difference open continuously, must remember his subservience to God.

> And yet with holy night the father will veil
> Our eyes, that still we may not perish. Untamed
> Excess he loves not. Power
> Expands but cannot suborn heaven.
>
> Nor is it good to be too knowing. Gratitude
> Knows him. Yet to keep and contain it alone
> Is a hard burden, others the poet
> Gladly joins who help understanding.[31]

Then, mindful of his stature as mediator, the poet seeks what will not melt, wither, change, or decompose. The poet seeks what will abide and remain, and he thereafter seeks to bring to the people, in the words of his song, what will not perish, as the concluding verses of *Andenken* witness:

> But memory
> Is taken and given by the ocean,
> And the eyes of love do not waver in their gaze,
> But poets establish what remains.[32]

With this introduction in mind, I can turn to Empedokles, a man who precisely forgot his mortality and his finitude and, in the presence of his fellow citizens, proclaimed himself to be a god. I want to examine the tragedy as a work that manifests Hölderlin's indebtedness to idealistic philosophy and his important attempts to transcend the division that idealism created between the subject and the object, a division that Hölderlin thought had ruptured the primordial oneness with nature, which rupture the poet himself could not sufficiently heal at the staging of his play.

In November 1794, Hölderlin had gone to Jena, where Johann Gottlieb Fichte had been lecturing, and he attended Fichte's lectures until May 1795. Those few months spent under the powerful authority of Fichte's personality and thinking constituted possibly the most formative period of Hölderlin's restless, questioning existence. For it was under the guidance of Fichte that Hölderlin had studied a philosophical interpretation of man's relationship to nature that would eventually provoke within him his most acute spiritual struggle. Nevertheless, the youthful poet's later rejection of Fichte's analyses notwithstanding, the *Wissenschaftslehre* penetrated deeply into his thinking. In fact, as Ernst Cassirer argues, Hölderlin proved to be perhaps the first of Fichte's students who knew how to survey the total range of his master's teachings and how to appreciate and evaluate their ultimate goals.[33]

Indeed, Hölderlin's correspondence offers important support for Cassirer's thesis. Writing to his friend Neuffer, for example, Hölderlin marvels not only at Fichte's ability to advance into the most remote regions of human knowledge and to discover therein the principles governing that knowledge but also at the power of Fichte's mind to draw the most audacious consequences from those principles—and to lecture on such intricate matters and write his derivations on the blackboard with fire and determination, heedless of the evening's darkness that had settled over the classroom before the lecture had ended:

> Fichte is now the soul of Jena. And praise be to God that he is. I have never before known a man of such depth and energy of spirit....Dear Neuffer, this is indeed certainly much, and, to be sure, not enough is said of this man. I hear him every day. Occasionally, I speak with him.[34]

Significantly, in January 1795 Hegel, in a letter to Schelling, takes explicit note of the enthusiasm their sensitive friend had for Fichte. "Occasionally, Hölderlin writes to me from Jena," Hegel wrote; "[h]e hears Fichte and speaks with enthusiasm of him as of a titan who fights for humanity and whose circle of influence will definitely not remain within the walls of the auditorium."[35] Furthermore, in another letter of the Jena period, Hölderlin recommends to Hegel Fichte's speculative writings on the question of the foundation of the entire doctrine of science, as well as his lectures on the meaning of the scholar's vocation, adding "His analysis of the reciprocal determination of the I and the not-I (to use his language) is definitely remarkable."[36] It is that thesis that announces the essential problematic of a vast amount of Hölderlin's work. In particular, *Der Tod des Empedokles* is precisely an attempt to think that thesis through and to assert an independence, if possible, over it.

Der Tod des Empedokles:Erste Fassung. What does the idealistic determination of the I and the not-I involve? How does Hölderlin give dramatic voice to that thesis? How does that distinctively modern question come to presence through a philosophical character of antiquity? In the first version of *Empedokles*, Hölderlin introduces us to Empedocles as to a man renowned not only for his teachings but also for his miraculous powers. Philosopher of the Parmenidean line, powerful orator, political activist, Empedocles reportedly enjoyed certain magical powers over nature, the exercise of which won for him unmatched honor and popularity. Diogenes Laertius transmits one story according to which Empedocles gained considerable admiration when he ordered bags, made from the skins of flayed asses, to be stretched out across the land to catch and check the violence of the estesian winds, whose blowing force had been damaging the crops. For that extraordinary feat, he became known as the "wind-stayer."[37] Diogenes also reports that Empedocles miraculously cured Panthea, whose health none of the other physicians had been able to restore. That miraculous healing brought Empedocles esteem and distinction which few mortals have yet to enjoy.[38]

Indeed, Hölderlin's Panthea says that not even Jove's eagle could be prouder than Pausanias, Empedocles' famulus, who is privileged to visit his master daily; and Delia wonders at the fact that the Athenians, who regarded Sophocles with awe, never quite lost their hearts "in such painfully transported homage" as they have to Empedocles.[39] The man in whose every syllable all of nature's melodies ring out (IV, 5) commands from men and even from nature notice and admiration that formerly was reserved for Orpheus alone:

> They say the plants themselves take note of
> Him, notice where he walks, and the waters under the earth
>> Strained upwards to where his staff would touch the ground!
>> All that might well be true!
>> And when, during storms, he looks up to the sky
>> The clouds part and out gleams the
>> Bright day.—(IV, 3)

Yet great fame is a mixed blessing, for what is awe-inspiring is often also invidious. The celebrated, according to Hölderlin's portrayal, provoke not only admiration but fear and wrath as well, encomiums but also calumnies. In fact, the historical Empedocles was allegedly not without his enemies, and in Hölderlin's work those enemies are the representatives of the religious and the political communities—Hermokrates and Kritias, respectively—who fear the dazzling command Empedokles exercises over the people. Hermokrates and Kritias regard Empedokles with alarm and resolve to discredit him because his charismatic spirit has transformed the citizens of Agrigent into drunken, anarchic and frenzied admirers. And men in such contumacious, transported—and, in a sense, liberated—conditions lack that readiness to obey that legalistic religions or authoritarian politics demand. Desirous of retaining religious and political control, Empedokles' enemies accuse him of irreverence and sedition because he has scorned convention, prohibited peace and challenged the past (cf. IV, 26-27). Therefore, as he accepted the tributes, so must he respond to the accusations.

Plato, to whose works Hölderlin devoted a lifetime of attention, teaches that everything great carries within itself the risk of a great fall,[40] and Hölderlin's Empedokles provides a dramatic instance of that principle. Hölderlin portrays Empedokles as a man extraordinarily gifted, divinely favored and empowered, and even Hermokrates acknowledges that the gods had loved Empedokles specially (IV, 11). Empedokles compares himself to Tantalus (IV, 15), to whose transgressions his own bear a striking similarity. In a letter, written to Böhlendorff years after *Empedokles*, Hölderlin mentions Tantalus as one to whom the gods had granted more than he was able to endure.[41] Empedokles' experience is exactly analogous to Tantalus' because Empedokles finds it increasingly unendurable to support the tension between his mortal nature and his immortal powers (IV, 17, 85):

> poor Tantalus,
> You have defiled the holy place and broken
> The lovely bond in insolent pride.
> Wretch, when the world's kind spirits
> Full of love forgot themselves in you, you
> Thought of your petty self and believed, as a fool would,
> That they were sold to you and served you, they
> The heavenly ones, like stupid serfs. (IV, 15, ll.335-342) (Constantine trans., p.358)

That tension pushes Empedokles into the extremities of decision because the abundance of his divine endowments—exactly that which made him great—causes him to forget his humanity and his divine benefactors. His tragic offense, which comes out of his response to that tension and which Hermokrates rightly perceives, is precisely the crime of forgetfulness, forgetfulness of the difference between God and mortals.

> The gods have loved him greatly, but
> He is not the first they've then
> Cast into senseless night
> From the summit of their trust and kindness
> Because he was too forgetful of distinctions
> In excessive happiness and felt
> Only himself; so it happened to him and now
> He is punished with boundless desolation. (IV, 11, ll.209-216) (Constantine trans., p.358)

Empedokles fails to remember that although the divine presence suffuses his being, he is, nevertheless, not himself a god. Forgetting the distinction between humanity and divinity, Empedokles forgets his origins, thereby losing sight of what those origins essentially originated, publicly claiming to be a god. Instead of struggling to be as god-fearing and divine insofar as a human being can possibly be, to use Plato's formulation[42]; instead of exercising in gratitude to the gods and in their honor the powers they showered on him; instead of cultivating a sense of deep humility by attributing his greatness to those sources from whom it came and who continued to nourish its excellence; Empedokles takes himself as ultimate source, as *causa sui*. Calling himself a god, he seeks to immortalize mortality and neglect the existential fact that he is of human estate. Therefore, violating the ancient wisdom of Delphi, Empedokles becomes accountable to the justice of divine retribution: "For the gods / Have taken his power away / Since he, drunk on himself, / Before the people said he was a god" (IV, 10, ll.185-188). (Constantine trans., p.358) "His mind has been darkened. / Because, in your presence, he made himself into a god" (IV, 24, ll.561-562).

Additionally, Hölderlin interprets Empedokles' forgetfulness in such wise that it bears crucial implications on his attitudes toward humanity. Grown unsolicitous and vainglorious, Empedokles cultivates the exclusive company of his flowers, walking contumeliously among them, scornfully indifferent toward the destinies of others. Indeed, Panthea tells us that Empedokles has driven himself back into himself so unapproachably that even the winds hesitate to disturb him; she says that "the unneedy one wanders in his own world" (IV, 5, ll.73-74).

Empedokles' solitude and serenity are won at a great cost, however. Reigning as "the lordly pilot" (IV, 6, l.90) over the universe, Empedokles defines a sovereignty that severs its mooring to the earth. Consequently, what is of the earth floats off into insignificance. Concretely, to the rule of the one reigning in such isolation from man, the world seems little more than "a soulless shadow-image" (IV, 4, l.45) and humanity nothing more than the "dream" (IV, 6, l.102) of the ruler's life. In short, Empedokles' exaggeration of the ego leads him to evaluate humanity, the human other, as essentially reducible to the activity of the *cogito*. The human other, too, is the non-I.

Empedokles' negation of humanity flows from the same abundance that causes him to offend the gods. In his presentation of the formal nature of Empedokles' excess, Hölderlin draws on a tradition essentially older than modernity. For he takes over the concept of the tragic hero as one who desires too much, understanding, as Plato does, the dangers involved in any human enterprise that disregards due proportion "by giving anything what is too much for it." The political nature of Plato's argument aside, too much authority in a soul leads, as it does with Hölderlin's Empedokles, to a spiritual kind of excess: presumption. Concerning presumption, Plato argues:

> ... its issue is crime.... No soul of man, while young or accountable to no control, will ever be able to bear the burden of supreme social authority without taking the taint of the worst spiritual disease, folly, and so becoming estranged from its dearest intimates. When this happens, that soul very soon suffers ruin and the loss of all its powers.[43]

Although Plato's insight sketches out the formal nature of the pride that fills Hölderlin's hero, the material character of Hölderlin's interpretation of excessive authority, folly and estrangement remains bound to the later tradition of idealism that derived finally from Descartes. Impelled by presumption as he clearly is, (IV, 11-12, ll.209-238), Empedokles perpetrates a modern crime precisely because his presumption is essentially modern. For instance, Empedokles uses the language of modernity rather than that of antiquity to articulate his presumption and to acknowledge the justice of his punishment. He is punished, he explains, because he has taken his inner life—his breast and his heart, the source of his former capabilities—to be "out of himself alone / And no other" (IV, 15, ll.313-314). At the roots of Empedokles' hubris lies modern subjectivity.[44]

For Hölderlin, modern hubris derives from the I. Specifically, it grows out of the claims of the *cogito* to lord itself over all nature as the measure for all that is. Swelled by that hubris, Empedokles collapses the difference between the sacred and the profane because his hubris motivates him to reduce nature and nature's gods into his service. Although the literature of antiquity is replete with accounts of presumptuous hostilities against nature and the gods, it does not speak of a hubris that endeavors to master the world totally, to assume absolute dominion over all reality, or to trace all reality wholly and exhaustively back to the subject. Such a will to totality, a will to absolute power, is unknown in antiquity.

The presumption that characterizes Hölderlin's Empedokles stands in essential contrast to that presumption which antiquity attributes to its great tragic personages because the I of modernity declares itself through a hubris which the I of antiquity had no experience of: the I of modernity endeavors to have all beings accommodate itself to it and, in turn, to be accountable to no other. To modern subjectivity, primacy in all things belongs to the subject, and for that reason Hölderlin positions the subject's insolent utterances in one of the most crucial discourses of the drama:

> EMPEDOKLES: ... sacred nature!
> Virginal maiden, who has flown from crude sense!
> I despised you, and set myself alone
> Up as lord, an overdaring
> Barbarian! To your simplicity I held you,
> Your pure ever-youthful powers!
> Who raised me with joy, with delight nourished me,
> And because you returned to me ever the same,
> You good ones, I honored not your soul!
> I indeed knew it, I learned it well,
> The life of nature, how it should have been
> Still sacred to me, how once! The gods
> Had now become serviceable to me, I alone
> Was God, and expressed it in impudent pride.
> O believe me, I would rather not have been
> Born!
>
> PAUSANIAS: What? For the sake of one word?
> How can you be so despondent, bold man!
>
> EMPEDOKLES: For the sake of one word? Indeed. And the gods
> Might annihilate me, as they have loved me.
>
> PAUSANIAS: Other people do not speak as you do. (IV, 20-21, 11.470-489)

"The bold word...with One syllable" (IV, 21, l.494), "the imperiously cold word" (IV, 38, l.882) that tore Empedokles from his intimacy with the gods, is the word "*Ich*." "*Ich*" is precisely the word that conveys modernity toward totality and absoluteness. Saying "*Ich*" audaciously and defiantly, Empedokles profanes the sanctuary of his sacred benefactors, nature, desecrating it with words of hubris that the blasphemies of old could not have enunciated. Indeed, two marginal notations render those issues clear as they identify Empedokles' hubris as the *peccatum originale* of *superbia* and emphasize the radical modernity of that crime (IV, 464, 446).[45]

Since Empedokles' crime is to perpetrate hubris, swelled up with which he assaults his origins, it can be seen as an origin-al sin of a double order. Speaking through Hermokrates, the gods vent their indignation, explaining that although they would suffer many violations in silence they are not willing to tolerate Empedokles' radically origin-al blasphemies and ingratitude. Their judgment is that the blasphemer be cast "backwards down into the bottomless dark" (IV, 25, l.591) and "senseless night" (IV, 11, l.211), and that he remain "soulless in the dark" (IV, 10, l.10). Once illuminating the ways of men as their privileged *lumen gentium*, Empedokles tumbles into unrelieved darkness because the gods have withdrawn, taking in their withdrawal the sources of all light.

Furthermore, although such darkness afflicts the inner man primarily, extinguishing his own interior lights, it also enervates him in his dealings with others. Because Empedokles had severed the covenant binding him and the gods, he had cut himself off from the sources of his power. In their flight, therefore, the gods reclaim the strength and power they had granted him, leaving him to lament and to warn: "O, give also to nature, before she takes from you" (IV, 65, l.1553).

Moreover, the flight of the gods denies man access to an intelligible world; for, according to Panthea, the world appears to waver and reel around the sun like a soulless shadow-image. Empedokles himself notices that the once-fertile land has become arid (IV, 31), that the world intrinsically and deeply rich in life spreads before him like his own lost property (IV, 11), that night reigns even during the day (IV, 14). One ironic consequence of the withdrawal of the world's meaning is that there is, finally, something like a mutual, reciprocal interplay between man and nature, even though such an interplay is not that of an I/not-I reciprocity (IV, 44, ll.1017-1023).

Banished into such darkened desolation, Empedokles is sentenced to wander as a beggar (IV, 15, 40), "the all-forsaken" (IV, 18), and "the God-forsaken" (IV, 59), and to remain nowhere because love, which binds and holds together, dies, immediately the gods flee (IV, 19). Uprooted by the gods and excommunicated by men, Empedokles experiences the punitive nature of his solitude. For the self, abandoned to itself, falls under the sway of disorientation, alienation and ambiguity. Consequently, hubris darkens not only the self but the self's relationship with every non-self as well; "poison is between us," Hölderlin poetizes in *Chiron*.[46]

As a branch can bear no fruit apart from the vine, the self cannot accomplish anything independently of a ground more ultimate than it, because it is neither absolutely self-sufficient nor absolutely originative. The I's claims to be something self-sufficient and originative lead inexorably to radical isolation, as they do in Empedokles, who prepares to end his life estranged from men and disinherited by nature (IV, 27-30).

Despite his inability during his final hours to establish any sense of genuine solidarity with his fellow men, Empedokles makes his peace with the gods. Indeed, the inner conversion that transforms his attitude towards the gods appears to result directly from the redeeming efficacy of his punishment. However, the flames of punishment have no value in and of themselves since their significance consists in the service they render to sacred ends, resolutions, or commitments beyond themselves. Their status is, therefore, that of necessary but not sufficient conditions. In particular, they cleanse and make ready, burning away one's stain of guilt, thus preparing one for hallowed obligations. In such a way, they purify.

Penitent, contrite, Empedokles commits himself to healing the wounds between himself and nature. "Today is my autumn day and the fruit falls / By itself" (IV, 65, ll.1514-1515). "The time of purification has arrived," he says (IV, 70, ll.1681-1683). Since Empedokles' presumption has worked to divide and to scatter, the purification to which he submits will serve the ends of unity and reconciliation. Concretely, Empedokles' purification, the fruit of punishment, prepares him to die. For Empedokles, death alone can propitiate his crime; only through death can the I transcend its separateness from the not-I because death denies the self. Through death, then, Empedokles obtains something like a full mystical identification of the self with the non-self since, as Binder formulates it, through death "consciousness returns back into Being"[47] and retrieves nature's embrace.

Empedokles approaches his death as his profoundly "sacred hour" (IV, 56, l.1279), a time which the banality, hypocrisy and lovelessness of Hermokrates' legalistic religiosity would only degrade were it allowed to partake in the solemnities of the moment (IV, 22-24, 53-54). Accordingly, he rejects with scorn Hermokrates' offers of forgiveness and repatriation (IV, 57) because Hermokrates—the "cold priest" (IV, 59, l.1361) "who knows everything" (IV, 25, l.581) and who "carries on sacred matters like a business" (IV, 23, l.535)—represents a divinity and a religiosity long since deceased. Empedokles says of Hermokrates that "his countenance is false and cold and dead, /As are his gods" (IV, 23, ll.536-537). Final reunification of man and nature, then, imbued as it is by a deep religiosity, must issue from an experience of renewal, and renewal must come from death. Thus Empedokles, having atoned for his sin, likens himself to "the golden fruit/And flower and seed that flows from the dark earth" (IV, 70, ll.1666-1667).

Empedokles maintains that his death is his happiness, his privilege, and his self-chosen path (IV, 79). Yet there attaches to his death a necessity—it "must" eventuate (IV, 56, 73, 85)—that places it beyond the sphere of human freedom. For that reason his death remains essentially Grecian and pre-Christian. In the *Frankfurter Plan* for the play, Hölderlin writes that Empedokles responds to his death "as a necessity that follows from his innermost essence," (IV, 148, ll.8-9) thereby resembling the death of Achilleus (IV, 65) or Oedipus (IV, 540).

The necessity of the death notwithstanding, Empedokles desires to consummate it in joy, in festive expectation of the recrudescence of a new order of peace, unity and love, "as after the time of hopelessness" (IV, 68, l.1608). In particular, Empedokles' death yearns for a renewed epiphany of the Saturnalia (IV, 68-69, ll.1625-1642), when all had hung together and nothing had stood apart and when persons had lived in friendship and communion and in the presence of the Most High (IV, 60, ll.1403-1412). It is, therefore, in the name of a primordial covenant, of a unity that will take up and dissolve every dissonance, harmonizing every-thing discordant and cacophonous, that the "son of Urania" (IV, 77, l.1843) defines himself as an oblation and plunges to his death into the volcanic fires of Mt. Aetna, a burnt offering, a holocaust.

Although two brief scenes follow Empedokles' final mono-logue and death, they are essentially anticlimactic. Therefore, I can ask whether Empedokles' death succeeds in bringing Hölderlin to terms with the problems he both inherited and created for himself as a student of idealistic metaphysics. Was Empedokles able to "put an end to the eternal conflict between our Self and the world?"[48]

Empedokles' final word is "joy" (IV, 81, l.1942) and he likens himself to a rainbow, the biblical manifestation and guarantee of God's presence. Although the play is permeated with a deep de-sire to bring about a new religiosity and a new politics, com-mencing a renewed sense of eternity and of history, the question remains whether Empedokles suffices to realize that renewal. The play remains unfinished, and it seems that within the limits of the first version of the play, Hölderlin remains decisively puzzled by idealistic philosophy. He neither transcends the subject-object di-chotomy nor recovers from the metaphysical point of view of subjectivity.

Der Tod des Empedokles: Erste Fassung comes to presence as an idealistic tragedy, a modern tragedy, and its hero is a metaphysi-cally modern hero, characterized by a distinctly modern hubris and godlessness.[49] Indeed, precisely in its attempts to liberate Hölderlin's commitments to idealism, the play in fact deepens the philosophical difference between the human subject and nature as the object. Indeed, months after he left Jena and assumed his po-sition as tutor in Frankfurt with the family of Susette Gontard, Hölderlin acknowledged that "the echo from Jena" had continued to resound all too powerfully within him; he wrote, "Philosophy is a tyrant."[50] And although he also wrote to Hegel that "the spir-its of the air, with their metaphysical wings, that accompanied me out of Jena, have left me since I've been in Frankfurt,"[51] it seems that he remains importantly bound to their inward trajectories.

Hölderlin will eventually transcend the level of reflection attained in the first version of his tragedy, but he will not do so as a tragedian or through the mediation of the regal Empedokles. Indeed, anticipating another tragedian and another tragedy—Nietzsche and *Also Sprach Zarathustra*—Hölderlin himself clearly realizes the provisional nature of his early attempts in *Empedokles* to resolve the problems of subjectivity:

> This is no longer the age of kings. (IV, 62, 1.1449)[52]
>   You should be ashamed
> Still to wanting a king, you are
> Too old. In your fathers' day
> It would have been different. You can't
>
> Be helped if you won't help yourselves. (IV, 63, 11.1460-1464) (Constantine trans., p.359)

In this article, I have limited myself to a study of the first version of *Der Tod des Empedokles*. Hölderlin's thinking upon the subject-object division would evolve through a second and a third draft of the play, although each subsequent version remains as unfinished as the first. A careful textual and formal comparison of the three versions would clearly yield a greater comprehension of Hölderlin's attempts to address the Cartesian problematic, especially as that issue had matured into the idealism of Fichte. At the stage of *Empedokles*, Hölderlin formulated the I/not-I problematic in terms of an opposition between the organic and the aorgic, the particular and the universal, the human individual and the world, art and nature. In his reflections upon the essence of a tragic dramatic poem, he wrote that the mutual tension between the organic and the aorgic will find reconciliation only at the point of their extreme opposition:

> ...so that at this moment, *at this birth of the highest hostility the highest reconciliation appears to be the case.* Yet the individuality of this moment is only the product of the highest struggle, its universality only the product of the highest struggle ....[53]

In *Der Grund des Empedokles*, Hölderlin writes that "[i]t is the most profound inwardness which is expressed in the tragic dramatic poem."[54] Although he clearly identifies Empedokles as the site of the highest struggle, he expressly restricts Empedokles to being a representative of the classical world. He writes:

> Thus Empedocles is a son of his heaven and his time, of his fatherland, a son of tremendous oppositions of nature and art in which the world appeared before his eyes. A man within whom those oppositions are united so intimately that they become one within him, that they discard and reverse their originally differentiating form ....[55]

Thus, Hölderlin wrote that Empedokles was "the result of his time, and his character points back to it just as it emerged from it."[56]

Hölderlin's preoccupation with the decline of the classical world and his poetics of waiting, expectation, and hope in the name of a new and different order found important foundation in his reflections on Empedokles, for in those reflections the difference between the two worlds is explicitly articulated in terms of the requirements of the ancient world and those of the present world:

> ... the destiny of his epoch, the tremendous extremes out of which he grew, did not demand a song where the pure is still easily conceived in an idealistic presentation which rests between the appearance of destiny and the original, if time has not yet too much moved away from it; neither did the destiny of his epoch demand the true action which takes effect and helps immediately, to be sure, though also more one-sidedly and all the more the less it exposes man; it demanded a sacrifice where man in his entirety becomes real and visible as that wherein the destiny of his epoch seems to dissolve, where the extremes seem to unite truly and visibly in one but therefore are united too closely; and where in an idealistic action the individual perishes and must perish ... .[57]

At the stage of the first version of his play, Hölderlin did not succeed in reconciling the organic and the aorgic. That reconciliation, if it was to eventuate at all, would need to wait for his later poetry. Hölderlin's thinking upon this subject-object relationship, his desire to reconcile the opposites without dissolving the inherent tension between them, had necessitated his going beyond the form of the drama into the greater freedom of the poetry. Empedokles forgot his nature as mediator, his hubris blinding him to the necessity of measure and propelling him out of the space between God and man. By declaring himself publicly to be a god, Empedokles rejected the very nature of mediation. Yet to be a mediator, to stand in the *Zwischenzeit*, to hold fast to the middle between the past and the future, between God and man is of the very essence of the poet. The element within which a future can be articulated for Germany, one that is its own and not a mere imitation of the foreign world of the Greeks, and within which a new reconciliation between art and nature can be realized is the interval of the *Zwischenzeit*.

Neither Descartes' *cogito* nor Fichte's I can assist, at the birth of the highest hostility, the highest reconciliation of the opposites, for they stand opposed to nature as to the *res extensa* and the not-I. Truth will come to pass only in the between, where the poet affirms the peculiarity of that interval as the field out of which new gold will upglitter from the dark land. Between day and night, the poet waits. Between day and night, a truth will appear. The poet stands in the meanwhile, in the meantime, in the middle of time. It is a time of night, but also a time of promise. In *Germanien*, the song of Germany, the poet sang:

> *Wo aber überflüssiger, denn lautere Quellen*
> > *Das Gold und ernst geworden ist der Zorn an dem Himmel,*
> > *Muss zwischen Tag und Nacht*
> > *Einsmals ein Wahres erscheinen.*[58]

Finally, it is perhaps somehow fitting that the poet had expressed this most metaphysical matter in the most direct and simple terms in a letter that he wrote from Homburg, dated January 1799, and that he addressed not to Schelling or to Hegel but to his mother:

> *Aber gerade wie nach dem Winter der Frühling kömmt, so kam auch immer*
> *nach dem Geistestode der Menschen neues Leben, und das Heilige bleibt immer*
> *heilig, wenn es auch die Menschen nicht achten.*[59]

Paddling Against Ethics: Huck Finn as Moral Quagmire

Elizabeth Morgan
Eastern University

"In a barrel of odds and ends it is different; things get messed up, and the juice kind of swaps around, and the things go better." ---Huck

If superlative epithets were a virtue, *Adventures of Huckleberry Finn*, would be the most reputable book around. Mark Twain, somewhat disingenuously but simply, called it "another boys' book," but others have shown no such restraint. The Concord, Massachusetts, library declared it "the veriest trash" in the year of its publication, while the Springfield *Republican* railed against its coarse moral tone and bad grammar. In 1957 the New York City Board of Education, trusting that it *was* a boy's book, pulled it from their reading lists for elementary and junior high school students, joining other civic leaders in asserting that "no amount of intended irony or satire can erase the humiliation experienced by black children" in reading it.[1] Julius Lester, professor of Judaic and Far Eastern studies has proclaimed that while he is "opposed to book banning, I know that my children's education will be enhanced by not reading *Huckleberry Finn*."[2] Meanwhile Ernest Hemingway has declared that "all modern American literature stems from one book by Mark Twin called *Huck Finn*," and critic

Daniel Hoffman has labeled it "the most universal book to have come out of the United States of America."[3]

This article suggests that any absolutizing evaluation of the novel is irrelevant, that it is a narrative written against ethics and therefore neither racist nor anti-racist, neither utilitarian nor intuitive in its understanding of conscience, neither morally inspiring nor systematically derogatory—and that therein lies its genius. It tests the limits of ethical reasoning *and* of the "sound heart," despite Twain's assertion that in this work "a sound heart and a deformed conscience come into collision and conscience suffers defeat."[4] One wonders what conscience Twain might be talking about here and recognizes that to trust what any author says about a work, no matter how intriguing, suggests a gullibility on the part of the reader that can only cause trouble. Surely, only the misguidedly bookish Tom Sawyer would be tempted to believe Twain's warning that "Persons attempting to find a motive in this narrative will be prosecuted, persons attempting to find a moral in it will be banished; persons attempting to find a plot in it will be shot. By Order of the Author."[5] This is not to say that individual readers cannot be offended and cannot be transformed by reading the work, rather it recognizes the narrative as a testament to the moral quagmire that defines human reality in the post-bellum American south and elsewhere.

According to Mikhail Bakhtin, this is the transgressive beauty of any decent novel. In his 1981 introduction to Bakhtin's *The Dialogic Imagination*, Michael Holquist says that Bakhtin "loves novels because he is a baggy monster,"[6] which is his way of saying that the novel itself is a "baggy monster" of a genre. This, in fact, is what Bakhtin celebrates about the novel—its eclectic, folkloric, multivoiced, multiclassed, disruptive, and overfull nature.

Bakhtin describes the novel as a hybrid genre, as uncanonic and plastic, forming itself out of bits and pieces of other genres, "ever questing, ever examining itself and subjecting its established forms to review."[7] Thus he sees it as the perfect genre for a changing, emerging world, "because it best of all reflects the tendencies of a new world still in the making."[8]

Such a view of the novel welcomes its enriching "heteroglossia," its multiple voices, both social and psychic. Bakhtin claims that the novel, of all literary genres, resists monologism and, in its breadth and complexity, keeps alive the multiple discourses of a given society. It assumes all persons are internally dialogic, no groups in society are voiceless (for even if they are illiterate, their nuanced speech can be heard and reproduced), and all culture centers around multiplicity of conflict. Characters and readers alike are in the position of discovering their own language within the languages of others, of discovering their own ideological horizons within the ideological horizons of others. Otherness itself becomes both contingent and illusory.[9] Thus the novel is, by its very nature, different from didactic politics: it is "an anti-authoritarian, democratizing art form,"[10] simultaneously teasing out and ultimately trumping singularity of thought.

Reading *Adventures of Huckleberry Finn* through the prism of Bahktin's dialogic imagination is to encounter a world where the disruption of assumed binaries proliferates.

Romance vs. Novel

In the course of his life, Twain wrote several types of works: tall tales, travel books,[11] narratives celebrating romantic freedom and imagination,[12] and deterministic parables.[13] What of *Huck Finn*? In many ways, it too is a frontier romance, involving flights of the imagination, wild chases on the river, and raft fantasies. Tom Sawyer's early and late antics form the model for Huck's adventures in the mid-section, prompting him to say such things as "I reckoned Tom Sawyer couldn't a done it no neater himself. Of course he would a throwed more style into it."[14] But soon into the narrative one discovers that Tom Sawyer's romance is all by the book, about as free as the Calvinist doctrine Ms. Watson preaches. In fact, it's Tom who cautions Huck that he can't really expect to join his robber gang unless he agrees to live with the widow Douglas and Ms. Watson and act "respectable."[15]

When Tom proposes an oath for his gang, the rag-tag members ask in awe if he "got it out of his head," to which he responds that it came "out of pirate books, and robber books," and that all gangs that are high-toned have such an oath.[16] Defending the practice of ransoming captives, although no one seems to know what that entails, Tom declares with no little frustration "Why blame it all, we've *got* to do it. Don't I tell you it's in the books? Do you want to go to doing different from what's in the books and get things all muddled up?"[17] Shaping a categorical imperative for the right kind of romance, Tom continues to use words like *regular* and *correct*, and where his romantic games center around stealing the escaped slave Jim from his down-river captors, Tom becomes increasingly dictatorial, narcissistic and cruel, making up tasks and torturous challenges for Jim that turn out to be totally beside the point, in that Ms. Watson has already freed Jim. It is the romantic game for its own sake that interests Tom, the game in which he risks nothing, crosses no irrevocable lines, and ultimately shows very little imagination. So the narrative turns into a satiric dismantling of romance as a genre, all the while embodying the promise of romantic freedom.[18]

Twain further complicates this shift by utilizing the satiric thrust of the realistic novel to critique many other aspects of nineteenth century Southern culture, from mob rule to undertakers, religious rigidity, and family violence. The major target of his satire, throughout, seems to be mindless cruelty. When Aunt Sally asks Huck if anyone got killed in a steamboat wreck, he answers, "No'm. Killed a nigger," and she replies, "Well, it's lucky; because people sometimes do get hurt," the reader is plunged into a rural idyll where learned candor is vile and humanity up for grabs.

Romantic Adolescence vs. Static Adulthood

If Twain escapes aesthetic binaries by refusing to give up options, so does Huck refuse psychological binaries in his rites of passage. Tom Sawyerism offers an escape from the physical confinement both the widow Douglas and Pap want to inflict on Huck, but it is at the expense of personal freedom. As a form of scripted adolescent behavior, Tom's "halfway-house of rebellion where all irrevocable decisions are magically held in abeyance"[19] must be outgrown. But adulthood looks equally unappealing. "Sivilization" is a place of multiple perversions—ranting Calvinists, rigid schoolmarms, abusive alcoholic fathers, blind legal systems, feuding families who cannot remember the initial offense, and grubby charlatans—which must be avoided at all costs. "Light[ing] out for the Territory" is a transient solution to be sure; the frontier is just about gone, but, in the end, it buys Huck time. To that extent, we're all buying time of some sort, and there are no decent endings, only expectations.

River vs. Shore

Lionel Trilling and T. S. Eliot turn the river in *Huck Finn* into a hermeneutical god. It is the fluid medium, the uncharted waters in which Huck returns to nature and discovers basic affections. It is where he and Jim plan their futures, where Jim becomes mother/father to the orphaned Huck, constructing home out of a teepee on a raft, calling Huck "honey," confronting him with moral conundrums. It is a place where Huck can accept affection without embarrassment, because no one from shore is there to see him in the company of an escaped slave. When he runs back to the raft after a close call on shore, he cries "They're after us!"—not you or me, but "us." Compared with this freedom to be and be together, life on shore, where cruelty reigns, is highly suspect. But one soon discovers that there is no real shoreline; attitudes from land penetrate sacred raft space, giving Huck existential nausea over how he "ought" to feel about Jim, and Jim terrible fears about his fate. The Duke and Dauphin, shameless con men, invade life on the raft and make it the platform for their corrupt schemes. A steamboat threatens to cut the raft in half and sends Huck and Jim on a terrified search for the other. This is not a god many of us would readily embrace.

Heaven vs. Hell

Nor is heaven much of a boon. Early on Huck has a very hard time figuring out what providence is supposed to be and to offer. For one thing, the widow Douglas and Ms. Watson, partners in other things, seem to describe different providences. The widow's sounds kind of nice, but the idea of entering Ms. Watson's paradise makes Huck long for hell: "Well, I couldn't see no advantage in going where she was going, so I made up my mind I wouldn't try for it."[20] Further alienating Huck from providence, and validating his choice of going to hell rather than do the "right" thing and turn in Jim, is the Duke's claim that providence is looking out for him and giving him the breaks: "This-yer comes of trust'n to Providence. It's the best way in the long run. I've tried 'em all, and ther' ain't no better way."[21] Repugnant as this may sound to ears trying to keep heaven and hell in different spheres of the universe, Huck too comes to claim that providence keeps him safe "Providence always did put the right words in my mouth, if I left it alone."[22] So whose heaven is claimed at any given point and whose hell is hazarded as Huck navigates the mine field of mid-nineteenth-century slave-owning Mississippi?

Free vs. Slave

At first glance, this binary would appear to hold fast: people never assume that Huck can be ransomed for a fee, and they all want a piece of Jim. Yet ironically, Huck, having feigned his death and renounced his old life, including his trust fund held by Judge Thatcher, is penniless (poor white trash) and without clear goals, while Jim knows he is worth $800, a value he respects and hopes to barter into the freedom of his family in the free territory, should he ever get there. That's revolutionary thinking. As Hilton Als comments in a review of Randall Kennedy's book *Nigger: The Strange Career of a Troublesome Word*, "if Jim—Every nigger— were to buy his wife and children back, what then?" In addition to having some ironic sense of his worth, Jim has had the vision to escape in the first place, and while Jim, a man, a husband and father, seems painfully submissive at times to this white boy who clings to him one moment and mocks him the next, Jim is not afraid to "talk back." When Huck expresses his contentment with the life they are leading, Jim reminds him "Well, you wouldn' a ben here, 'f it hadn'ben for Jim."[23] Later when Huck, escaping the world of the Grangerfords, asks Jim how he recaptured the raft, Jim finds the question ridiculously stupid and says so: "How I gwyne to ketch her, en I out in de woods?"[24] It is not a matter of Huck freeing Jim as is sometimes asserted, but of Jim having already freed himself. Yet he is not legally free; he is still terribly vulnerable after they pass Cairo and head south into the slave holding states, and he knows it.   The reader knows it too and cringes every time someone comes up with a new way to use Jim for his/her own profit. Perhaps the greatest insult, the greatest reminder of Jim's enslavement comes after he is declared free, and Tom tips him $40 for being the subject of a gratuitous escape scheme. Ironically, Tom may be more enslaved to capitalist, white patriarchy than anyone else at this juncture in the plot.

Black vs. White

The black/white binary is far older than slavery in the United States.   It is a categorization of good vs. evil that covers centuries of literary and religious metaphors. Jim plays right into this when he tries to explain to Huck the moral complications of Pap, claiming that Pap has a good white angel on one shoulder and a black bad angel on the other, both of which claim his loyalty.   It is a wonderful irony that two short paragraphs later, we find that Pap is a study in black and white, such that white carries the most sinister content: "There warn't no color in his face, where his face showed; it was white, not like another man's white, but a white to make a body sick, a white to make a body's flesh crawl—a tree-toad white, a fish-belly white."[25] And the reversals continue, until Huck, in a burst of affirmation of Jim, asserts the ultimate privileging of difference, "I knowed he was white inside."[26]

It may well have been this painful irony that inspired Shelly Fishkin to question the assumed sources for Twain's characters. If we are to trust her research, and many do, neither Huck nor Jim are racially pure.[27] The language used by Twain's characters tells her that Huck is modeled not just on Tom Blankenship, the son of the town drunk, but also on Jimmy, a "bright, simple, guileless little darkey boy" (Twain's description) who waited on Twain in a hotel in the Midwest,[28] and on Jerry, a "gay and impudent and satirical and delightful young black man—a slave—who daily preached sermons from the top of his master's woodpile, with me for the audience."[29]

In addition, Fishkin claims that Jim combines aspects of Patrick McCleer, a gentlemanly white man, and John Lewis, "a black man who was for Twain a model of supererogatory altruism."[30] Given the prevailing "scientific" notions of racial superiority of Caucasians at the time Twain was writing, this genealogy is particularly transgressive, although his failure to claim mixed racial models suggests that to do so might have been publishing suicide. Readers often suffer ambiguity better when it is not named.

Law vs. Outlaw

Closely related to issues of language are issues of legality. Overt law in this novel is murky, at best. The judge who affirms Pap's guardianship over Huck knows nothing of the family situation.[31] Laws governing the sale of human beings are exposed at many turns. Pap, the moral outlaw, turns out to be more legalistic even than Ms. Watson when it comes to slave law, arguing vociferously that it is absurd to delay the sale of a free black man living in a slave state for six months.[32] But it is Ms. Watson's attempt to assert her will over Jim's family's fate by selling him away from his wife and children that gives him the moral courage to escape. Later in the plot, Mary Jane Wilks and her sisters weep over their slaves that are to be separated and sold, while accepting the law as a given. Huck makes himself an outlaw in order to be with Jim, but ironically, it is Ms. Watson who legally frees Jim. One could argue that Huck has been an outlaw all along and, in fact, feely chooses outlaw culture, stealing what he needs and wants, including Jim for companion.

Language may be the place where this is best played out. Huck is confrontational, even flamboyant in his declaration of the non-standard forms of dialect he intends to use, and his failure *ever* to spell "sivilization" correctly seems totally deliberate. After all, it's his story, and he's belligerently unschooled, always staying several steps in front of the "gramama-r wolf" as Helene Cixous refers to the rules of mainstream discourse. In this sense he makes good use of "signifying": speech on the wild side, often used by oppressed groups, including slaves, to talk around the master's language—subverting it, teasing out new meanings, going underground with coded phrases. Henry Louis Gates describes it as "all of the rhetorical play in the black vernacular," and Fishkin reminds us that, through his association with slaves on his uncle's farm, "Mark Twain was fortunate enough to be exposed to brilliant and memorable 'signifying' on a daily basis during his adolescence."[33] So whether Huck's seemingly racist commentary is a realistic reflection of a young white boy's socialization, or, through Twain's borrowing (conscious and unconscious) of the rhythms and idioms of black vernacular, an act of signifying on that socialization, or a crazy mix of both, it is an embodiment of "heteroglossia" that Bakhtin would certainly applaud.

Utilitarian vs. Intuitive Ethics

Ultimately the disruption of binaries in this tale takes one to conscience(s). Twain was well aware of the debate between utilitarian and intuitive notions of conscience in his day.[34] The utilitarian view that the conscience is an "association of ideas" acquired through social interaction seemed to complement his observations of the world. Yet notions of a "sound [intuitive] heart" continued to appeal to him. Huck's narrative may be more of a refutation of moral clarity than the victory of one theory over another. One has to admit that Huck is hardly subject to a unified "association of ideas." He has no mother to pass on cultural tradition to him in the home. The widow and Ms. Watson are mostly disciplinarians. Pap takes him off to a home where radically different notions of "comfort" (usually connoting moral as well as physical well-being for Huck) and discomfort prevail. When Huck leaves these conflicting worlds behind, he feigns his own death, desiring to start over. But of course, no one ever escapes a past, especially a terribly mixed one, so while Jim offers a new moral prism by which to view the world, one where relationality, both dangerous and nurturing, drives choice, Huck still carries a variety of conditionings with him.

Early on he pledges loyalty to Jim in order to get Jim to tell him his story: "'But you wouldn' tell on me ef I'uz to tell you, would you, Huck?' 'Blamed if I would Jim.'"[35] So when Huck comes to his first real case of conscience, where he considers paddling to shore to turn Jim in, it's Jim who reminds him of that pledge: "Dah you goes, de ole true Huck, de on'y white genlman dat ever kep' his promise to ole Jim."[36] And it works. Huck loves and needs Jim more than he needs to be right in an old way of being right, but this in no way suggests that Huck understands or embraces abolitionism, or in any way generalizes his feelings about Jim to all slaves, much less to all black people.

The second crisis comes when he has to decide whether or not to write Ms. Watson (he has no idea yet that she has died and set Jim free) to tell her that Jim is at the Phelps farm. No association of ideas that he has imbibed so far—neither the Calvinist god watching his every action, nor the social code that determines private property, nor the shame of being seen as an abolitionist, nor his attempts to understand his poor beleaguered heart—are reliable here. Huck must choose against all clear ethical options and accept a muddy choice which in itself gives him a kind of freedom: "And for a starter, I would go to work and steal Jim out of slavery again; and if I could think up anything worse, I would do that too; because as long as I was in, and in for good, I might as well go the whole hog."[37] He responds to his desire for Jim's company and to the call of this other who makes a rightful claim on him. He's making it up as he goes along. And so was Twain, and so are we.

If one is looking for a clear moral perspective on mid-nineteenth century, or early twenty-first century racial thinking, he/she won't find it in this book. So maybe the book *should* be kept out of the hands of children. But if one is seeking the search itself, with all of its muddled moral anxiety, with all of its erasures and surprises, *Huck Finn*'s a beauty.

Exploring Ambiguities in the Political Implications of Freud

Bruce Lapenson
Temple University

The "political" Freud is not the first thing that often comes to mind when thinking about the work of the inventor of psychoanalysis. Freud did not devote so much as an entire chapter to the study of political life; however, psychoanalysis provided a lens to view and analyze culture, so it must have implications for politics. Psychoanalysis teaches that individuals cannot eliminate, but rather learn to endure[1] ambiguities and uncertainty. The cultural analysis done by Freud presents ambiguity around the question of humans' social progress. Freud's voice loses his characteristic certainty in his most widely read book, *Civilization and Its Discontents*, and he ends this work with a question: "The fateful question for the human species seems to me to be whether and to what extent their cultural development will succeed in mastering the disturbance of their communal life by the human instinct of aggression and self-destruction."[2] Freud's certainty that " . . . they [humans] are . . . creatures among whose instinctual endowments is to be reckoned a powerful share of aggressiveness"[3] predisposed him to be skeptical of any political form. However much he cast a cold, discerning eye on ideals, Freud was too concerned with human destructiveness to deny the need for political authority. The ambiguity in the "political" Freud will be the focus of this paper. This analysis will attempt to identify the political form Freud would find most effective for fostering human happiness.

Ambiguity in Freud

The ambiguities of Freud are especially evident in his cultural analysis, and are rooted in his notion of ambivalence. Freud stated that, " . . . liberty . . . is no gift of civilization. It was greatest before there was any civilization, though then, it is true, it had for the most part no value, since the individual was scarcely in a position to defend it."[4] One can take from this that men would be grateful to civilization because of the security it provides; however, in the same text it is stated, "[c]ivilized man has exchanged a portion of his possibilities of happiness for a portion of security."[5] The developing line of thought culminates with the view that humans develop hostility toward civilization[6] but also recognize that its existence is essential.[7] Humans would not be comfortable in the state of nature, and they are not so comfortable in civil society either. What results, according to Freud, is ambivalence toward institutions.

Freud believed that ambivalence was experienced early in the individual's life. The Oedipus Complex for males results in ambivalent feelings toward one or both parents since the boy's wishes are banned or their aim is restricted.[8] The female child's aims are also thwarted because she cannot possess her father in the same way her mother does, and she cannot have the anatomy of the male.[9] For both genders early wishes are feared by others and not allowed to achieve aims. The pleasure principle " . . . is at loggerheads with the whole world, with the macrocosm as much as with the microcosm."[10] Life begins with instinctual needs for pleasure coming face to face with institutional barriers.

Marx and Locke did not view man's nature and the corrective institutional responses to it as the root of his problems. For Marx humans find themselves participants in a limiting class structure. To Locke tyrannical governments severely limit the personal pursuit of happiness. For both thinkers liberation comes about only when socio-political conditions allow individuals to reclaim a freedom that originally existed.[11] Freud only wants man to revisit and become aware of his origins, to acknowledge the powerful force of his drives but not to totally reclaim them. To do the latter, for Freud, would inevitably create problems for self-regulation. Opposing Freud here is the confidence that Marx had in his liberated individual, "species being" and Locke had in the "rational and industrious" man making use of property rights and liberal democracy.[12] Self-regulation would naturally follow from the particular types of individual liberation Marx and Locke envisioned. We know that Freud had no such confidence in human behavior, but what does the liberated person look like to Freud?

To attempt to answer this question means being haunted by ambiguities of which Freudian ambivalence is the source. Freud was an essentialist, he did not view the mind as a blank slate at birth, but he believed humans possessed strong instincts, which continually sought gratification. Ambivalence has much to do with the coerced re-direction of instincts. Children develop ambivalent feelings for their parents as a result of the Oedipal event, and so too do adults feel ambivalent toward civilization and authority figures. It is due to this double view that ambiguity in Freud's overarching implications exist:

> A good part of the struggles of mankind center round the single task of finding an expedient accommodation—one, that is, that will bring happiness—between this claim of the individual and the cultural claims of the group; and one of the problems that touches the fate of humanity is whether such an accommodation can be reached by means of some particular form of civilization or whether this conflict is irreconcilable.[13]

The essence of the struggles that Freud refers to evolve from the fact that an individual is also a group member. Within all of us the repressed anarchic part of the self seeks perfection of our external encounters, to enjoy relentlessly, but the "writings" of institutions also exist internally. Readers of Freud are left as he left them, with a great uncertainty; mankind's efforts should go on, but the struggle may be eternal. Perhaps Freud would note that some measure of liberation exists when one accepts the ambiguity.

The Liberated Individual

To Freud, since humans naturally seek pleasure and they had more freedom prior to civilization, it is not outlandish to suggest that as neurotics are limited in their capacity for happiness, man inflicts a similar fate onto himself by becoming civilized. When one considers the mass popularity of the use of legal and illegal substances in our society and the other objects of addiction, credit cards, materialism, etc., Freud's statement "[i]t seems certain that we do not feel comfortable in our present-day civilization . . ."[14] seems accurate. However, Freud knew the necessity and inevitability of repression since he proclaimed that man minus restrictions could not enjoy his natural freedom. Still, unlike Plato, Aristotle, Hobbes, and Locke, Freud believed that we paid a great price for repression. Three noted theorists of the "Freudian Left," Wilhelm Reich, Herbert Marcuse and Erich Fromm agree that repression was destructive to individuals' fulfillment, but, in varying ways, did not agree with Freud that repression was fixed and inevitable.

Reich theorized that repression of the sexual instincts began in the family although the family is actually transmitting the repressive ideals of patriarchal authoritative systems such as capitalism to the individual member. Rebellious thinking was squelched, according to Reich, by the same learned inhibiting tendencies, which repressed sexuality, and it is the task of psychoanalysis to foster the individual's letting go of self-limiting traits, especially sexual ones.[15]   Freud might agree with contemporary left-Freudian scholar Stephen Frosh who charges Reich with a libertarian and highly individualistic theory.[16] Freud's concern with instinctual aggression would have him criticize Reich as one who desires for man to return to his original state of total instinctual freedom. While Freud did not explore the inhibiting tendencies of any particular economic or political system, Reich's lack of concern for human relations in an environment where the id is given a free rein even gives socialists such as Frosh pause:

> This form [Reich's] of politics returns to the individual rather than to the transformation of social structures. Consequently . . . politics is reduced to biology . . . leaving only sex (good) and society (bad).[17]

Marcuse is more sophisticated and nuanced regarding repression tha Reich since he noted a necessary and positive type of repression, 'basic repression,' and a destructive type, 'surplus repression.' *Basic repression* adds to pleasure and gratification because it allows individuals to focus on chosen objects for fulfillment rather than just haphazardly gratifying a primitive need.[18] However, *surplus repression* results from and reflects the dominant interests of a society. Surplus repression becomes interlaced with basic repression in history; deological illusions become entrenched and therefore suppress the human potential for liberation from instinctual repression and need. Yet, Marcuse believed that repressed instincts could always revolt and set the stage for '*the return of the repressed.*' Marcuse proclaimed that " . . . the full force of the pleasure principle not only survives in the unconscious but also affects in manifold ways the very reality which has superseded the pleasure principle."[19] Such a rebellion had the potential to make individuals abandon the illusory manifestations of surplus repression—performance, work ethics and guilt—allowing men to collectively focus on the elimination of need and to increase the time for leisure activity. Marcuse dealt with Freud's concerns about aggression by claiming that a freer libido would work in the service of *Eros* becoming a force to counter destructiveness.[20]

Freud was well aware of the power of repressed instincts, but he would be wary of optimistic accounts of their collective expression. According to Philip Rieff, Freud felt revulsion toward " . . . collective idealisms . . ." believing that they represented ". . . a response to pressure from the unconscious."[21] Freud advocated less restriction for the sexual morality of his day,[22] but he did not imply as Marx, Marcuse, and Reich do that liberation would achieve and maintain a social *homeostasis*. Instead of equilibrium Freud implied that the instincts had a dynamic nature,[23] which, gave Marcuse cause for optimism, but for Freud cause for concern. To Freud periods of freer libidinal expression might be good, but they could also lead society back to aggression and subsequently greater restrictiveness. Frosh pointed to the lack of concern in Marcuse and Reich for "the *internal* contradictions of the individual subject . . ." and ". . . of the difficulties engineered into the psyche by the complexities of personal encounters in all envisionable worlds . . ."[24] As individual development and social interaction are to varied and complex to expect a permanent or near-permanent solution to conflict, so too we cannot expect societal and political changes to erase conflict on the micro or macro level.

Erich Fromm's use of Freud with Marx comes across as much less radical, but just as optimistic, as Reich or Marcuse. Fromm viewed the effects of capitalist culture, e.g. consumerism as distorting the positive personal and social activities and relations of individuals. Although Fromm believed human behavior to be culturally conditioned,[25] he saw man as " . . . *primarily* a social being . . ."[26] Fromm also differed from Freud through his claim that ideals like "truth, justice, freedom . . . can be genuine strivings . . ."[27], as opposed to Freud's view of such things as necessitated by the difficulty of individuals trying to satisfy instinctual desires. Fromm thought, unlike Freud, that a character structure was the causal factor in social relationships not just instincts. Much opposed to Reich and Marcuse, Fromm proclaimed that the individual had the power to change the quality of his life by changing her/his self-limiting orientations toward others regardless of the economic or political system they lived under.[28]

Fromm's optimism opens up an interesting debate about Freud. Rieff argued that "[p]sychoanalysis is the doctrine of the private man defending himself against public encroachment."[29] Rieff acknowledged that Freud understood authority and social coercion to be necessary, but "even in an atmosphere of conformity, inner freedom is possible."[30] Fromm went beyond Rieff's view of Freud by positing that empowered individuals held great hope for macro-level change. Freud never analyzed economic or political systems, but he knew the effects of the power of widespread beliefs and institutions on the ego's difficult struggle for self-mastery. Knowing the super-ego to originate in the Oedipal event and then to unleash its force on the ego through societal institutions, Freud stated "[I]n the severity of its commands and prohibitions it [super- ego] troubles itself too little about the happiness of the ego."[31] Fromm side-steps the friction Freud was so aware of, which occurs when the moral cultural conditions (super-ego) overwhelm individual strivings for some measure of auton-omy and freedom. How much freedom Freud thought possible turns our inquiry to less radical readers of Freud who acknowl-edged the friction between the ego and institutions but still saw the possibilities for freedom in the political implications of psy-choanalysis.

Paul Roazen's, *Freud: Political and Social Thought* and Philip Rieff's, *Freud: The Mind of the Moralist*, both written decades ago, are much more aware than the radical thinkers previously dis-cussed of the problem of aggressive drives in social life but at-tempt to put Freud somewhere in the corner of liberalism. Roazen acknowledged Freud's concerns about " . . . the intensity of de-structive urges and . . . [that] societal coercions can be psychologi-cally necessary."[32] But, Roazen also pointed out that underneath Freud's wariness existed ". . . an Enlightenment dream of free-dom."[33] Roazen knew that "[t]he trouble with the liberal tradition . . . was its narrowness of understanding, its difficulties . . . treat-ing issues of human emotions."[34] However, Roazen stayed on Freud's view that individuals should contribute to society " . . . with the least possible sacrifice of [their] own activity."[35] Taking Roazen a little further, Freud did not want the optimism of any positive-sounding political ideology—democracy, liberalism, so-cialism all come to mind—to cloud men's thinking about impor-tant decisions and expectations of social life or understanding irrationality, but he was not whole-heartedly rejecting the indi-vidual desire for a better quality of life:

> We may expect gradually to carry through such alterations in our civili-zation as will better satisfy our needs and escape our criticisms.[36]

The next sentence, in *Civilization and Its Discontents*, as we may ex-pect by now highlights the ambiguity in Freud's political implica-tions:

> But perhaps we may also familiarize ourselves with the idea that these are difficulties attaching to the nature of civilization, which will not yield to any attempt of reform.[37]

Rieff does more than open up room for Freud in the liberal canon; he places him squarely there and thus attempts to resolve some of the ambiguity. Rieff claims that psychoanalysis has contributed to modern skepticism about politics by subjecting political life to psychological inquiry.[38] The jaded attitude of contemporary man toward government, groups and leaders is encouraged by Freud's view that groups suppress individual rationality and regime change amounts to the replacing of one authority with another.[39] Rieff acknowledges Freud's need for coercive authority in society and the positive uses of " . . . knowledge of the irrational . . ." by possibly rational leaders for democratic means.[40] Rieff comes down however on the side of strong classical liberalism for Freud, and calls him anti-political and "[t]he prophet of disengagement."[41] One can picture Freud's liberated man, from Rieff's view, as vigorously pursuing private life, and although self-controlled showing an interest in politics only if absolutely necessary.

Rieff's view of Freud is appealing for its attempt at being unambiguous and its classical liberal ideal. However, it is hard to see Freud not thinking Rieff's view incomplete and dismissive of the bedrock belief of psychoanalysis that civility masks the irrational. As much as Rieff used this belief to make Freud significantly reject political life, Freud's concerns about irrationality do not end with fascism or communism; they extend to all ideologies, as Rieff ironically points out.[42] The final paragraph of *Civilization and Its Discontents* shows Freud observing modern man's agitation about the unsteady condition of domestic and international peace. Unquestionably, he shared this anxiety. Disengagement may have been the last thing Freud would advocate.

The Good Society

The ego, influenced by a largely unconscious id, seeks unlimited freedom, but the super ego, also partly unconscious, doesn't feel secure about social life. Human interests in the psychoanalytic view are divided; the Enlightenment dream assumes a healthy balance of id and super ego, but such a neat framework has had troubles even in societies supposedly founded on ideals of freedom and liberation. To Freud, unconscious ambivalence upsets the conscious goals and political inclinations of the rational man of the Enlightenment. Attempts to place Freud in an unqualified, known political camp run smack into his ambiguities. Freud seemed to be the prophet of yes and no: yes, greater equality of property would improve the quality of life, but no, communism would not significantly decrease aggression.[43] Yes, societies should ask as little of an individual's freedom as possible, but no, the leveling effect of freedom may not produce the most rational political leaders.[44] The knowledge of the irrational, Freud might have said, must be taken into account in any political ideology. Human nature, both pleasure principle and aggression, individual and cultural narcissism, the wish to repeat and ambivalence can work both for and against Enlightenment goals.

Ironically, the possible resolution of Freud's political ambiguities may also be something of an ambiguity. Writing about the practice of psychoanalysis and its need to reject a worldview, Alan Bass proclaimed:

> . . . any life in Freud's conception, is a constantly resisted encounter with a differentiating, tension-increasing reality with internal division and with double-binds. And if there is no life that can avoid such encounters, then like Freud it has to embrace being "haunted" by them.[45]

Bass' point can be related to political life. Embracing the knowledge of the irrational may help societies avoid the limiting results of rigid ideologies. Politics may be best if guided by the need for freedom *and* order, and leaders and citizens should question dominant beliefs with regards to the specific political events thrust upon them.

The Enlightenment dream of freedom to Freud had to overcome the tendency of all related political ideologies to bypass human psychology and the knowledge of the irrational. Freud thought that " . . . 'the psychological poverty of groups'"[46] would haunt democracies, resulting in the most fit to lead being hampered from leading or doing so effectively; irrational attachments to not-so-fit leaders or policies would rule the day. Freud knew that communal ties had to be strong for social order to exist, but he also claimed that human nature always waits for some provocation,[47] so it can be assumed that freedom in its liberal or democratic forms would have to be developed with caution. Communal ties and individual pursuits could become as irrational as tyranny or fascism. Contemporary political theories have much remarked that liberalism is quite capable of dissolving communal bonds.[48] When one considers that psychoanalytic interpretations reject the false security of social order and the rational man of the Enlightenment, it is hard to think of Freud as the prophet of political disengagement.

Freud implies that we embrace and deal rationally with the ambiguities of Enlightenment-inspired ideologies. Freud may have had a liberal slant, but it was a cautious one. Machiavelli's *Prince* comes to mind in a qualified sense. The Prince knows that political life is the product of man; man's nature is full of drawbacks, and therefore an astute vigilance is constantly necessary to respond rationally to the dynamic nature of politics; ideals and ideologies must at times be put aside. For Freud, we just need to extend this orientation to the citizen. Such a perspective may help us, at least a little, deal with the ambiguity in the political implications of Freud.

Ambiguities in Nietzschean Philosophy: Problems for Feminism

Elizabeth Kaufer Busch
Berry College

Is Feminism Dead? Several scholars have recently commented on the embattled state of feminism, noting the paradox that roughly three-fourths of women reject the feminist label despite their dedication to many of its egalitarian principles.[1] Kay Hymowitz even declares: "Feminism is not simply suffering from a P.R. problem. It's just over. As in finished."[2] This is news to groups like NOW, the Feminist Majority, Ophelia Project, and the Ms. Foundation, who passionately dispute Hymowitz's claim. These groups warn of feminism's unfinished work, as "two hundred years of American 'enlightenment' have failed to deliver the goods to women—we cannot even pass the Equal Rights Amendment."[3] Given these contradictory views, it's worth pondering why women are abandoning the feminism that afforded them unprecedented rights and opportunities.

The first account, propounded by "equity feminists," holds feminism a victim of its own success: its vast achievements have rendered the movement obsolete. They furnish as evidence the fact that women now make up over 46 percent of the work force in the U.S.; workingwomen may outnumber workingmen by 2025[4]; the number of women running their own business firms increased at a rate twice the growth rate for all firms[5]; women outnumber men at Ivy League universities like Harvard,[6] and the gender pay gap is narrowing, or disappearing altogether.[7] The second, voiced by vocal interest groups, college administrators, and Women's Studies departments, denies that feminism is over on the grounds that women still suffer an inferior status. Political leaders, cultural norms, and societal institutions, they claim, continue to oppress women by perpetuating stifling gender norms. Christina Hoff Sommers coined the term "gender feminism" to describe the latter perspective that strives to transcend all gender roles and argues that this new feminism has replaced mainstream liberal feminism.[8] Gender feminists no longer seek "an equal partnership between the sexes," but *empowerment* to create "a world where patriarchal culture and male dominance no longer oppress us or the earth."[9] This abandonment of equal rights protection as a goal engendered the crisis in which feminism is currently embroiled. Sommers, a self-described equity feminist, who seeks equal opportunity for women, traces the rejection of *feminism* but not *feminist principles* to gender feminism's divergence from its liberal democratic origins. Women, in her view, do not denounce *feminism* in total; they reject *gender* feminism.

This paper argues that the evolution from equity to gender feminism is connected to an unlikely source, Friedrich Nietzsche. Conspicuous similarities between Nietzsche's will to power doctrine and gender feminist conceptions of power, or "empowerment," uncover the limitations of gender feminist goals—difficulties that may account for women's flight from the movement. Unlike traditional liberal feminists, gender feminists perceive the nature of politics solely as power, specifically as male-domination, which leads to their goal of *"overthrow[ing] …oppressive power structures set up by nature and reinforced by man."*[10] This shift leads to serious ambiguities within the gender feminist goal of empowerment.

After outlining the key features of Nietzsche's will to power teaching, the paper details striking similarities between it and the gender feminist conception of empowerment. These parallels, however, will be shown to be inadvertent, as Nietzsche never intended to befriend feminists, and feminists, for the most part, are unfamiliar with or simply reject him as a misogynist.[11] The feminist appropriation of Nietzschean ideas is generally a consequence of their affinity for Michel Foucault's work. Though interesting and important work could be done on the Foucaultian roots of gender feminism, turning to Nietzsche is sensible because he is *the source* of both Foucaultian and gender feminist conceptions of power. Turning to Nietzsche sheds light on feminism's current theoretical crisis in a way that Foucault's work alone could not.

Nietzsche's affirmation of the will to power was intimately tied to his condemnation of egalitarianism and feminism. The foundation of Nietzsche's rejection of feminism is his disagreement with the very core of democratic morality, which is based on the notion of universal equal rights. Egalitarianism, which treats unequals as equals, homogenizes the population and stifles much-needed human creativity, in Nietzsche's view. This is why Nietzsche argued that all democratic ideologies and feminism, in particular, failed to empower men or women in the fullest sense. Ironically, gender feminism may be following a less democratic path—i.e., moving toward the very things Nietzsche suggested— by invoking "empowerment" as its goal, and yet despite this turn, the movement is faltering still. Examining Nietzsche will therefore help clarify why gender feminist theory is in crisis today.

The article next considers whether gender feminists' shift of emphasis from equal rights to empowerment ultimately undermines feminism's own goals. Nietzsche's endorsements of hierarchy, inequality, and concubinage[12] make an alliance between the two highly problematic: if the will to power cannot be divorced from Nietzsche's anti-egalitarian politics without fundamentally altering its meaning, which I argue it cannot, the assumed egalitarian stance of gender feminism is called into question. Second, gender feminists' debt to Nietzsche, a patriarch, would mean that they have failed to break free from the bonds of male dominion. Any "empowerment" achieved would have to be incomplete. Even more problematic, however, is the possibility that gender feminism may sabotage its principled stance by availing itself of Nietzschean psychology. Once power becomes the only graspable goal, as key gender feminists imply, all claims to moral justification, including their own, are uprooted.

If gender feminists are to solve these problems, as they must if feminism is to survive, they need to confront the ambiguities inherent in Nietzsche's and their own conceptions of power and empowerment. Under the direction of gender feminists, the movement's future strength remains unclear. Given its current influence, gender feminism may bear the ultimate responsibility for feminism's future. The paper concludes by considering the lessons that feminists might draw from examining the theoretical tensions within their movement.[13]

The Will to Power: How Men Create Truth

By positing the will to power, Nietzsche replaces the Enlightenment teaching of self-preservation (or fear of violent death) as the chief human motivator and foundation of social contract theory. The will to power is a basic explanation for why humans, or even, why all living beings, behave as they do. "A living thing seeks above all to *discharge* its strength—life itself is *will to power*; self preservation is only one of the indirect and most frequent *results*."[14] Deeper than the lust for mere life (survival) lies the ever-present agitation toward augmenting one's (feeling of) power. Though Nietzsche admits that the will to power is only "*one* basic form of the will,"[15] he derives all instinctual drives from it: "our entire instinctive life [is] the development and ramification of ... the will to power."[16] Willing is inextricably linked to the instincts because humans cannot help but will what their instincts propel them to will. As a reflection of each individual's idiosyncratic drives, the will is also radically individualistic; no two wills are alike.

The will is best understood as an internal striving to influence oneself, others, and the world; it is both an internal struggle against oneself as well as an external struggle to shape people and things outside oneself. Willing means affecting a change, striving to leave an imprint on the world, pushing against opposing forces, transcending oneself, and wanting to be different.[17] The will's constant struggle manifests itself simultaneously in commanding and obeying: "That the weaker should serve the stronger, to that it is persuaded by its own will, which would be master over what is weaker still: this is the one pleasure it does not want to renounce. And as the smaller yields to the greater that it may have pleasure and power over the smallest."[18] Power is not only experienced in commanding others, but also in commanding oneself. An accumulation of power can even be experienced even in heeding others' commands, for in submitting to the stronger force, the weaker individual envisions one weaker over whom he can establish dominion. As essentially will to power, humans perpetually strive to dominate themselves and others, which means they are characterized internally and externally by tyrannical drives.

Exploitation, war, and oppression become nothing more than the means by which the will expresses itself, according to Nietzsche's characterization.[19] At their base, even egalitarian societies are powerdriven and tyrannical, for even they "do to other bodies what the individuals within it refrain from doing to each other: it will have to be an incarnate will to power, it will strive to grow, spread, seize, become predominant—not from any morality or immorality but because it is *living* and because life simply is will to power."[20] Or, as Foucault sees it, the will to power doctrine reverses Clausewitz's theory by conceiving politics as "a war continued by other means."[21]

The will to power reduces all human longings and drives, noble and ignoble strivings, and even the most seemingly apolitical activities, to the desire to predominate. This means that no activity is utterly selfless, including the most erotic activities (philosophy and love). Philosophers have never innocently searched for meaning; instead, each egoistically sought to create the world, to tyrannize nature to suit his idiosyncratic will.[22] Similarly, the lover never fundamentally seeks to bring happiness to the beloved but rather to dominate and ultimately to exercise "*unconditional power over the soul and over the body of the beloved.*"[23] Consequently, as both are rooted in the power dynamic, love and hatred become virtually the same.[24]

Nietzsche's attribution of all ideals to man's will has far-reaching implications. First, the doctrine affirms a greater authority to human creativity than had ever been conceived, a power traditionally attributed only to gods. The will to power affirms man's ability "to become master over the many vain and overly enthusiastic interpretations and connotations that have so far been scrawled and painted over that eternal basic text of *homo natura*".[25] By creatively willing a new interpretation of the world, humans have the power to alter the entire species (human nature). The feminist goal of empowerment aims to harness this creativity in order to transcend patriarchal values. Next, the will to power only becomes sensible after Nietzsche acknowledges the death of God, the declaration which signifies the death of *all ideals*, including "nature," and "truth."[26] One result of the death of God is radical relativism, the belief that truth varies depending on cultural, historical, and social circumstance, a consequence that could, if taken to its logical extension, lead to nihilism. Well aware of this threat, Nietzsche furnished will to power as *the* tool with which humans could fight the impending threat of nihilism and determine the future. Without an absolute standard by which humans can take their bearings, only the human will can empower humanity by consciously creating meaning. As the doctrine denigrates the origin of all truths to emanations of the human will, man, it seems, is responsible for humanity's great accomplishments as well as its colossal failures. This last point gives gender feminists the ammunition with which to condemn patriarchs' historical oppression of women.

The Nietzschean Root of the Gender Feminist Conception of Power

Why Gender Feminists Pledge Allegiance to Foucault Instead of Nietzsche: As tyrannical and impious as Nietzsche's doctrine may sound, the will to power has had widespread influence on postmodern democratic and feminist thought. Postmodern thinkers, however, generally lack an awareness of the extent to which their multidimensional conception of power is Nietzschean. In a few instances, feminist scholars acknowledge the Nietzschean root of their thought.[27] Jana Sawicki, for example, credits Nietzsche with granting "philosophical legitimacy to inquiries into sexuality, desire and power," issues which she regards as "central ... to feminism."[28] Where other gender feminists speak of Nietzsche, however, it is almost always to attack him.[29] Nietzsche's writings are overtly critical of feminism; he abhorred women's liberation, referring to it as the primary cause of mankind's diminution.[30] Thus, the rarity of feminists' acknowledgement of Nietzsche's influence on their work is not altogether surprising.

The source gender feminists much prefer is Foucault, the radical liberationist and egalitarian postmodernist thinker. [31] Foucault's focus on the history of sexuality gives the impression that he is sensitive to the plight of women and the problems of sex and sexuality. Judith Butler, for example, credits Foucault with uncovering "sex" as a social construction, "which effectively extends and disguises the power relations responsible for its genesis."[32] The Foucaultian idea that values are socially constructed has its roots in the Nietzschean declaration that "God is dead." This recognition has given rise to a radical reconstitution of feminist goals: "A feminist theory of sexuality would locate sexuality within a theory of gender inequality, meaning the social hierarchy of men over women."[33] Gender feminists are also attracted to Foucault's liberationist language: Foucault offered women a "more optimistic view of the relationship between language and power. He would have rejected the view that the power of phallocentric discourse is total."[34] Thus, he appears to offer women a re-definition of and means of achieving empowerment. "Freedom, Foucault maintained, must be understood as resistance to the impositions of power, as the antimatter of power.... Recognition of one's entanglement in the webs of power/knowledge, Foucault's defenders maintain, is a form of liberation in itself."[35] By uncovering the historical root of power structures, women can come to understand and liberate themselves from them.

What these feminists generally fail to acknowledge, however, is Foucault's own debt to Nietzsche,[36] a dependence that Foucault himself admits.[37] Though Nietzsche is not concerned with empowering women, his affirmation of human creativity is an obvious source of Foucault's deconstruction of social norms. Like Nietzsche, Foucault places power at the center of his system. Leslie Paul Thiele explains; "there is no absolute freedom from which power is absent. According to Foucault, there is no realm of freedom in which we may escape power to assert our nature: we might change our positions on the web, but there is no jumping off."[38] In addition to their central focus on power, both also lack a clear normative framework for their respective systems;[39] however, Foucault is often identified with democratic ends,[40] whereas Nietzsche is more aptly described as a radical aristocrat.[41] This divergence has led to a spirited debate regarding the coherence of Foucault's use and abuse of Nietzsche. As this has been competently debated by others,[42] my concern is to examine the consequences of the manifestly Nietzschean notions of empowerment for feminism.

What is Gender Feminism? Gender feminists' aversion to Nietzsche's chauvinism does not mitigate the fact that Foucault's ideas, and consequently their own, are Nietzschean to the core. But before analyzing the Nietzschean roots of feminist "empowerment," the meaning of gender feminism should be made clear. Gender feminists understand the world wholly in terms of gender, an oppressive institution imposed on boys and girls by parents, teachers, and authoritative institutions. In other words, gender feminists believe the concept of "nature" itself to be a false creation arbitrarily imposed on men and women. This extreme environmentalism finds no essential differences between the sexes, and, consequently, all gender roles to be unjust. Second, and most relevant for our purposes, genderists believe that "humans possess a single social motive—power—and that social life can be understood only in terms of how it is exercised."[43] Indeed, they generally acknowledge, as does Nietzsche, that "life itself is *will to power*."[44] Third, gender feminists understand political life as arising from the deliberate actions of groups rather than individuals, "in this case, the male gender dominating the female gender."[45] This view corresponds to the dichotomy Nietzsche draws between masters and slaves.

The clearest Nietzschean thread running through gender feminism is their conception of power, which has three essential components. First, just as Nietzsche uses the will to power as a single comprehensive explanation for how the world operates, gender feminists provide a similarly broad account: the "essence of politics is power."[46] Power alone explains individual human behavior and also the origin of all political laws, social norms, and cultural mores. Second, like Nietzsche, gender feminists redefine the entire history of the world in terms of this finding. They use the term "patriarchy" to describe all past societies, which they see as creations unjustly imposed by oppressor (all males) on the oppressed (all females). And because every society so far has been patriarchal, they view the boundary between public and private as an artificial construct of males for the purpose of subordinating females. Gender feminism's mantra, "the personal is political," reflects this recognition.

The Essence of Politics is Power: The gender feminist conception of politics, illustrated in the writings of Catharine MacKinnon, Kate Millet, Shulamith Firestone, Marilyn French, Judith Butler, Naomi Wolf, and others, reflects the Nietzschean view that all public and private life is essentially will to power.[47] Kate Millet begins with a seemingly simple point that power is "the essence of politics," which means that society is nothing but "a relationship of dominance and subordination."[48] Catharine MacKinnon elaborates: "By political, I mean here questions of power...[F]eminism is a theory of how the eroticization of dominance and submission creates gender, creates woman and man in the social form in which we know them."[49] Specifically, the conscious or unconscious battle between the sexes leads males to create laws, "gender roles," and institutions that reinforce them so they may capture and maintain power over women. Though Daly and Butler do acknowledge Nietzsche's authority in a few instances,[50] Butler, MacKinnon, and others more frequently credit Foucault's.[51]

The political power to which MacKinnon refers is, in the first place, the political authority to make laws, but as such laws generally follow the moral or immoral intentions of their authors, the meaning of power goes much deeper. As power is the defining feature of politics, the only way to understand the social network of public and private relationships is to consider the intentions of those who hold the power. When gender feminists examine those intentions, they come to see all public institutions, including language, as traceable to an underlying system of male domination. Thus, power also refers to the ability of patriarchs to shape the way others think, the ability to create the unwritten laws that reinforce the established order, and actually form the way we think.

All human activity, down to the minutia of life, can be derived from the will to power of individuals (males).

To say that the essence of politics is power is to say that the essential motive of *all humans* (male and female) is predominance, though most gender feminists tend to see only males in this way. They argue that men have been the only full actors in the political realm so far, while women have perpetually been exiled to the less prestigious domestic sphere. The only way to discover what women are and what society could be like would be to remove the oppressive structures that have always been in place. Though some gender feminists recognize difficulties associated with their appropriation of this view of power,[52] many do not.

Women Are Universally Oppressed by the Patriarchy: Because they believe that only males have held political power, gender feminism's next position logically follows: all societies, past and present, have been patriarchies, "a familial-social, ideological, political system in which men—by force, direct pressure, or through ritual, tradition, law, and language, customs, etiquette, education, and the division of labor, determine what part women shall or shall not play, and in which the female is everywhere subsumed under the male."[53] Combine this with their comprehensive understanding of power and we get Butler's recognition that "Power, rather than the law, encompasses both the juridical (prohibitive and regulatory) and the productive (inadvertently generative) functions of differential relations."[54] Even if males did not hold the juridical power, they would still be empowered by the lasting effects of the laws other males previously instituted. Such laws arose from the wills of males, who citing their legal, "natural," or "divine" authority shaped the character of the world. As *"commanders and legislators"*[55] they imposed laws on the world (forced the world to bend to their wills), and, as creators, they affirmed their idiosyncratic natures to the detriment of women's natures.

Gender feminists characterize all past and present societies as oppressive entities dichotomized into master and slave: man as the universal oppressor and woman as the universal victim. Their dichotomy flows directly from Nietzsche's distinction between master morality and slave morality.[56] The gender feminist characterization of patriarchy traces all injustice from the unequal distribution of power. In their hopes to maintain and justify their hegemony, men invented "hierarchy, slavery and private property... predicated upon, the initial subjugation of woman."[57] Gender feminists hope to bring death to patriarchy by uncovering the unjust underbelly of patriarchal norms, just as Nietzsche undermines previous standards by declaring God's death. They recognize all categories, with "gender" as foremost among them, to be socially constructed by the masters (males) for the sake of subordinating the slaves (females).[58] For them, "Gender is a matter of dominance, not difference"[59] in which "bi-sexual infants are transformed into male and female gender personalities, the one destined to command, the other to obey."[60] We do not know if the sexes are innately different, we only know that the system of patriarchy forces them to believe in their different "natures" in order to perpetuate male superiority. Gender feminists hope that revealing the origin of "masculinity" and "femininity" will empower women to redefine or eliminate those roles.

The perpetuation of patriarchy is not a result of the "might makes right" principle, but of a subtle, spiritual, and intimate form of oppression, though physical force is also used in the form of rape or domestic violence, according to genderists. This characterization perfectly coincides with Nietzsche's description of the philosopher or scientist, both of whom tyrannize through the creation of ideas. The only difference is that gender feminists stress *males'* ability to mold *females*. Nietzsche would likely agree that such power has been exclusively male, though he would certainly not lament that fact.[61]

The Personal Is Political: Just as Nietzsche's will to power attributes to man the great authority to create human nature, so too does the feminist doctrine, "the personal is political." To say that the personal is political is to say that the essence of *everything* is power. The basic idea behind "the personal is political" is the common sense point that private relationships have political dimensions. Gender feminists originally chose this as their battle cry in order to uncover the hidden injustices of rape and domestic violence that occurred behind the "silken curtain" of the master bedroom.[62] The identification of the personal with the political is simply an elaboration of the extent to which patriarchal oppression, that is, man, shapes life. The gender feminist denial of a boundary, natural or otherwise, between the personal and political implies that not only do men hold power politically but that power extends to all facets of life. Andrea Dworkin calls this "the power of naming, a great and sublime power. This power of naming enables men to define experience, to articulate boundaries and values, to designate to each thing its realm and qualities, to determine what can and cannot be expressed, to control perception itself."[63] Thus, just as Nietzsche describes the thousand and one tablets as products of the human will, gender feminists similarly depict all institutions, innovations, and creations as products of patriarchs' ulterior motive of increasing power for themselves.

The identification of the personal with the political intends to uncover the vast tools that males have at their disposal, for "virtually every institution is intractably man-made."[64] As Susan Moller Okin adds, even the boundaries between institutions are manufactured; "to the extent that a more private, domestic sphere does exist, its very existence, the limits that define it, and the types of behavior that are acceptable and not acceptable within it all result from political decisions—decisions by men.[65] Such political, social, and spiritual power implies that men need not use physical violence in order to dominate women. Dworkin explains; "men, because they are intellectually and creatively existent, name things authentically. Whatever contradicts or subverts male naming is defamed out of existence; the power of naming itself, in the male system, is a form of force."[66] The proposition that the personal is political, taken to its logical conclusion, means, even in the absence of a single physical assault, men are insidiously assaulting women every moment of every day through their masculinist institutions.

The evidence of gendered institutions that support women's alienation is vast and varied, including beauty myths, rape and domestic violence, sexual harassment, and cultural backlash.[67] For example, Brownmiller describes rape as "a conscious process of intimidation by which *all men* keep *all women* in a state of fear."[68] Men, she claims, have created the institution of rape to indoctrinate women with the "victim mentality."[69] And any man who inadvertently benefits from another's dereliction is complicit in such oppression, which for gender feminists means that all men op-press all women when a single rape is committed. Similarly, many see the concept of "love" as a tool of oppression, claiming, as does Nietzsche, "love is not altruistic" but "a cycle of envy, hostility and possessiveness."[70] Indeed, Firestone sees love as "the pivot of women's oppression today" because it teaches her to be satisfied to be less than man.[71] In sum, according to these authors, "The reality of male physical strength in an absolute sense is less important than the ideology that sacralizes and celebrates it."[72]

Ambiguities within the Gender Feminist Conception of Power

The gender feminist adoption of the will to power thesis ex-plains why many feminists see man as the enemy, for they view history as a conscious or unconscious "war against women."[73] It also helps explain the goals of feminist organizations like Gloria Steinem's Ms. Foundation that seek to "change the way the world works."[74] But there are theoretical problems with the empowerment sought by gender feminists, problems that indicate inconsistencies in their theory and a lack of clarity regarding which societal changes they hope to evoke. In particular, I will fo-cus on three fundamental ambiguities. First, their focus on vic-timization leads to a vagueness regarding gender feminist goals: it is not clear whether they seek empowerment or empathy. Not only do they inconsistently seek these divergent and potentially incompatible goals, but by fixating on woman's victim status, gender feminists beg the question of whether women are in fact the weaker sex. This first problem leads to a second: gender femi-nist theory places feminists in the difficult position of maintaining that women *have* and *do not have* fixed natures. Their diagnosis of the problem (patriarchy) posits men and women as different by social convention alone; but the world they envision as its re-placement (female empowerment) implies differences between the sexes by nature. These inconsistencies lead to a final, and perhaps most fundamental, difficulty: gender feminism's dual use of the concept "empower" both as a *means* to equal rights and an *end* in itself may undermine their assumed egalitarian stance. And if power turns out to be the fundamental goal of gender feminists, their moral foundation may be uprooted. I will discuss these in turn.

Is "Victim Feminism" Empowering?　Gender feminists' first problem is their "women under siege"[75] mentality, which leads them to seek "power through an identity of powerlessness."[76] This emphasis on female victimization perpetuates a debilitating view of women: "The majority are naifs who are in one way or another pawns of the patriarchy that shapes their minds and desires. The sophisticated minority of aware women can be divided into two classes: those who have not sold out to the patriarchy and those who have."[77] This depressing account embraces the weak, but alienates the strong, for it insists that such women must either be co-conspirators of the patriarchy or its ignorant victims. Gender feminist, Naomi Wolf, warns that this "victim feminism" has "slowed women's progress, impeded their self-knowledge, and been responsible for most of the inconsistent, negative, even chauvinistic spots of repressive thinking that are alienating many women and men."[78] The celebration of women's harassment, torture, and alienation cultivates resentful, indignant, angry women—character traits not generally associated with feelings of "empowerment."

The focus on victimization and the weak has the potential to undermine their goal of empowering women. Nietzsche's description of the differences between master and slave morality helps to clarify this problem:

> While every noble morality develops from a triumphant affirmation of itself, slave morality from the outset says No to what is "outside," what is "different," what is "not itself"; and this No is its creative deed. This inversion of the value---positing eye---this need to direct one's view outward instead of back to oneself--is of the essence of resentment: in order to exist, slave morality always first needs a hostile external world; … its action is fundamentally reaction.[79]

For Nietzsche, the problem of slave morality is not that it fails to be creative, but that its influences are degenerating rather than empowering. Masters are different from slaves because masters love and affirm themselves through their spontaneous creation. Slaves create because they cannot affirm themselves. Gender feminists adopt the Nietzschean language of empowerment, which Nietzsche equates with mastery, but they also take the side of the slaves, thus abandoning what Nietzsche would consider true power. Now, gender feminists might admit that theirs is a slave morality that intends to reject all oppression and protect the weak from the dominating, fearful influences in the world. But again, this central focus on women's fear and resentment diverges from their central goal of empowerment.

Gender feminists often highlight victimization because they feel it justifies their moral claim to power, but this portrayal of women actually undermines that claim because it creates the impression that men are superior to women. After all, couldn't male superiority explain why women have been so consistently and thoroughly crushed by men? Gender feminists would adamantly disagree, of course, for they believe their definition of patriarchy adequately explains why women have perpetually lost to men: these men got a head start, initially through the physical terrorism of women, and later through the psychological oppression that forced women into stifling gender roles. Men's conscious or unconscious tyranny over women explains all unequal achievements of women politically, socially, and economically. Because of their delayed start, women will forever be the underclass until the patriarchy is overturned.

But this theory fails to discredit two other viable accounts of women's victim status, which gender feminists generally dismiss mainly because they find them unpalatable. The first suggests that women's subordination may be due not to men's evil nature, but to a fundamental weakness of women, that is, women may, by nature or human convention, be physically, intellectually, and spiritually inferior to men. This account, if true, could justify male hegemony. A second explanation suggests that women lack power politically and metaphorically because their innate desires differ from men's; women seek goals other than predominance. This second position suggests that women (and the female will) are of a fundamentally different character than men (and the male will). Nietzsche would argue that these two accounts are more persuasive than gender feminist theory. Though he believes men and women to be animated by essentially the same force, the will to power, Nietzsche does in fact affirm male hegemony. "Man should be educated for war, and woman for the recreation of the warrior."[80] He does not, however, give clear evidence why men and women should take these divergent paths. This vagueness in Nietzschean theory opens the door for gender feminists' alternative account of sex inequality. Neither account is satisfactorily proven or disproved.

Whether their dismissal of these alternative explanations is willful or inadvertent, gender feminists are well aware of the threat each of these arguments poses for gender feminism and feminism simply. Both natural and social differences have been used to justify unequal treatment of the sexes, and, they believe, such unequal treatment is always to the detriment of women. Nevertheless, if gender feminism is unable to disprove either position, their theory of patriarchy remains merely speculative. And even if gender feminists were legitimately able to dismiss alternative accounts of women's enslavement, their focus on women's universal subordination still begs the question of whether men and women are naturally equal.

Is "Nature" Socially Constructed? A second fundamental difficulty for gender feminist theory is their inconsistent use of the concept "nature" both as a standard to establish female superiority and as an arbitrary social construction by males to oppress women. This contradiction mirrors a problem inherent in Nietzsche's own use of "nature" both as a fixed standard and changeable concept.[81] This contradiction leads gender feminists inconsistently to hold at least four different positions: (1) men and women are *naturally the same* and therefore capable of equal rights with men, (2) men and women are *different by nature,* which enable women to be more capable rulers, (3) men and women are different *by social convention,* which has led to the patriarchal belief that women are inferior, and (4) men and women *are equal (i.e., fundamentally the same), but not by "nature,"* because the very concept of "nature" is a fiction created by males to justify their oppression of the female sex. Each one of these positions is problematic by gender feminists' own standards.

Though gender feminists perceive the concepts "nature," "sex," and "gender" to be socially constructed by patriarchs, i.e., false "truths," their identification of politics as power comes close to presenting a universal definition of human nature. By identifying all human relationships as political and all politics as power, gender feminists equate human nature with the will to power, which implies that *men and women have fundamentally the same nature.* Some gender feminists might disagree by suggesting that only males are constituted by the will to power. This position is not sustainable, for if, as they contend, man's drive to oppress is innate, "women must share in it too as they receive a full complement of genes from one power-mad creature, their biological fathers."[82] In this regard women would be similarly driven to grasp power, though historically they either chose not to or failed to oppress others. They would have to accept that they are innately no better (or worse) than men. And if men and women do have fundamentally the same nature, there is no reason to believe that the overturning of patriarchy would create a better world or that women have any moral claim to do so.

However, gender feminists often claim a legitimate right to overturn patriarchy on the assumption that the world would be a more peaceful, pleasant, and just place under female rule.[83] "Since men have historically wielded power, and with power have come war, holocaust, and planetary destruction, men, it claims, innately promote those negative qualities while women promote their opposites."[84] In other words, they argue, the sexes have *different natures,* and women's superior nature justifies both the overthrowing of patriarchy and its replacement with female-centered rule. Yet this argument based on nature contradicts their belief that "nature" does not exist as an absolute standard, but only as an arbitrary creation of men. By gender feminist theory itself, any difference between men and women would have to be socially constructed, and women would have no natural claim to moral or political power.

One way to resolve this difficulty could be to argue that women's victimization has given them an enlightened perspective—*they are superior to men by nurture*—what didn't kill them made them stronger. This position would at least be consistent with their description of the arbitrariness and falsity of all standards created by patriarchs. But even if gender feminists were to maintain that women are morally superior to males by nurture rather than nature, it would imply two conclusions. First, they would need to praise men for victimizing women, because it was out of this subordination that women became superior. If gender feminists were to maintain that their superiority arises from their experiences as oppressed beings, they would then have to admit that patriarchs were responsible for evoking women's admirable qualities. They would also need to recognize that their superiority would be an arbitrary and temporary standard. Women's superiority over men could be maintained only within a patriarchal context, as there is no reason to suspect such traits would be fostered under other regimes.

Moreover, both explanation of sexual difference—nature and nurture—are potentially problematic from the standpoint of sex equality. Fundamental sex differences, whether natural or not, may imply the superiority of one sex over the other, which could render egalitarianism an inappropriate or undesirable political goal. And if equality were not the goal of gender feminism, this would seem to indicate that they are simply grasping at power. Gender feminists need to set straight whether they believe that the sexes are different and whether those differences have any social, political, or moral significance.

There are good reasons to suspect that the gender feminist position on the natural sex differences is not accidentally, but willfully, ambiguous. If gender feminists want to argue that men and women are naturally the same, or the same by nurture, the problem of gender feminists' lack of a moral grounding rears its ugly head. They would then have to accept that women are no better innately from men and therefore no more entitled to rule than are men. However, if gender feminists were to consistently maintain that men and women are innately different, and women are more capable leaders, the goal of sexual equality may be undermined. Finally, if there were no standard, no "nature," by which to determine what the sexes are or what they can be, there would be no fixed reason or moral ground for preferring one sex over the other. As in Nietzsche's philosophy, human will would be the only remaining determinant.

Are Gender Feminists Anti-Democratic Immoralists? Jean Bethke Elshtain terms this final problem the "antidemocratic impulse" within gender feminism.[85] This difficulty has three dimensions: it is unclear whether gender feminism (a) seeks equal rights, power over others, or both, (b) is morally justifiable, (c) is sustainable without a moral foundation. Though the movement initially presents itself as seeking the equality that liberal feminists sought, without a genuine distinction between public and private, there remains no non-arbitrary basis for establishing any political order. All that remains is "pervasive force, coercion, and manipulation; power suffusing the entire social landscape, from its lowest to its loftiest points."[86] Gender feminist rule, whether egalitarian or otherwise, would merely be the same regime with a change of dictators. By gaining power they would now have the ability to create institutions that shape the very nature of people's thinking.

But most gender feminists insist that they do not seek "domination and hierarchy ... at the expense of intimacy, wholeness and connection."[87] Instead, they aim to seize power from men in order to "embrace equality."[88] Despite their characterization of the world as dominated by amoral forces, gender feminists maintain a distinction between the rightful and wrongful use of power, without providing a basis for such distinction. Naomi Wolf, well aware of gender feminism's antidemocratic tendencies, urges women only to exert their "will to power," toward democratic ends. She explains that there is both a doctrine of empowerment, "No one should stand in my way because of my gender, and no one should stand in anyone's way because of my race, gender, orientation," and humanism, "As a humanistic movement its parameters are these: no hate. ...[It] is okay to work on behalf of women because female humans are oppressed in ways unique to their gender. But working on behalf of women does not allow one ever to deify them as better than, or socially separate from, their male counterparts."[89] Women are entitled to take power for themselves, but they may not act like patriarchs: they cannot be judgmental of or hateful towards others. Their central assumption must be that all individuals are of equal worth.

Wolf's vision of a non-oppressive end might be the ideal goal of many gender feminists, but it is by no means the only one suggested by their worldview. By grounding politics wholly on power, feminists lose all moral ground for saying that one group should or should not rule over another. They correspondingly lose all legitimate basis for criticizing patriarchy, Nazism, or any societal arrangement, and under their reasoning, men have absolutely no reason to relinquish authority to women. Further, they lack any basis for arguing that equality is a worthy goal. Why ought they to stop once they achieve equality; why not seize full power over men? And even if gender feminists were to insist that they would only use power to establish full sexual equality, this would merely be their conception of justice, which they would force upon others who may disagree.

Gender feminism would like to embrace the will to power as an explanation of male domination and woman's victimization, and use this will to power as a means to overcoming past oppressive regimes, but they do not want to accept the consequences of that Nietzschean doctrine, namely its antiegalitarianism and moral relativism. Wolf and other gender feminists think that their empowerment need not be as brutal as Nietzsche's; it can instead mean the actualization of equal rights and mutual respect. But this position belies their characterization of the world. Their communitarian end goal would be unrealistic in an innately antagonistic and exploitive world. Wolf herself seems to recognize this when she urges women not to seek permission to create the society they envisage.[90] In the harsh world of power politics, the most realistic option for women would be to turn the tables and exploit men for the first time in history, i.e., female "empowerment" would mean taking power to tyrannize others rather than being tyrannized oneself. One cannot help but notice that despite their egalitarian leanings, gender feminism's goal of empowering women, which rarely entails any discussion of the empowerment of men or any other social group, implies that *women in particular* deserve power, perhaps to the detriment of others.

In sum, the description of the social world presented by gender feminists could lead to a conclusion other than an egalitarian society as the solution to woman's woes. Their conception of politics as essentially will to power leads to their ambivalence regarding the natures, or lack thereof, of men and women. The goals that follow their ambiguous stance on natural differences are similarly unclear. In a world understood as will to power, female hegemony would be no more or less legitimate than equality between the sexes.

From Ambiguity to a Clear Future

By turning back to Nietzsche we can make sense of feminism's current crisis, since the ambiguities in gender feminism mirror ambiguities in Nietzsche's own thought, the most fundamental of which surround the questionable moral status of the will to power. The consequence of Nietzsche's recognition of the human will as the only producer of valuations would appear to be that one value system is as good as the next. But Nietzsche does not take this position. He clearly values master over slave morality and even strives to produce radical, hierarchical aristocracies over tolerant, egalitarian liberal democracies.[91] Nietzsche also appears to use some type of moral standard (1) to distinguish the "natures" of man and woman[92] and (2) to determine what the future path of society ought to be (toward the Ubermensch). In these instances, it is not clear whether Nietzsche utilizes a fixed standard or whether he merely exercises his own idiosyncratic preference, his "this is I" deep down.[93] This fundamental ambiguity accounts for the fact that gender feminists adopt the language of master and slave without his corresponding valuations. Nietzsche's ability to justify his own doctrine morally is also questionable. Nietzsche believes that the eternal recurrence of the same solves this difficulty, but the doctrine itself is of questionable persuasiveness. Similarly, gender feminists utilize an amoral doctrine to justify a moral cause, a fundamental flaw about which gender feminists are generally unaware. Like Nietzsche, gender feminists want to use the will to power teaching to debunk patriarchy (and all previous "truths"), but they also want to maintain that women *deserve* power for the sake of retribution—justice demands their situation be rectified. They remain morally indignant, without a clear grounding of their value system.

Because Nietzsche's reasoning for preferring the masters to slaves is somewhat opaque, gender feminists' selective appropriation of Nietzschean ideas is not surprising. And, it should be said, that Foucault's revisionist readings of Nietzsche are largely responsible for this turn. Taking to heart Zarathustra's command to *go your own way*,[94] Foucault believes the only "valid tribute to thought such as Nietzsche's is precisely to use it, to deform it, to make it groan and protest."[95] And, it is not altogether clear that such bending toward egalitarian goals, ends that Nietzsche would have despised, is inconsistent with the Nietzschean system.

Nevertheless, when it is placed alongside Nietzsche's parallel doctrine of the will to power, gender feminism shows itself to be replete with fundamental ambiguities—ambiguities that undermine the moral claims of feminism itself. If gender feminism is to be defended, it would need to explain how those difficulties can possibly be solved. Frankly, I fail to see how they can without a radical re-conception of the nature of the political world. And if they cannot, there is really only one other option: to abandon the position that so closely follows what one of the most notorious misogynists saw fit to propound, and instead consider, or reconsider, a feminism whose principles are coherent and sound. In my view, that feminism would be a non-partisan feminist doctrine of equal rights and protection.

On a practical level, one can understand why the feminist movement would gravitate toward the polemical language of empowerment, a rallying cry that certainly stirs the imagination. But since empowerment is not just a word, but an anti-democratic reductionist worldview, its depiction of reality simply may not resonate with the everyday experiences of many women today, who believe they enjoy more freedoms than did their mothers or grandmothers. As long as gender feminism is replete with assumptions, ambiguities, and contradictions regarding their goals, women will have difficulty identifying with the movement. A return to a more traditional philosophy, akin to equity feminism, would not only enjoy greater success among the women of today, what is at least as important, it would deserve that success. And that is something a Nietzschean-inspired feminism could never do.

An Afterthought on Ambiguity

Marc Stier
Temple University

What results, then, when interpreters of texts are asked to bring the equivocal notion of ambiguity to their reading of classic works? In our introduction my fellow editors and I have suggested that the notion of ambiguity can help us understand these texts. Has our suggestion been vindicated by the essays in this volume? How? And, what broader conclusions, if any, can we draw from this collection of essays about the contentious issues that arise when we ask how we can or should interpret texts?

It is not just a taste for symmetry and irony that leads me to say that our answers to these questions are likely to be uncertain and ambiguous. But it is, perhaps, useful to offer some reflections at the end of this volume about the implications of this work for these issues.

Ambiguity and the Middle Ground

Most of our authors do not directly address the broadest debates about hermeneutics and interpretation. Nor should they have been expected to do so. Our charge to them was to bring the notion of ambiguity to a rereading of one of the classic texts of our tradition. But, taken collectively, the practice of interpretation found in these essays leads to a certain distance from the extreme claims that have often marked these debates.

None of these essays insists that the texts they consider must be read in one way or for one purpose. Nor do they make the rigid and sterile claim that these texts necessarily have one fixed and unchanging meaning. Nor do they suggest that the "Great books" must be seen as utterly coherent works. For the most part, our authors are open to multiple readings of these texts. They encourage us to bring alternative perspectives to them, and they recognize that even the greatest books might have internal tensions or discontinuities.

While the ambiguity of texts opens up the possibility that we might find a variety of coherent or plausible ways of reading a text, none of our authors take the further step of denying that some interpretations are better than others. They do not defend the view I am going to call radical textual indeterminacy. Even those who find tensions and problems within the texts they study do not conclude that these texts are wildly incoherent.

These essays are mostly located in a middle ground between the extremes that characterized the *methodenstreit* of the eighties and nineties. This outcome, I would suggest, is not a product of our authors having all been persuaded by some philosophical account of the nature of hermeneutics. Some of the authors of these papers have studied or written on these matters. But others have not, and only a few of them have addressed these general issues in their papers. I would suggest, however, that the urge to find a middle ground in the conflict over the nature of interpretation is a consequence of the act of interpreting texts itself, and it is an urge, curiously enough, stimulated by our focus on the problem of ambiguity.

Varieties of Ambiguity

Prior to the twentieth century, interpreters of texts typically assumed that a good interpretation is one that shows a text at its best, and this was most often taken to mean that the text was coherent and consistent. More recently, however, interpreters of texts have been more willing to recognize—or have been eager to find—tension and inconsistency in texts. Interpreters are likely to read the text in a way that stresses one or another of these clusters of ideas. But each may give a plausible reading of the text. Further, openness to the ambiguities in texts—a willingness to see texts as something less than entirely coherent—may lead to a third, plausible reading, one that tries to bring the rough edges of texts out into the open rather than smoothing them over.

The multiple intentions with which texts are written are another source of ambiguity and multiple interpretations. While our essayists would mostly insist that the meanings of texts go beyond the intentions of the author, few of them would deny that it is often useful to seek to elucidate those intentions.

The authors recognize that texts are only meaningful when situated within some context of thought. As a result, texts can only be interpreted, and reinterpreted in light of the different traditions of thought that come before and after them. Here, too, ambiguity is possible because texts are the result of, or can be seen in the light of, more than one tradition of thought. Again, the multiple contexts in which we place texts can lead to multiple readings of them.

Some writers in this volume point to another source of ambiguity in texts: Ambiguity at one level is sometimes the product of a clarity of purpose at another. A writer might, for example, deliberately create a text that is ambiguous in various ways. Straussian interpreters have often pointed to the hidden or esoteric meanings of texts that lie beneath the surface or exoteric view. But one need not be a Straussian to recognize the layers of meaning and intention that sometimes characterize texts.

Ambiguity and Indeterminacy

Surveying all these ways of being ambiguous, one can understand the temptation to say that in textual interpretation "anything goes." What I have called radical textual indeterminacy would seem to be the rule. Texts can, from this point of view, be read in an essentially unlimited number of ways, and in choosing between interpretations, we might well conclude "there be no good or bad but that thinking makes it so."

This, however, is not a conclusion reached by most of our authors. Of course, most of the papers in this collection are not focused on general issues about hermeneutics but, rather, on the particularities and peculiarities of the texts themselves. At our request, these essayists have tried to make use of the notion of ambiguity in addressing these texts. Yet, one might find it curious that our encouragement to employ the fashionable notion of ambiguity has not led our essayists to embrace the equally fashionable notion of radical textual indeterminacy.

I would suggest that we can explain this result in terms of the task we set for our authors. Radical ideas about interpretation are, I would contend, mostly the result of writers who theorize about interpretation, not practitioners of this important art. Or, perhaps, I should say that radical textual indeterminacy is the doctrine of interpreters of texts whose theoretical reflections rise too far above their own practice of interpretation. Down on the ground, where textual interpretation is done, radical indeterminacy is simply not a real option.

Bernard Williams once criticized the argument that leads from the variety of moral beliefs to moral indifference by saying that it took a "mid-air" position between moral views.[1] That I would suggest is what some defenders of radical textual indeterminacy do as well.[2] They take a kind of mid-air position between different views of the text and conclude from the variety of interpretations that one view is as good as another. But that theoretical claim is just another interpretation of the text itself. The search for tension and ambiguity in texts leads us to recognize the depth of texts and the consistency and clarity of their meaning. At a more prosaic level this occurs when what we had initially taken to be an inconsistency or incoherence in a text drives us deeper into it and helps us see just how good it is. For the most central—and original—ideas of many texts are precisely those that seek to overcome old alternatives, most often by finding new ways to state old problems. Attention to ambiguity in our texts, then, can help us locate not just tension and vision but originality and brilliance.

Notes

In Praise of Ambiguity by John D. Caputo

1   Augustine, *Confessions*, X.33.   This text is also famously cited by Martin Heidegger, *Being and Time*, trans. J. Macquarrie and E. Robinson (New York: Harper & Row, 1962),§9, 69 and was a touchstone for the "existential analytic."

2   G. S. Kirk and J. E. Raven, *The Presocratic Philosophers* (Cambridge: Cambridge University Press, 1962), 271 (Parmenides, Fr. 345).

3   As a purely formal matter, Aristotle, who will ultimately be a defender of ambiguity in the sense which I want to champion, complained that ambiguity represents an error in reasoning. In the Middle Ages, Thomas Aquinas wisely conceded that we cannot say a thing about God if we insist upon speaking about God in absolutely univocal terms, but that was no license for ambiguity, Thomas warned. While we must be prepared to admit a certain analogical quality into our language about God, nonetheless *analogia* must never be allowed to degenerate into *aequivocatio*, a wily equivocation.

4   Heidegger, *Being and Time*, §37, 217.

5   Friedrich Nietzsche, *The Birth of Tragedy*, ch. 13, in *The Birth of Tragedy and Other Writings*, ed. R. Geuss and R. Speers (Cambridge: Cambridge University Press, 1999).

6   Jacques Derrida, *Edmund Husserl's "Origin of Geometry,"* trans. John Leavey (Boulder: John Hays Co., 1978), 101-103.

7   Hans Georg Gadamer, *Truth and Method*, 2nd rev. ed., trans. Joel Weinsheimer and Don Marshall (New York: Crossroad, 1989), 386.

8   Occasionally, to be sure, a translation can itself become a classic, which occurs when its own deployment of the resources of the target language becomes an event in its own right. So even though modern readers will always need modern translations--the *New Revised Standard Version*--we will forever treasure the flavor and suggestiveness of the King James Bible. That means that a good translation can enrich the original, adds to its history, extends its suggestiveness, multiplies its valence in such a way that the original is not distorted but enriched and made more complex. The original and the translation are, in that case, related then, not as model and copy, but as root and branch, parent and child, forming together a greater whole in which the original has acquired an enlarged life.

9   Jean-François Lyotard and Jean-Loup Thébaud, *Just Gaming*, trans. Wlad Godzich (Minneapolis: University of Minnesota Press, 1985), 10.

10   On the idea of "metaphronesis," see John D. Caputo, *Radical Hermeneutics* (Bloomington: Indiana University Press, 1987), 261-62

11   Jacques Derrida, "Circumfession: Fifty-nine Periods and Periphrases" in Geoffrey Bennington and Jacques Derrida, *Jacques Derrida* (Chicago: University of Chicago Press, 1993), 155.

12   For Derrida on the secret, see Jacques Derrida, *On the Name*, ed. Thomas Dutoit (Stanford: Stanford University Press, 1995), 27-31.

13   Emmanuel Levinas, *Otherwise than Being or Beyond Essence*, trans. Alphonso Lingis (The Hague: Martinus Nijhoff Publishers, 1981), 20, 94, 167.

Tragic Ambiguity in the Oedipus Tyrannos by Robert Guay

1   A. Hug, "Der doppelsinn in Sophokles Oedipus könig," *Philologus* 31(1872): 66–84.

2   Thirlwall, "On the Irony of Sophocles," *The Philological Museum* 2 (1833): 483–xx, cited by A. Hug, "Der doppelsinn in Sophokles Oedipus könig," *Philologus* 31(1872): 68.

3   W. B. Stanford insists that the term "Sophoclean Irony" be restricted to instances in which the intended meaning "runs quite counter to the actual state of affairs as the audience and author knows it," and such a restriction seems sensible, but whether or not one observes it is irrelevant to the discussion of this paper; cf. W. B. Stanford, *Ambiguity in Greek Literature* (New York: Johnson Reprint Company, 1972), 68.

4   Cited by Stanford, *Ambiguity in Greek Literature*, 167.

5   Quotations from *Oedipus Tyrannos* are from the text of H. Lloyd-Jones in *Sophocles I* (Cambridge, MA: Harvard University Press, 1994). Translations of the text are also from this edition, except where it is obvious that the translation is mine.

6   For a comparable use of *phanô*, cf. line 1063.

7   J. P. Vernant, "Ambiguity and Reversal: On the Enigmatic Structure of *Oedipus Tyrannos*," in *Myth and Tragedy* (Cambridge, MA: 1988), 118.

8   Hug, "Der doppelsinn in Sophokles Oedipus könig," 66. Translation mine.

9   Stanford, *Ambiguity in Greek Literature*, 165.

10   Stanford, *Ambiguity in Greek Literature*, 76.

11   O. Müller, *Griechische Literaturgeschichte*, 140. Translation mine. Cited by Hug.

12   C. Segal, "Time and Knowledge in the Tragedy of Oedipus," in *Sophocles Tragic World: Divinity, Nature, Society* (Cambridge, MA: Harvard University Press, 1995), 141. Cf. also Vernant, "Ambiguity and Reversal," 120–5.

13   B. Knox, "Why Is Oedipus Called *Tyrannos*?" *Classical Journal* 50 (1954): 97–102.

14   J. Lear, *Open Minded: Working out the Logic of the Soul* (Cambridge, MA: Harvard University Press, 1998), 50.

15   Cf. Vernant, "Ambiguity and Reversal," 121: "Man is not a being that can be described or defined; he is a problem, a riddle the double-meanings of which are inexhaustible."

16   E. R. Dodds, "On misunderstanding the *Oedipus Rex*," in E. Segal ed., *Oxford Readings in Greek Tragedy* (New York: Oxford University Press, 1987).

17   Cf. D. Bain's comments on the "Oedipus the stupid" interpretation, in "A Misunderstood Scene in Sophokles, *Oidipous* (*O.T.* 300-462)," in *Greek Tragedy*, ed. I. McAuslan and P. Walcot (Oxford: Oxford University Press, 1993), 82ff.

18   Cf. M. C. Nussbaum, *The Fragility of Goodness* (New York: Cambridge University Press), 1986.

19   Cf. W. Kaufmann, *Tragedy and Philosophy* (Princeton: Princeton University Press, 1968), 154 *inter alia*.

20   Cf. R. Bittner, "One Action," in *Essays on Aristotle's Poetics*, ed. Amélie Rorty (Princeton: Princeton University Press, 1992).

21   *Rep.* 479bc, trans. G. M. A. Grube, revised by David Reeve (Indianapolis: Hackett Publishing, 1992).

22   Cf. A. Nehamas, "Plato on the Imperfection of the Sensible World," *American Philosophical Quarterly*, 12(1975): 105–17.

23   J. C. Kamerbeek, *The Plays of Oedipus; Commentaries IV: Oedipus Tyrannos* (Leiden: Brill, 1967), 84; R. Jebb, *The Oedipus Tyrannos of Sophocles*, (Cambridge: Cambridge University Press, 1958), 42.

24   Kamerbeek, *The Plays of Oedipus*, 84, emphasis added.

25   Cf. Vernant, who cites the *Agamemnon* of Aeschylus in "Ambiguity and Reversal," 429n10. Zeus has a similar role in *The Iliad*: he fulfills Achilles' wish, and thereby brings death to Patroclus and to Achilles himself. Note as well that every instance of *teleos* in the *Oedipus Tyrannos*, save one, involves death or Oedipus' fate. The exception is the ironic (from the audience's perspective) promise of *kerdos* at line 232.

26   Cf. Lear, *Open Minded: Working out the Logic of the Soul*.

27   Cf. Diogenes' famous remark: "Oedipus bewails the fact that he is both father and brother to his children and husband and son to his wife; but that is something that neither cocks nor dogs nor birds complain about."

28   I have rendered Lloyd-Jones's "close" (*isa*) as "equal" here.

29   Oedipus offers a number of reasons why death is not suitable for him, following his recognition: cf. 1271ff, 1334ff, 1374ff.

30   Cf. Lear, *Open Minded: Working out the Logic of the Soul*, xx.

31   Cf. B. Williams, *Shame and Necessity* (Berkeley: University of California Press, 1993), 58f.

32   Stanford, *Ambiguity in Greek Literature*, 76.

33   Dodds, "On misunderstanding the *Oedipus Rex*," 187.

Is Socrates a Model? Ambiguity in the Symposium of Plato by Marc Stier

1   Or, more accurately, has been recovered as some early interpreters of Plato took this same view. The way I read Plato is most closely associated with the

name of Leo Strauss. See, among many other works, *The City and Man* (Chicago: The University of Chicago Press, 1990). But there are many read who read Plato in this non-traditional way and yet do not share Strauss's hermeneutic (or political) views. In reading the *Symposium* as I do, I have been most influenced by Stanley Rosen, *Plato's Symposium* (New Haven: Yale University Press, 1987); Martha Nussbaum, *The Fragility of Goodness* (Cambridge: Cambridge University Press, 2001) and Allan Bloom, "The Ladder of Love" in *Plato's Symposium*, (Chicago, Chicago University Press, 2001) all of whom take the dialogue form of Plato's writing seriously. Although my focus on and conclusions about the text are different from that found in these three works, I am very much indebted to them for both the manner in which I read the text and for some of the particular interpretative points I make.

2   At least that was the state of humankind in the ancient world. With the explosion of productivity in the modern world things are now different and the struggle over material goods is not quite as intense. Still, that struggle is not entirely over, and, as we shall see, there are other sources of tension between human beings.

3   But the desire for sex is clearly not the same as the desire to procreate. In the love of bodies there is a greater gap between desire and product than in the love of soul.

4   209b.

5   209c.

6   209c.

7   Perhaps plays and poems are immortal only to the extent that they have a philosophic dimension. For it is that which makes them available to people in different times and places.

8   As Allan Bloom points out, this is precisely the point of Socrates saying that it would be unfair for Socrates to trade his wisdom for Alcibiades good looks (Bloom, "Ladder of Love," 162).

9   Still, we know from the Apology that Socrates reads the books of natural philosophers.

10   Political theorists rarely recognize our politicians have access to the concerns of others that is not available to most people. People come to politicians with their troubles. And politicians have a license to go to complete strangers and ask about their concerns.

11   Author's note: This paper is not directed toward specialists on Plato but to all who have some familiarity with the basic elements of text and, especially, the speeches of Aristophanes, Socrates, and Alcibiades. As such, my argument does not turn on any disputes about the meaning or translation of particular passages. So it has not seemed necessary to point the reader to the particular passages I paraphrase. Only specific quotes are referenced. They are given by Stephanus numbers and are to the translation by Seth Bernadete, *Plato's Symposium* (Chicago, Chicago University Press, 2001). Thanks to Patrick Messina, Craig de Paulo, Daniel P. Tompkins and Robert Guay for helpful questions that have

shaped the revisions of this paper. This paper is part of a larger project on the nature of erotic desire. Discussions with Isaac Balbus have done much to shape my ideas on this issue. As always, Diane Gottlieb and Katja Gottlieb-Stier have helped immeasurably.

Augustine of Hippo on Seeing with the Eyes of the Mind by Roland J. Teske, S.J.

1   A previous version of this paper was delivered as the inaugural lecture for the Donald J. Schuenke Chair in Philosophy at Marquette University in October of 2002.

2   See P. Courcelle, *Recherches sur les Confessions de saint Augustin* (Paris: de Boccard, 1968), 157-167. For an example of the lively continued debate of this question, see the articles by Robert J. O'Connell, S.J. and Frederick Van Fleteren in *Augustinian Studies* 21 (1990): 83-152.

3   *De ordine* II, 3, 10: *"Menti hoc est intelligere, quod sensui videre."*

4   *Soliloquia* I, 6, 12: *"Sine tribus istis igitur anima nulla sanatur, ut possit Deum suum,"* and *Soliloquia* I, 7, 14: *"Ergo cum animae Deum videre, hoc est Deum intelligere contigerit, videamus utrum adhuc ei tria illa sint necessaria."*

5   *De vera religione* 19, 37: *"Hinc jam cui oculi mentis patent, nec pernicioso studio vanae victoriae caligant atque turbantur, facile intelligit, omnia quae vitiantur et moriuntur, bona esse, quanquam ipsum vitium, et ipsa mors, malum sit."*

6   *Epistula* 7.

7   *Confessiones* VII, 7, 11: *"Et haec de vulnere meo creverant, quia humiliasti tanquam vulneratum, superbum; et tumore meo separabar abs te, et nimis inflata facies claudebat oculos meos."*

8   *Soliloquia* I, 6, 12.

9   *Soliloquia* I, 6, 12: *"Non enim hoc est habere oculos quod aspicere; aut idem hoc est aspicere quod videre."*

10   *De quantitate animi* 27, 53: *"Ut ratio sit quidam mentis aspectus, ratiocinatio autem rationis inquisitio, id est, aspectus illius, per ea quae aspicienda sunt, motio."*

11   *Contra academicos* III, 17, 37.

12   *De ordine* I, 11, 32: *"Esse autem alium mundum ab istis oculis remotissimum, quem paucorum sanorum intellectus intuetur, satis ipse Christus significat, qui non dicit, Regnum meum non est de mundo; sed, Regnum meum non est de hoc mundo."*

13   *De diversis quaestionibus octaginta tribus,* qu. 46, 2: *"Sunt namque ideae principales formae quaedam, vel rationes rerum stabiles atque incommutabiles, quae ipsae formatae non sunt, ac per hoc aeternae ac semper eodem modo sese habentes, quae in divina intelligentia continentur."*

14   *De diversis quaestionibus octaginta tribus,* qu. 46, 2: *"Anima vero negatur eas intueri posse, nisi rationalis, ea sui parte qua excellit, id est ipsa mente atque ratione, quasi quadam facie vel oculo suo interiore atque intelligibili."*

15   *De diversis quaestionibus octaginta tribus,* qu. 46, 2: *"Et ea quidem ipsa rationalis anima non omnis et quaelibet, sed quae sancta et pura fuerit, haec asseritur illi visioni esse idonea: id est, quae illum ipsum oculum quo videntur ista, sanum, et sincerum, et serenum, et similem his rebus quas videre intendit, habuerit."*

[16]   *De diversis quaestionibus octaginta tribus*, qu. 46, 2.

[17]   *Soliloquia* I, 13, 23: *"Lux est quaedam ineffabilis et incomprehensibilis mentium. Lux ista vulgaris nos doceat quantum potest, quomodo se illud habeat."*

[18]   *Confessiones* XI, 11, 13: *"O Sapientia Dei, lux mentium."*

[19]   *In Joannis evangelium tractatus*, tr. 12, 5: *"Quia ergo non videbatur lux hominum, id est lux mentium, opus erat ut homo diceret de luce testimonium, non quidem tenebrosus, sed jam illuminatus. Nec tamen quia illuminatus, idco ipsa lux; sed ut testimonium perhiberet de lumine. Nam non erat ille lux. Et quae erat lux? Erat lux vera, quae illuminat omnem hominem venientem in hunc mundum."*

[20]   *Soliloquia* I, 8, 15: *"Ergo quomodo in hoc sole tria quaedam licet animadvertere; quod est, quod fulget, quod illuminat: ita in illo secretissimo Deo quem vis intelligere, tria quaedam sunt; quod est, quod intelligitur, et quod caetera facit intelligi."*

[21]   *Soliloquia* I, 1, 3: *"Deus intelligibilis lux, in quo et a quo et per quem intelligibiliter lucent, quae intelligibiliter lucent omnia."*

[22]   For the state of contemporary scholarship, see Ronald Nash, *The Light of the Mind: St. Augustine's Theory of Knowledge* (Lexington: University Press of Kentucky, 1969), as well as Nash's article, "Illumination, Divine," in *Augustine through the Ages: An Encyclopedia*, ed. A. Fitzgerald, O.S.A. (Grand Rapids: Erdmanns, 1999), 438-440. After more than thirty years Nash's book is still, in my opinion, the best study on the question. E. Gilson's *The Christian Philosophy of St. Augustine*, trans. L. E. M. Lynch (New York: Random House, 1960), of which the French original stems from 1929, also remains worth consulting.

[23]   For the sense of "ontologism," as it appears in the discussion of Augustine's position in relation to Malebranche and various 19th century thinkers, see "Ontologism" in the original version of the *Catholic Encyclopedia*.

[24]   See Robert J. O'Connell, *St. Augustine's Early Theory of Man, A.D. 386-391* (Cambridge, MA: Harvard University Press, 1968), 154-155. Also, see O'Connell's "Faith, Reason, and Ascent to Vision in St. Augustine," *Augustinian Studies* 21 (1990): 83-126, especially 101 and 108.

[25]   See my "Augustine on the Vision of God," in *Augustine: Mystic and Mystagogue*, ed. by F. Van Fleteren, J. Schnaubelt, and J. Reino (New York: Peter Lang, 1994), 287-308.

[26]   *In Joannis evangelium tractatus* tr. 2, 4: *"Illud potuerunt uidere quod est, sed uiderunt de longe."*

[27]   *In Joannis evangelium tractatus* tr. 2, 4: *"Noluerunt tenere humilitatem Christi, in qua navi securi pervenirent ad id quod longe videre potuerunt; et sorduit eis crux Christi. Mare transeundum est, et lignum contemnis? O sapientia superba!"*

[28]   See Gilson, *The Christian Philosophy of St. Augustine*, 92.

[29]   See, for example, *De trinitate* VIII, 2, 3 and *Epistula* 147, 17, 42.

[30]   *De vera religione* 64: *"Date mihi qui videat sine ulla imaginatione visorum carnalium."*

[31]   See Bernard Lonergan, *Insight: A Study of Human Understanding* (New York: Philosophical Library, 1957), 412.

[32]   See Thomas Aquinas, *Summa theologiae* I, qu. 84, a. 5 cor.

[33]   See *De libero arbitrio* II, 6, 14.

[34] *De libero arbitrio* II, 6, 14: "*Quae si nullo adhibito corporis instrumento, neque per tactum, neque per gustatum, neque per olfactum, neque per aures, neque per oculos, neque per ullum sensum se inferiorem, sed per seipsam cernit aeternum aliquid et incommutabile, simul et seipsam inferiorem, et illum oportet Deum suum esse fateatur constiterit.*"

[35] *De libero arbitrio* II, 7, 19: "*Proprium ergo et quasi privatam intelligendum est, quod unicuique nostrum soli est, et quod in se solus sentit, quod ad suam naturam proprie pertinet: commune autem et quasi publicum, quod ab omnibus sentientibus nulla sui corruptione atque commutatione sentitur.*"

[36] *De libero arbitrio* II, 8, 20: "*Age, nunc attende, et dic mihi utrum inveniatur aliquid quod omnes ratiocinantes sua quisque ratione atque mente communiter videant, cum illud quod videtur praesto sit omnibus, nec in usum eorum quibus praesto est commutetur, quasi cibus aut potio, sed incorruptum integrumque permaneat, sive illi videant, sive non videant.*"

[37] *De libero arbitrio* II, 8, 20: "*Ratio et veritas numeri omnibus ratiocinantibus praesto est. . . .*"

[38] *De libero arbitrio* II, 8, 21: "*Tamen, si tibi aliquis diceret numeros istos non ex aliqua sua natura, sed ex iis rebus quas sensu corporis attingimus, impressos esse animo nostro quasi quasdam imagines quocumque visibilium; quid responderes?*"

[39] *De libero arbitrio* II, 8, 22: "*Propterea nullum corpus vere pureque unum esse concedimus, in quo tamen non possent tam multa numerari nisi illius unius cognitione discreta.*"

[40] *De libero arbitirio* II, 8, 22: "*Ubi ergo novi quod non est corpus unum, quid sit unum novi: unum enim si non nossem, multa in corpore numerare non possem.*"

[41] *De libero arbitrio* III, 10, 28: "*Item, juste esse vivendum, deteriora melioribus esse subdenda, et paria paribus comparanda, et propria suis quibusque tribuenda, nonne fateberis esse verissimum, et tam mihi quam tibi atque omnibus id videntibus praesto esse communiter?*"

[42] *De libero arbitrio* II, 12, 33: "*Quapropter nullo modo negaveris esse incommutabilem veritatem, haec omnia quae incommutabiliter vera sunt continentem; quam non possis dicere tuam vel meam vel cujusquam hominis, sed omnibus incommutabilia vera cernentibus, tanquam miris modis secretum et publicum lumen, praesto esse ac se praebere communiter.*"

[43] *De Genesi ad litteram liber imperfectus* 16, 57: "*Castitas autem nullius participatione casta est, sed ejus participatione sunt casta quaecumque casta sunt. Quae utique in Deo est, ubi est etiam illa sapientia, quae non participando sapiens est, sed cujus participatione sapiens est anima quaecumque sapiens est.*"

[44] In BA 6 (Paris, 1952), 525, F. J. Thonnard appeals to the principle of participation. He distinguishes "*deux modes d'être des vérités éternelles: l'un participé, en notre esprit, où elles vivent sous la forme multiple des règles des nombres et de la sagesse; l'autre absolu, dans la source du Verbe, où elles vivent sous la forme parfaite de l'infinie simplicité de la Vérité divine; et des unes à l'autre, des participations à la Source, il faut s'élever au moyen du principe de causalité ou de raison suffisante, qui est, sous sa forme augustinienne, le principe de participation.*"

[45]   I have argued that what we have in *De libero arbitrio* is not so much a proof that there is a God as an argument that God is truly, that is, that he is immutable and non-bodily. See my "The Aim of Augustine's Proof That God Truly Is," *International Philosophical Quarterly* XXVI (1986), 253-268, as well as "The *De Libero Arbitrio* Proof for the Existence of God," *Proceedings of the Jesuit Philosophical Association* (1987), 15-47; in revised form in *Philosophy and Theology* 2 (1987) 124-142.

[46]   *De libero arbitrio* III, 5, 13: "*Potest ergo esse aliquid in rerum natura, quod tua ratione non cogitas. Non esse autem quod vera ratione cogitas, non potest. Neque enim tu potes aliquid melius in creatura cogitare, quod creaturae artificem fugerit.*"

[47]   *De libero arbitrio* III, 5, 13: "*Humana quippe anima naturaliter divinis ex quibus pendet connexa rationibus, cum dicit, Melius hoc fieret quam illud; si verum dicit, et videt quod dicit, in illis quibus connexa est rationibus videt.*"

[48]   *De libero arbitrio* III, 5, 13: "*Credat ergo Deum fecisse quod vera ratione ab eo faciendum fuisse cognovit, etiamsi hoc in rebus factis non videt.*"

[49]   *De libero arbitrio* III, 5, 13: "*Non enim cogitatione videret fuisse faciendum, nisi in iis rationibus quibus facta sunt omnia. Quod autem ibi non est, tam nemo potest veraci cogitatione videre, quam non est verum.*"

[50]   *De trinitate* XII, 14, 23: "*Manent autem, non tanquam in spatiis locorum fixa veluti corpora: sed in natura incorporali sic intelligibilia praesto sunt mentis aspectibus, sicut ista in locis visibilia vel contrectabilia corporis sensibus.*"

[51]   *De trinitate* XII, 14, 23: "*Ad quas mentis acie pervenire paucorum est; et cum pervenitur, quantum fieri potest, non in eis manet ipse perventor, sed veluti acie ipsa reverberata repellitur, et fit rei non transitoriae transitoria cogitatio.*"

[52]   In the last decade of his life Augustine wrote the four books of *De natura animae et ejus origine* in defense of his agnostic position on the origin of human souls. In his *Retractationes* I, 1, 3, he says regarding how the human soul comes to be in the body, "*nec tunc sciebam, nec adhuc scio,*" though such claims to ignorance do not, of course, mean that he did not once think that he knew. See Robert J. O'Connell, *St. Augustine's Early Theory of Man, A.D. 386-391* (Cambridge, MA: Belknap Press, 1968), 150.

[53]   *Epistula* 166, 2, 4: "*Porro si corpus non est, nisi quod per loci spatium aliqua longitudine, latitudine, altitudine ita sistitur vel movetur, ut majore sui parte majorem locum occupet, et breviore breviorem, minusque sit in parte quam in toto, non est corpus anima.*"

[54]   *Epistula* 166, 2, 4: "*Nam per omnes ejus particulas tota simul adest, nec minor in minoribus, et in majoribus major; sed alicubi intentius, alicubi remissius, et in omnibus tota, et in singulis tota est.*"

[55]   *Epistula* 166, 2, 4: "*Unde intelligitur anima, sive corpus, sive incorporea dicenda sit, propriam quamdam habere naturam, omnibus his mundanae molis elementis excellentiore substantia creatam, quae veraciter non possit in aliqua phantasia corporalium imaginum, quas per carnis sensus percipimus, cogitari, sed mente intelligi, vitaque sentiri.*"

[56]   *Epistula* 119, 1: "*si enim fides sanctae Ecclesiae ex disputationis ratione, non ex credulitatis pietate apprehenderetur, nemo praeter philosophos atque oratores beatitudinem possideret.*"

⁵⁷ On this point, see F. Masai, *"Les conversions de saint Augustin et les débuts du spiritualïsme en Occident,"* Moyen Âge 67 (1962): 1-40.

⁵⁸ *Epistula* 119, 3: "*credebam Deum . . . esse inaestimabilis cujusdam lucis infinitam magnitudinem, cujus nec qualitatem aestimare, nec quantitatem metiri, nec speciem fingere. . . .*"

⁵⁹ *Epistula* 119, 3: "*cui adsit incomparabilis forma, inaestimabilis pulchritudo, quam etiam carnalibus oculis saltem Christus aspiciat.*"

⁶⁰ *Epistula* 119, 3: "*Deus, inquam, unus est, et personae tres sunt. Deus indiscretus est, personae discretae sunt. Deus intra omnia, trans omnia est, ultima includit, media implet, summa transcendit, ultra universa et per universa diffunditur: personae autem sibi constantes, proprietate secernuntur, non confusione miscentur.*"

⁶¹ *Epistula* 119, 4: "*Deus ergo unus est, et ubique est; quia et alius praeter illum non est, et locus non est vacuus ubi esse alius possit. Plena sunt Deo omnia, et praeter Deum nihil est.*"

⁶² *Confessiones* VII, 1, 2: "*Ita etiam te, vita vitae meae, grandem per infinita spatia undique cogitabam penetrare totam mundi molem, et extra eam quaquaversum per immensa sine termino. . . .*"

⁶³ *Confessiones* VII, 5, 7: " *Te autem, Domine, ex omni parte ambientem eam [totam corporealem creaturam] et penetrantem, sed usquequaque infinitum: tanquam si mare esset ubique, et undique per immensa spatia infinitum solum mare, et haberet intra se spongiam quamlibet magnam, sed finitam tamen; plena esset utique spongia illa ex omni sua parte ex immenso mari: sic creaturam tuam finitam te infinito plenam putabam. . . .*"

⁶⁴ *Epistula* 119, 5: "*Ais non tanquam aliquod corpus debere cogitari Deum. Nam etiamsi quispiam animo lucem millies quam hujus solis clariorem intensioremque confingat, nullam illic Dei similitudinem comprehendi posse.*"

⁶⁵ *Epistula* 119, 5: "*ideoque non possum adhuc Deum, id est, viventem naturam, justitiae similem cogitare; quia justitia non in se, sed in nobis vivit. . . .*"

⁶⁶ *Epistula* 120, 3, 13: "*Intellectum vero valde ama.*"

⁶⁷ *Epistula* 120, 3, 13: "*Et quidquid tibi, cum ista cogitas, corporeae similitudinis occurrerit, abige, abnue, nega, respue, abjice, fuge.*"

⁶⁸ I pointed out another example of this move in "Heresy and Imagination in St Augustine," *Studia Patristica*, Vol. XXVII, ed. E. A. Livingstone (Leuven: Peeters Press, 1993), 400-404. See also O'Connell, *Early Theory of Man*, 58-60.

⁶⁹ *Epistula* 120, 3, 14: "*Nam etsi carnaliter acceperimus quod scriptum est, Coelum mihi sedes est, terra autem scabellum pedum meorum; et ibi et hic cum esse credere debemus: quamvis non totum ibi, quia hic essent pedes; nec totum hic, quia ibi essent superiores corporis partes.*"

⁷⁰ *Epistula* 120, 3, 14: "*Quam cogitationem carnalem, rursum illud nobis excutere, quod de illo scriptum est, potest: Qui coelum mensus est palmo, et terram pugillo.*"

⁷¹ *Epistula* 120, 3, 14: "*Quis enim sedeat in spatio palmi sui, aut in tanto loco pedes ponat, quantum ejus pugnus apprehendit? Nisi forte in tantum caro vana progreditur, ut ei parum sit humana membra substantiae Dei tribuere, si ea non etiam monstruosa confingat, ubi palmus lumbis, et pugillus ambabus palmis conjunctis sit latior.*" I interpret "*palmis*" as referring to the soles of the feet; perhaps the text should read "*plantis*."

[72] *Epistula* 120, 3, 14: *"Sed haec dicuntur, ut cum sibi non conveniunt quae carnaliter audimus, eis ipsis admoniti, ineffabiliter spiritualia cogitemus."*

[73] *Confessiones* VII, 10, 16: *"Intravi, et vidi qualicumque oculo animae meae, supra eumdem oculum animae meae, supra mentem meam, lucem incommutabilem; non hanc vulgarem et conspicuam omni carni: nec quasi ex eodem genere grandior erat. . . . Nec ita erat supra mentem meam sicut oleum super aquam, nec sicut coelum super terram; sed superior, quia ipsa fecit me, et ego inferior, quia factus sum ab ea."*

[74] Ibid. VII, 14, 20: *"cessavi de me paululum, et consopita est insania mea: et evigilavi in te, et vidi te infinitum aliter; et visus iste non a carne trahebatur."*

St. Augustine's Phenomenology of Confusion by Craig J. N. de Paulo

[1] Augustine, *City of God*, trans. Marcus Dods (New York: Random House, 1950), VIII.1.

[2] For the development of the term "Augustinian phenomenology" and its philosophical presuppositions, see my dissertation *Being and Conversion: A Phenomenological Ontology of Radical Restlessness* (Ph.D., Pontifical Gregorian University, 1995, reprinted under the title *Being and Conversion* by Xlibris Company in 2002.) Also, see my recent article "The Augustinian Constitution of Heidegger's *Being and Time*," *American Catholic Philosophical Quarterly* 77, no. 4 (fall, 2003).

[3] "Adam" is itself an equivocal term, referring to a) the first man created by God in the Garden of Eden, b) humanity itself, or the entire human race. Also, the term "Adam" has a double connotation: on the one hand, signifying the glory of creation, the man having been made "in the image and likeness" of God, while, on the other hand, the term is synonymous with disobedience and death. Further, Augustine follows St. Paul in referring to Christ as the "New Adam" in order to discuss the relationship of creation and the fall to the "restoration" of the Son of God.

[4] *City of God*.XV.22.

[5] The term "Jerusalem" is also used equivocally by Augustine, analogously referring to: a) the "Eternal Jerusalem" meaning the Heavenly kingdom and, at times, b) the Church, but this, too, can mean either the Church temporal on earth or the Church triumphant in Heaven.

[6] Cf. *City of God*.XIX.26.

[7] *City of God*.XVI.4, also, XVIII.41.

[8] *City of God*.XIII.10.

[9] Cf. *Literal Meaning of Genesis*, trans. John Hammond Taylor, s.j. (New York: Newman Press, 1982), XI.32.

[10] Cf. *Confessions*.XIII.1.

[11] Cf. *City of God*.XIII.1.

[12] Cf. *Confessions*.XI.2. Also, cf. *City of God*.XIII.15.

[13] *City of God*.XIII.21, citing St. Paul (1 Cor.XV.47-49).

[14] For more on my use of the term "dualities" in Augustine and for an original treatment of "silence" in Augustine, see Patrick A. Messina, "The Significance of

Silence in Augustine's Confessions" (Ph.L. thesis., Pontifical Gregorian University, 2002), 15-42. Also, see my *Being and Conversion*.

[15]   Galatians.V.17; also, Augustine, citing St. Paul, *Confessions*.VIII.5.

[16]   *Confessions*.VIII.5.

[17]   *Confessions*. VIII.11, Augustine cites Psalm 118: 85

[18]   *Confessions*. VIII.11, Augustine cites Ecclesiastes.1: 2.

[19]   Cf. *Confessions*. X. 30, Augustine cites 1 John.2: 16.

[20]   Augustine's use of these terms essentially refers to the human being's love of the world either for its own sake (*frui*) or, through grace, as a means to sanctification.

[21]   *Exposition of the Psalms*.XC.1, 8.

[22]   There are several instances of Augustine's use of the term *"animus"* in his examination of the etymology of "cogitation" (*unde dictum est cogitare*) in the *Confessions*.X.11. Also, in the *Confessions*.X.25: *"et veni ad partes eius, ubi commendavi affectiones animi mei, nec illic inveni te,"* where Augustine further suggests another confusion in his identification of the mind with affection.

[23]   Cf. *Confessions*.XI.8.

[24]   *Confessions*.XIII.11: *"Dico autem haec tria: esse, nosse, velle. Sum enim et scio et volo: sum sciens et volens et scio esse me et velle et volo esse et scire. In his igitur tribus quam sit inseparabilis vita et una vita et una mens et una essentia, quam denique inseparabilis distinctio et tamen distinctio."* Also, Augustine discusses the mind in this way throughout his work, *The Trinity*.

[25]   Cf. *City of God*.XIV.7, where Augustine himself addresses the ambiguity of the various terms in Latin that signify "love." He argues that while the term *"amor"* sometimes appears in St. Jerome's Vulgate to mean "holy love," in general the term *"caritas"* is more commonly used. Augustine contends that the terms *"amor," "diligis"* and *"caritas"* appear to be synonymous in the Scriptures. He further states that any term that denotes "desire" (e.g. *cupiditas, concupiscentia*) in general refers to something corrupt unless otherwise stated.

[26]   *Confessions*.X.6: *"Non dubia, sed certa conscientia, domine, amo te. Percussisti cor meum verbo tuo, et amavi te."*

[27]   The "concupiscence" (*concupiscentia*) is also discussed as lust, or corrupt love.

[28]   *Confessions*.XIII.9: "my love is my weight."

[29]   Cf.*Confessions*.IV.6., where Augustine discusses himself as his beloved, but unnamed friend's *"ille alter"* and also *"dimidium anime suae."* Elsewhere, he also uses terms like *"ego secundum"* and *"alter ego"* and, in each case, to describe friendship as he does here as "one soul in two bodies" (*nam ego sensi animam meam et animam illius unam fuisse animam in duobus corporibus*).

[30]   *City of God*.XIX.8.

[31]   *Confessions*.II.2: *"Et quid erat, quod me delectabat, nisi amare et amari? Sed non tebebatur modus ab animo usque ad animum, quatenus est luminosus limes amicitiae, sed exhalabantur nebulae de limosa concupiscentia carnis et scatebra pubertatis et obnubilabunt atque obfuscabant cor meum, ut non discerneretur serenitas dilectionis a*

caligine libidinis. Vtrumque in confuso aestuabat et rapiebat imbecillam aetatem per abrupta cupiditatem atque mersabat gurgite flagitiorum."

[32]   *Confessions*.IV.1.

[33]   *Confessions*.III.1.

[34]   *Confessions*.III.1: "I plunged headlong into love, whose captive I desired to be."

[35]   For example, to elucidate what we are calling here the "composite of confusion," let us look to Augustine's view of Rome. On the one hand, he frequently refers to Rome as "the second Babylonia" (*City of God*.XVI.17) in as much as it was founded by pagans and represents the worldly city yet, on the other hand, Augustine recognized the "new" Rome re-founded by the apostles and re-formed by the blood of the martyrs, representing *both* the Church *and* the heavenly city. Further, Augustine does not view this confusion (of Rome) in a temporal, linear way, but rather as an admixture of the two cities in this one great capital, itself turning from paganism to Christianity. Augustine also viewed Constantinople as the "second Rome," baptized and reborn by Christianity with a Christian Emperor (Cf. *City of God*.V.25).

[36]   *Confessions*.III.1.

[37]   *Confessions*.III.1.

[38]   *Confessions*.III.1.

[39]   Cf. *Confessions*.IV.6.

[40]   *Confessions*.IV.6: "*Credo, quo magis illum amabam, hoc magis mortem, quae mihi eum abstulerat, tamquam atrocissimam inimicam.*"

[41]   Cf. *Confessions*.IV.8.

[42]   *Confessions*.IV.6.

[43]   Aimé Solignac. "L'Existentialisme de Saint Augustin." *Nouvelle Revue Theologie*, 70 (1958), 10.

[44]   As I have already addressed elsewhere in my dissertation, *Being and Conversion*, 185.

Prudence in St. Thomas Aquinas: Certitude in Ambiguity by John M. Haas

[1]   Fabian Wendelin Bruskewitz et al., "Are Organ Transplants Ever Morally Licit?" *The Catholic World Report*, March 2001, 50–54.

[2]   The neurological criteria for determining death are continually being refined. See "The Diagnosis of Brain Death," *New England Journal of Medicine* 344, no. 16 (2001): 1215-1221.

[3]   Pope John Paul II, "Address to the International Congress on Transplants," Vatican City, August 29, 2000. The address can be found in *The National Catholic Bioethics Quarterly* 1, no. 1 (Spring 2001): 89-92.

[4]   Op cit., 55.

[5]   See Joseph Fletcher, *Situation Ethics: The New Morality* (Philadelphia: Westminster, 1966).

[6]   *Summa Theologica* (ST), Second Part of the Second Part (*Secunda Secundae* or 2a2ae), Question 47, Article 3.

7   Aristotle, *Nicomachean Ethics* (NE), trans. David Ross (New York: Oxford University Press, 1984), III3, 1112b11.

8   NE, I1.

9   1357, 23-7.

10   NE 1.3 1094b24. See also Thomas Aquinas, *Summa Contra Gentiles* 1, chap. 3.

11   Josef Pieper, *The Four Cardinal Virtues* (South Bend: University of Notre Dame Press, 1966), 3.

12   *Summa Theologica* (ST) 1a2ae, 66, 3.

13   "Things done are indeed the matter of prudence, in so far as they are the object of reason, that is, considered as true: but they are the matter of the moral virtues, in so far as they are the object of the appetitive power, that is, considered as good" (ST 2a2ae, 47, 5 ad 3).

14   *Quaestiones disputatae de veritate*, 1.

15   Op cit. 1, *respondeo*.

16   Op cit., 21, 3.

17   *Quaestio disputata de virtutibus in communi*, 9.

18   ST 1a2ae. 64, 3 ad 2.

19   ST 2a2ae. 48.

20   ST 2a2ae. 47, 9.

21   ST 2a2ae. 48, 16 ad 3.

22   NE VI, 9.

23   ST 2a2ae. 47, 9 ad 2.

24   ST 2a2ae. 49, 3.

25   *Questio disputata de virtutibus in communi*, 6.

26   ST 1a2ae. 1, 2.

27   ST 1a2ae. 3, 8.

28   ST 2a2ae. 151, 1.

29   ST 2a2ae. 47, 15.

30   Noldin-Schmidt, *Moral Theology*, Volume II, Precepts, #403.

31   NE II, 6, 1107a.

32   Neurological criteria for determining death led to a less frequent use of organs from donors judged dead using cardio-pulmonary criteria. Because of the need for more organs for donation, the medical community has begun to consider the use of "Non-Heart-Beating Donors" or DCD "Donors with Cardiac Death." Dying people on life support will have that support removed, resulting in the cessation of spontaneous breathing and heart beat. The prudential decision which then must be made, and which is currently being debated, is how long should the physicians wait before a declaration of death. See Axel Carlberg, O.P., "Transplanting Lungs from Non-Heart-Beating Donors," *The National Catholic Bioethic Quarterly* 2, no. 3 (Autumn 2002).

"Stay, illusion": Ambiguity in Hamlet by Camille Paglia

1 All quotations from *Hamlet* are from *The Signet Classic Shakespeare*, general editor, Sylvan Barnet (New York, 1963).

Leo Tolstoy, Russia's Greatest Heretic by Jaroslav Pelikan

1   For the sake of readers who do not have access to Russian, I shall cite Tolstoy's works on the basis of easily available English translations (using their systems of transliterating the Cyrillic alphabet).

2   *Anna Karenina* (New York: Modern Library, 1965), 236-37.

3   *War and Peace* (New York: Signet Classics, 1968), 130.

4   *Hadji Murád* in *Great Short Works* (New York, 1967), 623.

5   *Resurrection* (New York: Penguin Classics, 1966), 190.

6   *Resurrection*, 237.

7   *Resurrection*, 83.

8   *War and Peace*, 413.

9   *War and Peace*, 604.

10   *Hadji Murád*, 585.

11   *War and Peace*, 198, 210, 455.

12   *The Cossacks* in *Great Short Works*, 116.

13   *Cossacks*, 159.

14   *War and Peace*, 650.

15   *War and Peace*, 798-99.

16   *Anna Karenina*, 460-64.

17   *Anna Karenina*, 461.

18   *Anna Karenina*, 676.

19   *Anna Karenina*, 738.

20   *Anna Karenina*, 742-43.

21   *Father Sergius* in *Great Short Works*, 509.

22   *War and Peace*, 466.

23   *War and Peace*, 625.

24   *War and Peace*, 893.

25   *War and Peace*, 797.

26   *Resurrection*, 182-83.

27   *Resurrection*, 177.

28   Matt. 6:7.

29   *Resurrection*, 184.

30   *Father Sergius*, 521.

31   *Father Sergius.*, 523, 534.

32   *War and Peace*, 1107; cf. 994.

33   *War and Peace*, 1036-37.

34   *War and Peace*, 475.

35   *War and Peace*, 917-19.

36   *War and Peace*, 1225.

37   *War and Peace*, 998.

38   *War and Peace*, 1013.

39   *War and Peace*, 1118.

40   *Resurrection*, 382-83.

41   *Master and Man*, 493-94.

42   *War and Peace*, 1225.

43   *War and Peace*, 1015.

44   *War and Peace*, 1161.

45   *Resurrection*, 157.

46   *Resurrection*, 178.

47   *Resurrection*, 325.

48   *Master and Man*, 493-94.

49   *Master and Man*, 500.

50   *Anna Karenina*, 522-23.

51   *The Death of Ivan Ilych* in *Great Short Works*, 300.

52   *War and Peace*, 104-6.

53   *War and Peace*, 793-95.

54   *War and Peace*, 1361.

55   *War and Peace*, 1177.

56   *The Cossacks*, 164.

57   *Family Happiness*, 39.

58   *War and Peace*, 213.

59   *War and Peace*, 891.

60   *The Death of Ivan Ilych*, 249.

61   *The Kreutzer Sonata* in *Great Short Works*, 357.

62   *Master and Man*, 472.

63   *War and Peace*, 835.

64   *Resurrection*, 382.

65   *Resurrection*, 366.

66   *Resurrection*, 533-35.

67   *War and Peace*, 706.

68   *Alyosha the Pot*, 673-74.

69   *Alyosha the Pot*, 677.

70   *War and Peace*, 578.

71   *War and Peace*, 865.

72   *Resurrection*, 43.

73   *Resurrection*, 184-87.

74   *Resurrection*, 364-66.

75   *Anna Karenina*, 821.

76   *Resurrection*, 382-83.

77   *War and Peace*, 117,660.

78   *War and Peace*, 1001, 1017.

79   *Resurrection*, 535.

80   *Anna Karenina*, 819.

81   *Anna Karenina*, 847.

82   *Anna Karenina*, 849-50.

83   *Anna Karenina*, 535.

84   *Father Sergius*, 530.

85   *The Cossacks*, 87.

86   *Resurrection*, 416.

87   *War and Peace*, 427-31.
88   *War and Peace*, 470.
89   *War and Peace*, 525.
90   *War and Peace*, 801-2.
91   *War and Peace*, 1208.
92   *War and Peace*, 1077-78.
93   *War and Peace*, 1320.
94   *Resurrection*, 565-66.
95   Matt. 5:39.
96   *Resurrection*, 557.
97   *Anna Karenina*, 299.
98   *Anna Karenina*, 415.
99   *Anna Karenina*, 430.
100   *Anna Karenina*, 434.
101   *Anna Karenina*, 453.
102   *Anna Karenina*, 537.
103   *Anna Karenina*, 754.
104   Matt. 5:30.
105   *The Devil* in *Great Short Works*, 331.
106   *Father Sergius*, 524.
107   *The Kreutzer Sonata*, 433-34, 449.
108   Matt. 6:26.
109   *War and Peace*, 1171.
110   *War and Peace*, 1159.
111   *Father Sergius*, 544-45.
112   *Resurrection*, 504.
113   *War and Peace*, 1163.
114   *War and Peace*, 1268.
115   *War and Peace*, 131.
116   *War and Peace*, 148.
117   *War and Peace*, 1341.
118   *War and Peace*, 473.
119   *War and Peace*, 144.
120   *War and Peace*, 359.
121   *War and Peace*, 393.
122   *War and Peace*, 584.
123   *War and Peace*, 978.
124   *War and Peace*, 1140.
125   *War and Peace*, 396, 859, 870, 879.
126   *War and Peace*, 393.
127   *War and Peace*, 758.
128   *War and Peace*, 393.
129   *War and Peace*, 1132.
130   *War and Peace*, 1135.
131   *War and Peace*, 1136.

132 *War and Peace*, 1381.
133 *War and Peace*, 1406.
134 *War and Peace*, 129-30.
135 *War and Peace*, 286-87.
136 *War and Peace*, 859.
137 *War and Peace*, 661.
138 *War and Peace*, 1374.
139 *War and Peace*, 1403.
140 *War and Peace*, 408.
141 *War and Peace*, 288.
142 *War and Peace*, 671-72.
143 *War and Peace*, 695.
144 *War and Peace*, 723.
145 *War and Peace*, 1167.
146 *War and Peace*, 1292-93.
147 *War and Peace*, 1407.
148 *War and Peace*, 1375.
149 *War and Peace*, 130.
150 *Anna Karenina*, 236-37.
151 *War and Peace*

Hölderlin's Der Tod des Empedokles: Erste Fassung by Arthur Grugan

1 See Martin Heidegger, *Zu Hölderlin: Griechenlandreisen* (GA 75) (Frankfurt am Main: Klostermann, 2000), 331-339.

2 Hannah Arendt, *Men in Dark Times* (New York: Harcourt, Brace & World, 1968), 23.

3 Friedrich Hölderlin, *Der Rhein*, in *Sämtliche Werke* (Grosse Stuttgarter Ausgabe), ed. Friedrich Beissner (Stuttgart: Kohlhammer, 1951), vol. II, 148, ll.216-221. (Hereinafter referred to a GSA, with volume number, page number, and line numbering.) Throughout this paper, I have used the following translations: Friedrich Hölderlin, *Hymns and Fragments*, trans. and intro. Richard Sieburth (Princeton: Princeton Univ. Press, 1984); Friedrich Hölderlin, *Poems and Fragments*, trans. Michael Hamburger (Ann Arbor: Univ. of Michigan Press, 1967); Friedrich Hölderlin, *Essays and Letters on Theory*, trans. and ed. Thomas Pfau, (Albany: State Univ. of New York Press, 1988). (Here, Sieburth trans., 81).

4 *Der Archipelagus*, GSA, II, 109, l.224 (Hamburger trans., 225).

5 *Germanien*, GSA, II, 129, l.27(Hamburger trans., 401).

6 "Das Gesichtspunct aus dem wir das Altertum anzusehen haben," GSA, ed. Friedrich Beissner (Stuttgart: Kohlhammer, 1961), IV, 221. (Pfau trans., 39).

7 *Id.*

8 *Id.*, (Pfau trans., 40).

9 Br.# 236, GSA, ed. Adolf Beck (Stuttgart: Kohlhammer, 1954), VI, 425-426. (Pfau trans., 149); cf. Sieburth, 11-14.

10 *Der Archipelagus*, GSA, II, 110, ll.241-256 (Hamburger trans.,227).

[11]   *Der Main*, GSA, II, 303, ll. 9-15 (Hamburger trans., 95).

[12]   *Der Mutter Erde*, GSA, II, 124-125, ll.51-60.

[13]   *Schlusschor des ersten Aktes (Entwurf), Der Tod des Empedokles: Dritte Fassung,* GSA, IV, 141 (Hamburger trans., 365).

[14]   "...die schaurige Nacht..." *Menons Klagen um Diotima*, GSA, II, 75, l.17 (Hamburger trans., 233).

[15]   "...in dürftiger Zeit?" *Brot und Wein*, GSA, II, 94, l.122.

[16]   "...in heiliger Nacht." *Brot und Wein*, GSA, II, 94, l.124.

[17]   "...bis Gottes Fehl hilft." *Dichterberuf*, GSA, II, 48, l.64.

[18]   *Thränen*, GSA, II, 58, ll.9-16. (Hamburger trans., 193).

[19]   *Germanien*, GSA, II, 149, ll. 27-28. (Hamburger trans., 401).

[20]   *Der Rhein*, GSA, II, 148, l. 221.

[21]   *Mein Eigentum*, GSA, II, 306, ll.21-22.

[22]   *Der Mutter Erde*, GSA, II, 124, ll.31-36.

[23]   *Die Heimath*, GSA, II, 19, ll.1-4 (Hamburger trans., 143).

[24]   *Menons Klagen um Diotima*, GSA, II, 77, ll. 57-58 (Hamburger trans., 237).

[25]   *Germanien*, GSA, II, 149, ll.1-16 (Hamburger trans., 401).

[26]   *Id.*, 149-150, ll.28-29 (Hamburger trans., 401, 403).

[27]   *Der Archipelagus*, GSA, II, 111, ll.278-280 (Hamburger trans., 229).

[28]   *Menons Klagen um Diotima*, GSA, II, 77, ll.69-82 (Hamburger trans., 237).

[29]   *Brot und Wein*, GSA, II, 93-94, ll.109-124. (Middleton trans., 43). Because of the importance of this stanza of poetry, we here provide an alternative translation for critical comparison and comprehension.
But, my friend, we have come too late. Though the gods are living,
Over our heads they live, up in a different world.
Endlessly there they act and, such is their kind wish to spare us,
Little they seem to care whether we live or do not.
For not always a frail, a delicate vessel can hold them,
Only at times can our kind bear the full impact of gods.
Ever after our life is dream about them. But frenzy,
Wandering, helps, like sleep; Night and distress make us strong
Till in that cradle of steel heroes enough have been fostered,
Hearts in strength can match heavenly strength as before.
Thundering then they come. But meanwhile too often I think it's
Better to sleep than to be friendless as we are, alone,
Always waiting, and what to do or say in the meantime
I don't know, and who wants poets at all in lean years?
But they are, you say, like those holy ones, priests of the wine-god
Who in holy Night roamed from one place to the next. (Hamburger trans., 249, 251).

[30]   Martin Heidegger, *Vorträge und Aufsätze,* (GA 7) (Frankfurt am Main: Klostermann, 200), 185; cf. Sieburth, 22.

[31]   *Dichterberuf*, GSA, II, 48, ll.53-60 (Middleton trans., 35).

[32]   *Andenken*, GSA, II, 189, ll.56-59 (Sieburth trans., 109).

[33] Ernst Cassirer, "Hölderlin und der Deutsche Idealismus," in *Hölderlin: Beiträge zu seinem Verständnis in unserem Jahrhundert*, ed. Alfred Kelletat (Tübingen: J.C.B.Mohr [Paul Siebeck], 1961), 79.

[34] Br. # 89, GSA, VI, 139-140.

[35] GSA, VI, 721.

[36] Br. # 94, GSA, VI, 156.

[37] Diogenes Laertius, *Lives of Eminent Philosophers*, trans. R. D. Hicks (London: William Heinemann, 1925), II, 375.

[38] Id., 383.

[39] *Der Tod des Empedokles; Erste Fassung*, GSA, IV, 7, 1.129. (All subsequent references to this play will appear in the body of the article.)

[40] Plato, *The Republic of Plato*, trans., with Notes and Interpretive Essay, Allan Bloom (New York: Basic Books, 1968), 177 (497d).

[41] Br. #6, GSA, VI, 427, ll.73-77.

[42] Plato, *The Republic*, 383c; cf. Richard Unger, *Hölderlin's Major Poetry: The Dialectics of Unity* (Bloomington: Indiana Univ., 1975), 54; and *Friedrich Hölderlin: Hyperion and Selected Poems*, ed. with Introd. by Eric L. Santner (New York: Continuum, 1980), xxv-xxvii.

[43] Plato, *The Laws*, trans. A. E. Taylor, in *The Collected Dialogues of Plato*, eds. Edith Hamilton and Huntington Cairns (New York: Bollingen Foundation, 1966), 1286 (691c-d).

[44] Emil Staiger, *"Der Opfertod von Hölderlins Empedokles,"* *Hölderlin-Jahrbuch*, 1963-1964, 7. Staiger's wording of Empedokles' ego-rooted hubris is directly to the point: *"Er lautet: Eigensinn.... Er selber klagt sich an wegen seines Eigensinns, seines eigenen Sinns, seiner Egoität, seiner ungebührlichen, frevelhaften Betonung des Ich."*

[45] In the second version of the play, that issue came forcefully to words:
Yes, I know everything, I can master everything. / Through and through, like the work of my own hands / I know what lives and like a lord of spirits / Conduct it as I choose. The world / Is mine, subject to me and in my service / Are all its powers. / Nature that wanted / A master is my handmaiden. / What honor she still has comes from me. / What would the sky be and the ocean, / The islands and the stars and everything / Men have before their eyes, what would they be, / These lifeless strings, without my giving them / Music and speech and soul? What are / The gods and the spirits of the gods if I / Don't make them known? (IV, 109, ll.501-516) (Constantine trans., 360).

[46] *Chiron*, GSA, II, 56, 1.22.

[47] Wolfgang Binder, "Hölderlins Dichtung im Zeitalter des Idealismus," *Hölderlin-Jahrbuch*, 1965-66, 68.

[48] *Fragment von Hyperion*, GSA, III, 64; cf. Constantine, 133-35.

[49] Cf. Friedrich Nietzsche, *Zur Genealogie der Moral*, III, 9 in *Friedrich Nietzsche, Werke in Drei Bände*, ed. Karl Schlechta (München: Carl Hanser Verlag, 1966), II, 854-55.

[50] Br. #117, GSA, VI, 202-03.

[51] Br.#128, GSA, VI, 222.

52   Cf. the return of these words in Nietzsche, *Also Sprach Zarathustra*, in *Werke*, II, 456.

53   *Der Grund des Empedokles*, GSA, IV, 153-154 (Pfau trans., 54).

54   d., 150 (Pfau trans., 50).

55   Id., 154 (Pfau trans., 54-55).

56   Id., 155 (Pfau trans., 55).

57   Id., 156 (Pfau trans., 56); cf. Pfau, 27.

58   *Germanien*, II, 151-152, ll.90-93.

59   Br. # 173, GSA, VI, 310, ll.87-90.

Paddling Against Ethics: Huck Finn as Moral Quagmire by Elizabeth Morgan

1   Peaches Henry, "The Struggle for Tolerance: Race and Censorship in *Hucklebury Finn*" in *A Case in Critical Controversy*, ed. Gerald Graff and James Phelan. (Boston: Bedford Books, 1995): 364. Herein refered to as Henry.

2   Henry, 342.

3   Henry, 317.

4   Justin Kaplan, "Born to Trouble: One Hundred Years of *Huckleberry Finn*" in *A Case in Critical Controversy*, 354. Herein refered to as Kaplan.

5   Mark Twain [Samuel Clemens]. *The Adventures of Huckleberry Finn* (Boston: Bedford Books, 1995): 27. Herein refered to as Twain, *Adventures*. The irony of this warning against meaning is enhanced by Twin's statement in his *Autobiography* that "Humorists of this mere sort cannot survive. . . .Humor must not professedly teach and it must not professedly preach, but it must do both if it would live forever." *The Autobiography of Mark Twain*. (New York: Washington Square Press, 1961): 298. Herein refered to as Twain, *Autobiography*.

6   Bakhtin, Mikhail. *The Dialogic Imagination: Four Essays*, ed. Michael Holquist, trans. Caryl Emerson and Michael Holguist. (Austin: University of Texas Press, 1981) : xviii. Herein refered to as Bakhtin.

7   Bakhtin, 39.

8   Bakhtin, 7.

9   Bakhtin, 365.

10   Bakhtin, 56.

11   *Life on the Mississipi, Roughing It, Innocents Abroad, A Tramp Abroad.*

12   *The Adventures of Tom Sawyer, The Prince and the Pauper, A Connecticut Yankee in King Arthur's Court, Recollections of Joan of Arc*

13   *Pudden'head Wilson*, "The Man Who Corrupted Hadleyburg," "The Mysterious Stranger," "What Is Man?"

14   Twain, *Adventures*, 187.

15   Twain, *Adventures*, 32.

16   Twain, *Adventures*, 37.

17   Twain, *Adventures*, 38

[18] Having once described Sir Walter Scott as the plague of the south – "Sir Walter had so large a hand in making the Southern character before the War that he is in great measure responsible for the War"--Twain's distrust of romance is no great surprise.

[19] Kenneth S. Lynn, "You Can't Go Home Again" in Adventures of Huckleberry Finn: A Norton Critical Editon. (New York: Norton, 1977): 401. Herein refered to as Lynn.

[20] Twain, *Adventures*, 33.

[21] Twain, *Adventures*, 164.

[22] Twain, *Adventures*, 207.

[23] Twain, *Adventures*, 70.

[24] Twain, *Adventures*, 121.

[25] Twain, *Adventures*, 46.

[26] Twain, *Adventures*, 251.

[27] In part, Fishkin plays off of an interview with Ralph Ellison in which he claimed that Twain's facility in working with southern dialects of all kinds "made it possible for many of us to find our voices." As Fishkin elaborates, the fact that "Twain allowed African-American voices to play a major role in the creation of his art. . . . may go a long way toward clarifying what makes this novel so fresh and so distinctive" (4-5).

[28] See Twain's sketch "Sociable Jimmy."

[29] Twain, *Adventures*, 54.

[30] Twain, *Adventures*, 67.

[31] Twain, *Adventures*, 48.

[32] Twain, *Adventures*, 53.

[33] Twain, *Adventures*, 54.

[34] He had his own copy of W.E.H. Lecky's *History of European Morals from Augustus to Charlemagne* (1896) and had both marked it up and commented on it.

[35] Twain, *Adventures*, 65.

[36] Twain, *Adventures*, 103.

[37] Twain, *Adventures*, 203.

Exploring Ambiguities in the Political Implications of Freud by Bruce Lapenson

[1] Paul Roazen, *Freud: Political and Social Thought* (New York: Alfred A. Knopf, 1968), 228-229.

[2] Sigmund Freud, *Civilization and Its Discontents*, trans. and ed. James Strachey (New York: W.W. Norton & Company, 1961), 111-112.

[3] Freud, 68.

[4] Freud, 49.

[5] Freud, 73.

[6] Freud, 38-39.

7   Peter Gay, ed., *The Freud Reader* (New York: W.W. Norton & Company, 1989), 692-693.

8   Gay, 640-641.

9   Gay, 665.

10   Freud, 25.

11   The view that Communism would return humans to their original freedom to express their essential powers is implied, if not overtly stated in Erich Fromm, *Marx's Concept of Man* (New York: Frederich Ungar, 1961), 29-30. The original freedom of man is discussed by Locke in John Locke, *The Second Treatise of Government*, ed. Thomas P. Pearden (New York: Macmillan, 1952), Chapter II.

12   For further discussion of Marx' "species being" see Robert C. Tucker, ed., *The Marx–Engels Reader* (New York: W.W. Norton & Company, 1972), 44-45. Further reference to Locke can be found in *Second Treatise of Government* (Chapter V).

13   Freud, 50.

14   Freud, 41.

15   Stephen Frosh, *The Politics of Psychoanalysis*, 2nd ed. (New York: New York University Press, 1999), 157-160.

16   Frosh, 160-163.

17   Frosh, 163.

18   Herbert Marcuse, *Eros and Civilization* (New York: Vintage Books, 1962), 35.

19   Marcuse, 15.

20   Frosh, 165-171.

21   Philip Rieff, *Freud: The Mind of the Moralist*, 3rd ed. (Chicago: University of Chicago Press, 1979), 250.

22   James Strachey, trans. and ed., *The Complete Psychological Works of Sigmund Freud* (London: The Hogarth Press and The Institute of Psychoanalysis, 1959), 9:181-204.

23   Gay, 563-568.

24   Frosh, 175.

25   Erich Fromm, *Escape from Freedom* (New York: Avon Books, 1967), 26-29.

26   Fromm, 317-318.

27   Fromm, 322.

28   Frosh, 176-177.

29   Rieff, 255.

30   Rieff, 260.

31   Freud, 108.

32   Roazen, 249.

33   Roazen, 298.

34   Roazen, 248.

35   Roazen, 278, quoting from James Strachey, trans. and ed., *The Standard Edition of the Complete Psychological Works of Sigmund Freud* (London: Hogarth Press, 1953), 10:146.

36   Freud, 74.

37   Freud, 74.

38 Rieff, 240-243.
39 Rieff, 246.
40 Rieff, 242, 246.
41 Rieff, 243.
42 Rieff, 246.
43 Freud, 109, 70-72.
44 Freud, 74.
45 Alan Bass, "Sigmund Freud: The Question of a Weltanschauung and of Defense", in *Psychoanalytic Versions of the Human Condition*, eds. Paul Marcus and Alan Rosenberg (New York: New York University Press, 1998), 445.
46 Freud, 74.
47 Freud, 69.
48 See, e.g., Alasdair MacIntyre, *After Virtue*, Second Edition (Notre Dame, Indiana: University of Notre Dame Press, 1981) and Michael J. Sandel, *Liberalism and the Limits of Justice* (London: Cambridge University Press, 1982).

Ambiguities in Nietzschean Philosophy: Problems for Feminism by Elizabeth Kaufer Busch

1 K. S. Hymowitz, "The End of Herstory," *City Journal* 12 (2002): 52.
2 Hymowitz, "End of Herstory," 1.
3 D. Patai and N. Koertge, *Professing Feminism: Cautionary Tales from the Strange World of Women's Studies* (New York: Basic Books, 1994), 116.
4 S. Pfeil, "Women in Corporate America 2002," *Employment Review Online*, <http://www.empolymentreview.con/2002-05/features/CNfeat02.asp_(accessed 21 August 2002).
5 D. R. Francis, "Behind a Surge in Firms Owned by Women," *Christian Science Monitor* (2002).
6 The Associated Press, "Harvard Women Undergrads to Outnumber Men," *USA Today*, www.usatoday.com/news/education/4004-04-02-harvard-women_x.htm (accessed 2 April 2004).
7 Christina Stolba argues that the figures given as evidence of a pay gap typically do not control for education, experience, choice, or field of expertise. When such factors are taken into consideration, the pay gap virtually disappears. For example, among people 27-35 without children, women earn 98% of men's salaries. (C. Stolba, "A Manufactured Crisis," *The Women's Quarterly* [2000]: 4-6).
8 C. Hoff Sommers, *Who Stole Feminism?* (New York: Simon and Schuster, 1994).
9 National Organization for Women, "Statement of Purpose" and "Declaration of Sentiments" in *E Pluribus Unum*, ed. D. McKenzie (Acton, Massachusetts: Copley Custom Publishing Group, 2002), 439-443. The first quote is excerpted from NOW's 1966 Statement of Purpose, and the latter is taken from their 1998 Declaration of Sentiments.
10 S. Firestone, *The Dialectic of Sex* (New York: Farrar, Straus & Giroux, 1970), 15.

11   Cf. Kaufmann's footnote BGE, 238, n. 31; M. Nussbaum, "Is Nietzsche a Political Thinker?" *International Journal of Philosophical Studies* (1997); L. Singer, "Nietzschean Mythologies: The Inversion of Value and the War Against Women" in *Feminist Interpretations of Friedrich Nietzsche*, eds. K. Oliver and M. Pearsall (University Park: Pennsylvania State University Press, 1998); D. B. Bergoffen, "Nietzsche Was No Feminist... " in *Feminist Interpretations of Friedrich Nietzsche*; M. Clark, "Nietzsche's Misogyny" in *Feminist Interpretations of Friedrich Nietzsche*. All subsequent references to *Beyond Good and Evil* (BGE), *The Gay Science* (GS), and *Human-all-too-Human* (HAH) will cite the aphorism only. References to *On the Genealogy of Morals* (GM) will cite to the essay number and aphorism. Other references to Nietzsche's texts (The Antichrist [AC], *Thus Spoke Zarathustra* [Z], *Twilight of the Idols* [TI], *Ecce Homo* [EH]) will cite the page number of the reference. All references are taken from the following translations: Friedrich Nietzsche, *The AntiChrist* in *The Portable Nietzsche*, trans. and ed. W. Kaufmann (New York: Penguin Books, 1982); *Beyond Good and Evil*, trans. and ed. by W. Kaufmann (New York: Vintage Books, 1989); *The Birth of Tragedy*, trans. and ed. W. Kaufmann (New York: Vintage Books, 1967); *Ecce Homo*, trans. and ed. W. Kaufmann (New York: Vintage Books, 1989); *Human-all-too-Human*, trans. by R. J. Hollingdale (Cambridge, New York: Cambridge University Press, 1993); *The Gay Science*, trans. and ed. by W. Kaufmann (New York: Vintage Books, 1974); *On the Genealogy of Morals*, trans. and ed. W. Kaufmann (New York: Vintage Books, 1989); *Twilight of the Idols* in *The Portable Nietzsche*; *Thus Spoke Zarathustra*, trans. and ed. W. Kaufmann (New York: Penguin Books, 1982); and *Will to Power*, trans. W. Kaufmann and R. J. Hollingdale, ed. W. Kaufmann (New York: Vintage Books, 1967).

12   For his praise of hierarchy see BGE 257-260, TI, 540; for his promotion of inequality see BGE, 263, 268, 271, 272, AC, 57, 646; for his praise of concubinage see BGE, 238.

13   A caveat is warranted at this point. Any attempt to categorize feminism as a whole is vulnerable to the criticism that feminism's rich diversity transcends categorization. Though there is truth to this assertion, my focus on gender feminism is both warranted and necessary. Gender feminism must be the focus of this inquiry because it has become the most vocal strand in political and educational spheres and is often (mis)taken to be the whole of feminism today.

14   BGE, 13.

15   BGE, 36. See his discussions of other forms of the will including the "will to ignorance" (Z, 227); the "Basic will of the spirit" (BGE, 24, 59); the "will to stupidity" (BGE, 230); the "will to the denial of life" (BGE, 259); and a "double will" (Z, 254).

16   BGE, 36.

17   Z, 227.

18   Z, 226-227.

19   BGE, 259.

20   BGE, 259.

21   M. Foucault, *Power/Knowledge* (New York: Random House, 1980), 90.

22   BGE, 9.

23   GS, 14, emphasis added.

24   EH, 267, cf. GS, 14.

25   BGE, 230.

26   Z, 191.

27   Very few books have been published on Nietzsche's influence on feminist thought. Here are the most significant: P. Burgard, *Nietzsche and the Feminine* (Charlottesville and London: University Press of Virginia, 1994); K. Oliver and M. Pearsall, eds., *Feminist Interpretations of Friedrich Nietzsche* (Univesity Park: Pennsylvania State University Press, 1998); P. Patton, *Nietzsche, Feminism & Political Theory* (New York: Routledge, 1995).

28   J. Sawicki, *Disciplining Foucault* (New York: Routledge, 1991), 4.

29   See footnote 11.

30   Cf. BGE 232-239; HAH I: 425; GS, 66, 363; Z, 177-179.

31   Here are some examples of gender feminists who cite Foucault's authority: J. Butler, *Bodies That Matter* (New York: Routledge, 1993); J. Butler, *Gender Trouble* (New York: Routledge, 1990); Jana Sawicki, *Disciplining Foucault* (New York: Routledge, 1991); C. Ramazanoğlu, ed., *Up Against Foucault* (New York: Routledge, 1993); C. A. MacKinnon, "Sexuality, Pornography, and Method: Pleasure under Patriarchy," *Ethics* 99, no. 2 (Jan. 1989): 314-346; E. A. Buker, "Hidden Desires and Missing Persons: A Feminist Deconstruction of Foucault," *The Western Political Quarterly* 43, no, 4 (Dec. 1990): 811-832; I. Diamond and L. Quinby, eds., *Feminism and Foucault* (Boston: Northeastern University Press, 1988); L. P. Thiele, "The Agony of Politics: The Nietzschean Roots of Foucault's Thought," *The American Political Science Review* 84, no. 3 (Sept. 1990): 907-925; L. McNay, *Foucault and Feminism: Power, Gender and the Self* (Boston: Northeastern University Press, 1992); M. Daly, *Gyn/Ecology: The Metaethics of Radical Feminism* (Boston: Beacon, 1978); M. Daly, *Pure Lust: Elemental Feminist Philosophy* (Boston: Beacon, 1984); M. Deveaux, "Feminism and Empowerment: A Critical Reading of Foucault," *Feminist Studies* 20, no. 2 (Summer 1994): 223-248; S. Phelan, "Foucault and Feminism," *American Journal of Political Science* 34, no. 2 (May 1990): 421-440; W. E. Connolly, "Taylor, Foucault, and Otherness," *Political Theory* 13, no. 3 (Aug. 1985): 365-376.

32   Butler, *Gender Trouble*, 92.

33   MacKinnon, "Sexuality, Pornography, and Method," 316.

34   Sawicki, *Disciplining Foucault*, 1.

35   Thiele, "The Agony of Politics," 907-908.

36   There are a few notable exceptions. Jana Sawicki, for example, notes that "Foucault borrows Nietzsche's hypothesis that power makes truth possible." *Disciplining Foucault*, 55

37   "It was Nietzsche who specified the power relation as the general focus, shall we say, of philosophic discourse…. Nietzsche is the philosopher of power, a philosopher who managed to think of power without having to confine himself within a political theory in order to do so." Foucault, *Power/Knowledge*, 53.

38   Thiele, "The Agony of Politics," 908.

[39]   McLaren, "Foucault and the Subject of Feminism," 109.   Also see my discussion of Nietzsche on pages 3-5 above.

[40]   Cf. C. Taylor, "Foucault on Freedom and Truth," *Political Theory* 12, no. 2 (May 1984): 152-183; McLaren, "Foucault and the Subject of Feminism," 109-129; McNay, *Foucault and Feminism.*

[41]   This has been conclusively shown by B. Detwiler in *Nietzsche and the Politics of Aristocratic Radicalism* (Chicago: University of Chicago Press, 1990) and F. Appel in *Nietzsche Contra Democracy* (Ithaca: Cornell University Press, 1999).

[42]   Thiele, "The Agony of Politics," 908. Frederick Appel, *Nietzsche Contra Democracy*, 3.

[43]   S. Pinker, *The Blank Slate* (New York: Penguin, 2002), 341.

[44]   BGE, 13.

[45]   Pinker, 341.

[46]   K. Millet, *Sexual Politics* (Garden City, New York: Doubleday, 1970), 25.

[47]   C. MacKinnon, *Sexual Harassment of Working Women: A Case of Sex Discrimination* (New Haven: Yale University Press, 1979); Millett, *Sexual Politics*; Firestone, *The Dialectic of Sex*; M. French, *The War Against Women* (New York: Ballantine, 1992); and N. Wolf, *Misconceptions* (New York: Anchor, 2001).   Others include Susan Brownmiller, Mary Daly, Andrea Dworkin, Gloria Steinem, Carol Gilligan, Rachel Simmons, Mary Pipher, Eleanor Smeal, Maureen Dowd, Judith Butler, Susan Moller Okin, Mary Field Blenky, Blythe McVicker Clinchy, Nancy Rule Goldgerger, and Jill Mattuck Tarule.

[48]   Millet, *Sexual Politics*, 25.

[49]   C. MacKinnon, *Feminism Unmodified* (Boston: Harvard University Press, 1988), 50.

[50]   Daly, *Gyn/Ecology*, 64, 109-110, 355; Daly, *Pure Lust*, 100-101; Butler, *Gender Trouble*, 20, 25, 57; Butler, *Bodies That Matter*, 14, 87.

[51]   Butler, *Gender Trouble*, 29, 32, 75, 91-106, Butler, *Bodies That Matter*, 9. 22, 33-35, 223-224; MacKinnon, "Sexuality, Pornography, and Method," 319.   See also footnotes 28-29.

[52]   Ramazanoğlu, *Up Against Foucault*; Fisher, "Should Feminists Forget Foucault?" *Studies in 20th Century Literature* 22, no. 1 (Winter 1998): 227-44; Buker, "Hidden Desires and Missing Persons," 811-832; Butler, *Gender Trouble*; M. Lloyd, "The (F)utility of a Feminist Turn to Foucault," *Economy and Society* 22 (Nov. 1993): 437-460.

[53]   A. Rich, *Of Woman Born: Motherhood As Experience and Institution* (New York: W.W. Norton, 1986), 57.

[54]   Butler, *Gender Trouble*, 29.

[55]   BGE, 203.

[56]   BGE, 260.

[57]   S. Brownmiller, *Against Our Will: Men, Women and Rape* (New York: Fawcett Columbine, 1975),18.

[58]   MacKinnon, "Sexuality, Pornography, and Method," 317.

[59]   MacKinnon, *Feminism Unmodified*, 51.

[60]   Quoted in Hoff-Sommers, *Who Stole Feminism*, 22.

[61] "A people is a detour of nature to get six or seven great men," (BGE, 126). Nietzsche's use of the term "Männer" instead of "Mensch," indicates he is referring to *males* specifically.

[62] National Organization for Women, "Statement of Purpose," 440.

[63] A. Dworkin, *Pornography: Men Possessing Women* (New York: G. P. Putnam, 1981), 17.

[64] N. Wolf, *Fire with Fire: The New Female Power and How to Use it* (Toronto: Fawcett Books, 1994), 144.

[65] S. Moller Okin, *Justice, Gender, and the Family* (New York: Basic Books, 1989), 129.

[66] Dworkin, *Pornography: Men Possessing Women*, 18.

[67] N. Wolf, *The Beauty Myth* (New York: Wm. Morrow, 1991); S. Faludi, *Backlash: The Undeclared War Against American Women* (New York: Bantam Doubleday, 1991); Brownmiller, *Against Our Will*; Butler, *Gender Trouble*; MacKinnon, *Feminism Unmodified* and *Sexual Harassment of Working Women*.

[68] Brownmiller, *Against Our Will*, 15.

[69] Brownmiller, *Against Our Will*, 309.

[70] Firestone, *The Dialectic of Sex*, 114-116.

[71] Firestone, *The Dialectic of Sex*, 113. It should be said that Nietzsche might agree with Firestone on this point. This may be the reason he insists on maintaining a sexual dichotomy; he hopes to keep women in their chains. Nietzsche does, after all, recommend concubinage.

[72] Dworkin, *Pornography: Men Possessing Women*, 14-15.

[73] This is the title and theme of M. French's book (New York: Ballantine, 1992).

[74] This is their subtitle (and goal) of the official Ms. Foundation website.

[75] "Women Under Siege" is the title and theme of Chapter 1 of Hoff-Sommers' *Who Stole Feminism?*

[76] Wolf, *Fire with Fire*, 135.

[77] Hoff-Sommers. *Who Stole Feminism*, 242-243.

[78] Wolf, *Fire with Fire*, 135.

[79] GM I: 10.

[80] Z, 178.

[81] Nietzsche often distinguishes between these two uses of the terms by italicizing the term or setting it off with quotes. Cf. BGE, 231-239.

[82] J. B. Elshtain, *Public Man, Private Woman: Women in Social and Political Thought* (Princeton: Princeton University Press, 1981), 208.

[83] Cf. C. Sylvester, *Feminist Theory and International Relations in a Postmodern Era* (Cambridge: Cambridge University Press, 1994), 84, 86, 212; Elshtain, *Public Man, Private Woman*, 221-223.

[84] Wolf, *Fire with Fire*, 146.

[85] Elshtain, *Public Man, Private Woman*, 219.

[86] Elshtain, *Public Man, Private Woman*, 217-218.

[87] Wolf, *Fire with Fire*, 148.

[88] Wolf, *Fire with Fire*, 235-260. The title and subject of chapter 15 is "Are We Ready To Embrace Equality?"

89   Wolf, *Fire with Fire*, 139-140.
90   Wolf, *Fire with Fire*, 52.
91   Cf. BGE 257; TI, 540; AC, 57, 646; WP, 981.
92   On one hand Nietzsche reduces his truths about "woman as such" to his idiosyncratic will: "these are after all only—*my truths*" (BGE 231). On the other hand, he speaks of the "Eternal-Feminine" and the "Eternal-Masculine" thereby suggesting that there are fixed masculine and feminine natures (BGE, 236).
93   BGE, 231.
94   Zarathustra reminds his followers: "*the* way... does not exist," (Z, 307).
95   Foucault, *Power/Knowledge*. 53-54.

An Afterthought on Ambiguity by Marc Stier

1   Bernard Williams, *Morality* (New York: Harper and Row, 1972).
2   Or perhaps I should say it is the critics of radical textual indeterminacy who present this view when constructing the bogeyman they then proceed to attack. On my reading of the debates about interpretation, defenders of radical textual indeterminacy are few and far between. Indeed, with a little distance, much of this debate seems to be between those who make the entirely reasonable claim that there are multiple, plausible ways to read most texts in a way that makes them seem far more radical than they really are. This shocks and provokes the traditionalists who then respond in a way that makes them seem far more rigid than they really are. The subtle thinkers on both sides are not all that far apart. It is the less subtle thinkers—and the graduate students—who tend to repeat the provocative slogans, thus generating much of the heat that keeps the pot boiling.

Index

•A•

Academics, 74
Anna Karenina, 132, 134, 140, 147, 230-233
Aquinas, St. Thomas, 2, 6, 101, 106-111, 115, 217, 222, 228-229
Arendt, Hannah, 233
Aristophanes, 4, 53-59, 62-63, 65, 67, 220
Aristotle, 6, 28-30, 73, 104-105, 107, 110-111, 115, 184, 217, 219, 229
Aristotelianism, 30
Augustine of Hippo, St., 2, 5, 15, 33, 72-87, 88-100, 107, 115, 217, 221-222, 224-228
Augustinian, 6, 221-222, 226

•B•

Babylon, 89, 93, 98
beauty, 66, 243
being, 7, 19, 66, 100, 107, 166, 217-218, 226-228
Busch, Elizabeth Kaufer 12-13, 239

•C•

Caputo, John D. 3, 217-218

caritas, 94-95, 227
Cartesian, 9-10, 149, 153, 168
Catholic, 6, 76, 101, 113, 118, 222, 226, 228-229
chaos, 149
Christ, 9, 74, 84, 89-90, 93-95, 132-133, 135, 141-143, 145-146, 226
Church, 95, 133, 136-137, 139-140, 146, 226, 228
City of God, 226-228
Civilization and Its Discontents, 181, 187-188, 237
concupiscence, 93, 96
Confessiones, 221-222, 225-226
Confessions, 2, 6, 33, 72-73, 84, 86, 89, 92, 97, 217, 221, 226-228
confusion, 5, 88, 90, 94, 96, 100, 226
conversion, 93, 226-228
Courcelle, Pierre, 72, 87, 221

•D•

death, 99, 102, 228-229, 231
deconstruction, 241
De diversis quaestionibus, 22-23, 221-222
De libero arbitrio, 23-25, 222-224
De ordine, 221
democracy, 124, 242
de Paulo, Craig J. N., 5, 220, 226
De quantitate animi, 221

Derrida, Jacques, 16-17, 21-22, 32-33, 217-218
De vera religione, 221-222
Descartes, Rene, 9, 19, 119, 148, 150, 162, 170
duality, 91

• E •

Empodokles, 9-10, 148, 152, 156, 158-169, 233-236
epistula, 221-222, 224-226
eros, 52-53, 60-61, 185, 238
evil, 240

• F •

faith, 31, 133, 222
Feminism, 13, 191, 198, 204, 239, 241-243
Feminist, 191, 196, 203, 240-243
Freud, Sigmund, 2, 11-12, 181-190, 237-239
Fromm, Erich, 184, 186, 238
Frosh, Stephen, 184, 186, 238

• G •

Gadamer, Hans-Georg, 26, 217
Galatians, 227
gift, 18
Gilson, Etienne, 76, 222
God, 5, 9-10, 15, 22, 31, 33-34, 72-77, 79-81, 83-87, 88-93, 95-96, 98, 100, 111, 118-119, 133-138, 141, 143-144, 149, 152-153, 156-157, 160, 163, 167, 170, 196-197, 201, 217, 222, 224, 226, 228
good, 61, 96, 107, 188, 240
Grugan, Arthur, 9-10, 233
Guay, Robert, 3, 218, 220

• H •

Haas, John M., 6-7, 228
Hamlet, 7, 117-130, 229
heart, 94,
heaven, 175, 226
Hegel, Georg Wilhelm Friedrich, 148, 157, 167, 170
Heidegger, Martin, 17, 19, 148, 156, 217, 226, 233-234
hell, 175
hermeneutics, 218
Hölderlin, Friedrich, 2, 9-10, 148-159, 161-163, 165-169, 233, 235
Homer, 60, 148
Huck Finn, 10, 171, 173, 175, 180, 236

• I •

idealism, 149
illusion, 229

• J •

Jerusalem, 89, 93, 226
Jesus, 93, 132, 135
Joyce, James, 9, 21-22

• K •

Kant, Immanuel, 108, 148
Kierkegaard, Søren, 16, 19
knowledge, 43, 83, 218, 222, 241-242, 244

• L •

Lapenson, Bruce, 11-12, 237

Levinas, Emmanuel, 34, 218
Locke, John, 182, 184, 238
Lonergan, Bernard, 76, 222
Louvain, 76
love, 95, 128, 153, 220
lust, 241-242
Lyotard, Jean-François, 27, 218

•M•

MacIntyre, Alasdair, 239
Marcuse, Herbert, 184-186, 238
Marx, Karl, 182, 185-186, 238
Messina, Patrick, 220, 226
mind, 1, 5, 72, 187, 221-222, 238
Morgan, Elizabeth, 10, 236

•N•

Nietzsche, Friedrich, 2, 13, 20, 168,
    192-201, 203-206, 208, 210-212, 217,
    235-236, 240-244
Nussbaum, Martha, 56, 69, 214, 219-
    220, 240

•O•

oedipal, 127, 183, 186
Oedipus, 3, 35-40, 42-49, 118, 123-124,
    127, 166, 182, 218-219
ontologism, 222
ontology, 100, 226
Orthodox, 9, 131-139, 144, 146

•P•

Paglia, Camille, 7, 229
Paul, St., 33, 76, 91-92, 187, 197, 226-
    227, 235, 237, 239

Pelikan, Jaroslav, 8, 230
phenomenology, 5, 88, 91, 226
philosophy, 12, 19, 62, 67, 167, 191,
    219, 221-222, 224, 239, 241
phronesis, 104
Plato, 2, 4, 8, 12, 51-53, 70-71, 73-74,
    77, 119, 159-160, 162, 184, 219-220,
    235
Platonic, 4-5, 39, 45, 51, 68, 73, 79
Platonism, 91
Pope John Paul II, 6, 101, 228
postmodern, 196, 243
power, 156, 194-196, 198-200, 203, 240-
    244
psychoanalysis, 181, 238

•R•

Reich, Wilhelm, 184-186
religion, 75, 76
Republic, 39-40, 58, 60, 65, 235
restlessness, 89, 226
Resurrection, 8, 133, 135-139, 141-143,
    230-232
Rieff, Philip, 185-188, 238-239

•S•

scriptural, 91
Scripture, 81, 119
seeing, 5, 70, 72, 221
self, 167, 241
sexual, 56, 62, 129, 242-243
Shakespeare, William, 7, 119-128, 229
Silentio, Johannes de, 16
Socrates, 4, 19-20, 39, 51-54, 57-61, 63-
    71, 219-220
Socratic, 19, 40, 58, 62, 67, 70
Solignac, Aimé, 100, 228
Soliloquia, 221-222
Sophocles, 3, 35, 37-38, 41, 47, 118,
    123, 148, 158, 218-219

soul, 82, 218-219
Stier, Marc, 4, 219, 244
Summa Theologiae, 2
Symposium, 2, 4, 51-52, 55, 58, 60, 63,
    68-69, 219-220

•T•

Teske, Roland, 5, 221
theology, 73, 224, 229
Tolstoy, Leo, 2, 8, 131-146, 230
Twain, Mark, 2, 10-11, 171-174, 177-
    180, 236-237

•U•

undecidability, 16, 32
univocity, 21

•V•

Van Fleteren, Frederick, 221-222
virtue, 6, 239

•W•

War and Peace, 8, 133-134, 136-138,
    140-141, 143-145, 230-233
will, 77, 194, 240, 242-243